With every increase in the population the world grows smaller. The planet will not support the wasteful practices that presently produce most of its meat-based protein supply. A better source of protein must be found, and thanks to Ellen Buchman Ewald and Frances Moore Lappé an alternative method of creating high-quality complete proteins is now a viable—and delicious!—reality.

Ms. Lappé's book, DIET FOR A SMALL PLANET, outlined the method and gave sample recipes. Ms. Ewald's book, RECIPES FOR A SMALL PLANET, expands the possibilities and gives both the broad, fundamental basics to work from and hundreds of specific recipes.

Needless to say, both books follow the principles inherent in natural food cooking and eating: both are dedicated to the concept that eating should be not only healthful but joyous.

The concept of meat complementarity—obtaining high quality complete protein by the right combinations of legumes, grains, seeds and dairy products—is not a fad: it is fundamental and original—a truly new approach to the idea of obtaining wholly delicious, totally health-giving food from nature's bounty—the good earth.

RECIPES FOR A SMALL PLANET

The Art and Science of High Protein
Vegetarian Cookery

Ellen Buchman Ewald

Illustrations by
Diane Coleman

BALLANTINE BOOKS • NEW YORK

ISBN 0-345-30871-9

Manufactured in the United States of America

First Edition: May 1973
Twenty-fourth Printing: October 1982

Cover art by Eva Cellini

To Frankie, who made it all possible

Acknowledgments

First I wish to thank my husband, Doug, who has unflinchingly withstood many an incredible meal, and has given his support throughout, not only by eating up all of the burnt sesame crackers but also by kneading the bread and making many beautiful meals from my recipes. His companionship in the kitchen helped give my culinary experiments the excitement and suspense of a science. We always prepare our meals together so that cooking is excitement for two.

Many friends have encouraged and helped me along the way by offering recipes and also giving specific suggestions for the book. I would like to thank Nancy Posselt for her help in editing, also Lou Todd, Judy Cook, Randy Alfred, my sisters, my mother, and all of my friends who have influenced my life and helped to put my head where it's at today.

EBE
Berkeley, California, 1972

CONTENTS

Foreword

When I began writing *Diet for a Small Planet*, I was asking one question: since a meat-centered diet so squanders the earth's limited resources, is there a viable alternative? After many long hours of research I finally came up with an answer. Yes, theoretically there is an alternative. It *is* possible to supply all man's nutritional needs from non-meat sources. But that's as far as I got. In my head I knew which plants were protein-rich and which combinations of non-meat foods create the highest quality protein. But was this alternative practical in the kitchen? Luckily for me, I knew Ellen Ewald.

She showed me that if you concentrate on plants rather than meat, many more dishes suggest themselves. When I turned to Ellen for recipe ideas using protein combinations that I knew to be "correct," she not only proved that the possibilities were practically infinite, but that they could become the basis of superb culinary creations as well. Simply put, she demonstrated to me that my *ideas* were more than textbook possibilities— they represented in fact a practical means of living daily in closer harmony with the earth's capacities to provide for the entire human family.

How often since then, when confronted by someone who doubts the appeal of a diet based on plant food, have I wished that I could introduce them to Ellen. I knew that I could convince even the most sceptical "meat and potatoes" person that eating directly from the earth is so much more stimulating and satisfying to *all* of the senses if I could only take him or her into Ellen's kitchen. Now, in this book, my wish has been fulfilled. Reading it is like walking into Ellen's kitchen. For in it Ellen has put so much of herself that you'll be able to smell the bread baking in her oven and perhaps even hear the crisp chopping sounds of her knife as she cuts the fresh vegetables from her garden.

Frances Moore Lappé
Hastings-on-Hudson, N.Y.
September, 1972

Introduction

This book is intimately and entirely related to the discoveries revealed in another book, *Diet for a Small Planet* by Frances Moore Lappé. *Diet for a Small Planet* is required reading for those who cannot find even one reason for limiting their intake of flesh in this world. It is essential reading for those vegetarians or semi-vegetarians who have a desire to get enough high-quality protein in their diets and want to understand how it can be done.

We had been eating natural foods for about two years when we introduced Frankie Lappé to this way of eating. After many months of work, Frankie had taken natural foods one step further in sensible eating. I learned from her that being a vegetarian does not mean the sacrifice of high-quality protein in one's diet; that with a little knowledge about the amino acids in vegetables, we can combine them in proportions that make the total usable protein greater than the sum of the protein in the individual foods. Once I became familiar with these combinations while helping Frankie with recipes for her book, I realized that I would not simply store this knowledge in the back of my mind as interesting information. I devised new recipes to fit these high-quality-protein combinations, and I altered old favorites to be just as delicious but higher in protein quality.

I hope that a collection of high-protein vegetarian recipes using natural foods will be valuable for vegetarians, natural-food freaks, and lovers of good food everywhere.

I. Protein Complementarity

What Is Protein Complementarity?

We are 18 to 20 percent protein by weight, and in order to support all of our body's vital processes we must renew part of our supply of protein every day. Proteins are made of amino acids. There are eight amino acids that our bodies cannot synthesize—these are called Essential Amino Acids (EAAs). The human body has a unique EAA pattern that must be filled out completely to make human protein. We must eat these EAAs in certain proportions in order to obtain maximum protein synthesis—any excess is merely catabolized for energy. If one amino acid is even partially missing from the pattern (called the "limiting amino acid"), the use of all the other amino acids for protein synthesis is reduced proportionately. This is true even when the limiting amino acid is eaten a few hours later, since there are no amino acid reserves.[1]

Every food that we eat can be rated in terms of how well its amino acid pattern matches the pattern required by the human body. This "biological value," along with

[1] "An acid hydrolysate of casein containing no tryptophane did not produce nitrogen balance when given intravenously. If tryptophane (and methionine) were added, nitrogen balance was achieved at once. In the course of these studies it was noted that if the tryptophane were injected several hours after the basic incomplete mixture its favorable effect on the retention of nitrogen is lost and that a negative nitrogen balance occurs, almost as if no tryptophane had been given." Robert Elman, "Time Factor in Retention of Nitrogen After Intravenous Injection of a Mixture of Amino Acids," *Proceedings of the Society for Experimental Biology and Medicine*, 40, p. 484, 1939.

the actual digestibility of the food, gives us its Net Protein Utilization, or NPU. That is, NPU tells us how much of the protein we eat is actually available to make human protein. What I call a "complete protein," or a food or meal containing "complete protein," would be one where all of the EAAs are present in the best proportions obtainable.

CHART I—THE LIMITING AMINO ACID

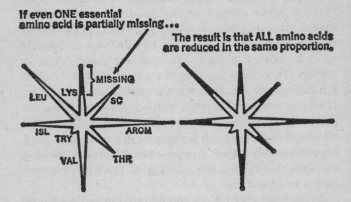

If even ONE essential amino acid is partially missing...

The result is that ALL amino acids are reduced in the same proportion.

LEU LYS MISSING SC

ISL TRY AROM

VAL THR

This amount of protein in the food............Becomes...This amount of protein for your body to use.

(From *Diet for a Small Planet,* p. 37)

One thing I realized once I had learned about usable protein was that protein and nutrition charts listing the amount of protein in foods are almost useless, because they do not take into account the NPU of the foods. For instance, a chart might tell you that 2 tablespoons of peanut butter has 8 grams of protein. This seems like a large amount of protein until you check the NPU for peanuts, which is 43, meaning that 43 percent of 8 grams is usable protein—or about 3 grams. However, once you learn to complement the peanuts (with milk, for instance), the protein quality improves. The combination of peanuts and milk in the proper proportions has an NPU of 67, an obvious improvement!

The higher NPU results from combining foods in such a way that the strengths and weaknesses of their amino acids match. For instance, beans generally have an abundance of lysine, but they are deficient mainly in the sulfur-containing amino acids. Wheat, on the other hand, is deficient in lysine but has abundant sulfur-containing amino acids. By combining the two we increase the protein availability by 33 percent over the amount we would get from eating the two foods separately. The following chart should make the concept of complementarity even more obvious.

I think that many people criticize vegetarian diets because they think vegetarians eat only lettuce and carrots, or that there isn't any protein in rice or beans, or that somehow the protein in vegetables is different from the protein in animal flesh. It is true that animal protein has a good balance of amino acids and a high NPU, but when vegetables are combined properly the NPU's are as good as, if not better than most animal products. (After all, animal protein *should* be high quality, since it takes 21 pounds of vegetable protein to make each pound of animal protein!) And remember, beef is not *all* protein. If you eat a one-pound steak, you ingest 4 ounces of protein, and slightly less than 3 ounces is actually usable protein.

The truth of the vegetarian diet is that if the proper amino acids are eaten together in the right proportions, there is no need to fear that vegetable protein might be inferior. Protein is protein and amino acids are amino acids whether they occur in roast beef or mung beans. It is important for the vegetarian to include foods from

CHART II—DEMONSTRATING PROTEIN COMPLEMENTARITY

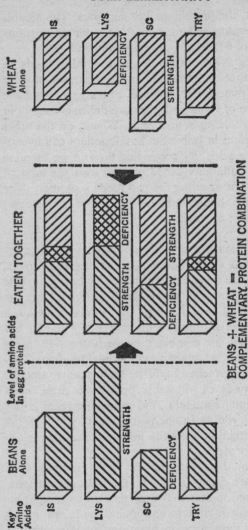

(From *Diet for a Small Planet*, p. 53)

four main food categories for "complete protein": grains, legumes, seeds, and dairy products. (And even the dairy products could be eliminated for those who are not ovo-lacto vegetarians. This would only reduce the complementary combinations by one-third.) So the criticism that vegetarians cannot get proper protein without adding some kind of animal products to their food is unwarranted.

Macrobiotics is highly criticized for its emphasis on brown rice (because rice is deficient in two of the EAAs: isoleucine and lysine). However, there are two foods that this "all rice" diet usually includes—sesame seeds and soy sauce. Sesame and rice is one of the tested high-protein combinations, and soy sauce, although it is mostly water, does contain a small amount of soy protein, which also complements rice. I am not advocating that anyone should try to exist on rice and sesame alone (or on any single-food diet). My greatest criticism of macrobiotic cooking is the lack of fresh, raw fruits and vegetables. Besides being delicious, raw fruits and vegetables supply the body with essential vitamins and minerals. Many diets relying heavily on meat and other flesh often exclude fresh fruits and vegetables. Perhaps that's why we have a multi-million-dollar synthetic vitamin industry in this country today!

It seems that a well-balanced diet would occur naturally when extremes of all kinds are avoided. After all, in my family we were vegetarians for two years before learning about protein complementarity, and we weren't sick or anemic. We were probably getting high-quality protein quite accidentally by eating a diet that included a variety of wholesome natural foods.

In *Diet for a Small Planet* Ms. Lappé discusses twenty-one tested high-protein combinations of vegetable and dairy foods. One can see by studying the tables in *Diet for a Small Planet* that you could theoretically put together many complete protein combinations by matching strong and weak amino acids. Unfortunately, only twenty-one combinations have been proven experimentally, so I have worked only with these for the recipes in this book. The usable protein in each recipe is calculated from the basic combination plus other high-protein foods that occur in the recipe, such as eggs, nutritional additives (wheat germ, brewer's yeast), and other vegetables that have a significant amount of protein (such as peas, corn, or mushrooms).

In each recipe I have listed the number of grams of usable protein per portion and the percent of average daily protein need that one portion would contain. For these figures to mean something to you when you plan your meals, I will briefly interpret them for you.

The grams of usable protein tells you, based on NPUs, how much protein is directly available for use by the body. But what does a body need? The percent of average daily protein need gives the range for average adults—154 pounds to 128 pounds. The lower percentage figure applies to the heavier weight. According to *Diet for a Small Planet,* we need 0.28 grams of *usable* protein per pound of body weight per day. Multiplying 0.28 by 154 pounds (the average male) we get a daily protein requirement of 43.1 grams of *usable* protein. For the average female (128 pounds) the requirement is 35.8 grams per day. You can easily calculate your own exact daily usable protein requirement by multiplying your weight by 0.28. Then if you are curious about the exact protein percentage provided by a given recipe, divide the grams of usable protein per portion by your own requirement. That is what I have done to get the percent figures for the average male and female.

But Eating All of Those Beans and Grains Is So Fattening!

After hearing many complaints about the "excessive calories" in our vegetarian diet, I decided to compare calories in a useful way. Since I am mainly concerned with protein, and usable protein at that, it seemed that the number of calories per gram of usable protein for each combination of foods would be useful information for those who are concerned with calorie intake. You can see in Chart III that the calories per gram of usable protein vary from a high of 62 calories per gram (for rice and sesame seeds) to 24 calories per gram (for beans and milk).

Suppose a 154-pound man decided to get all of his daily protein requirement from one source. He would need 43.1 grams of usable protein. If he chose the rice and sesame combination, at 62 calories per gram he would have to ingest 2700 calories, which would be slightly under the limit required to maintain a moderately active man. He would certainly lose weight if he picked beans and milk. At 24 calories per gram of usable protein, 43.1 grams would "cost" only about 1050 calories, far below the number of calories needed to maintain 154 pounds of weight.

Remember that a woman (or man) weighing less than 154 would need fewer grams of usable protein, and thus fewer calories. For instance, at 128 pounds the daily requirement is 35.8 grams of usable protein. At 62 calories per gram, the total calorie intake would be about

2200, or just about what would be required to maintain 128 pounds.

Naturally, these calculations are unrealistic as far as most normal eating habits go. It certainly would be dull to eat all of our protein or calories from the same source. What these figures suggest, however, is that it would be reasonable to obtain protein from any of the vegetable sources (even from the rice-sesame combination) as long as you didn't eat one combination all of the time, and you did include raw vegetables and fruits. There are single foods, too, that have very few calories per gram of usable protein. (See Chart IV: It becomes obvious why cottage cheese is such a widely used "diet" food.)

So in certain food combinations, and from some single foods, we can obtain enough protein and not too many calories. Also, remember when you observe the meat and fish protein figures that usually at a meal one does not eat just meat or fish; those foods are often accompanied by potatoes, rice, breads or rolls, which add calories but little protein if eaten uncomplemented (especially if they are white rather than whole grain products).

To further explain Chart III: where multiple quantities are listed for one food, you may use any alternative form. I included the NPUs because I thought it would be useful to see how the NPU is increased for combinations, as this is what the protein in the recipes is based on. You can see the increase if you compare the NPUs of the individual foods as listed in Tables I through VIII of *Diet for a Small Planet*. The Grams of Usable Protein column refers to the number of grams available from the given quantities of one combination. That is, if you prepared a simple dish of ⅔ cup of rice and ¼ cup of beans and you ate it all, you would have eaten 15 grams of usable protein. If you were curious about how many calories you had consumed, you could multiply the number of grams (15) by the calories per gram (43).

Remember that the quantities listed refer always to *uncooked* whole grains and dry beans.

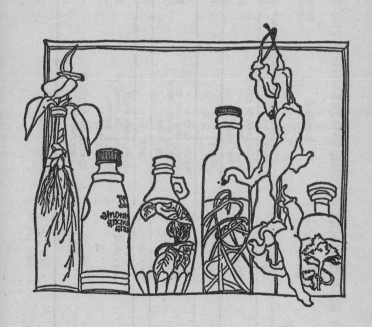

CHART III—HIGH-PROTEIN COMBINATIONS—THEIR PROTEIN AND CALORIES

Quantities[1] (footnotes are at end of chart)	Combination (: = combined with)	Quantities[1]	NPU for the Combination[3]	Grams of Usable Protein	Calories Per Gram of Usable Protein
2/3 cup	rice : beans	1/4 cup	70	15	43
2 1/2 cups	rice : soy	1/4 cup beans or grits or 1/2 cup flour or 6 oz tofu	73	37	53
1 cup	rice : brewer's yeast	1/4 cup	77	24	35
1 cup	rice : sesame	1/3 cup seeds or 1/2 cup seed meal or 3 tbsp sesame butter or Tahini	67	16	62
3/4 cup	rice : milk	1 cup[2]	83	17	42
1 cup	rice : wheat & soy	1/2 cup whole wheat (berries or kernel) or 3/4 cup bulgur or 1 cup flour 1/2 cup beans or grits or 1 cup flour or 12 oz tofu	72	41	34

¾ cup ½ cup whole wheat (berries or kernel) or ⅔ cup bulgur or ¾ cup flour	rice : peanut & & wheat soy	¼ cup nuts or ⅓ cup meal or ⅛ cup butter ⅓ cup beans or grits or ⅔ cup flour or 8 oz tofu	64	38	41
1½ cups bulgur or 2 cups flour or 1 cup macaroni or 5 slices bread	wheat : milk	1 cup[2]	67	28	34
1½ cups whole wheat (berries or kernel) or 2½ cups bulgur or 3 cups flour	wheat : beans	½ cup	64	46	33
½ cup whole wheat (berries or kernel) or ¾ cup bulgur or 1 cup flour	wheat : soy	⅛ cup beans or grits or ¼ cup flour or 3 oz tofu	72	16	28
2 cups whole wheat (berries or kernel) or 3 cups bulgur or 3¾ cups flour	wheat : peanuts & milk or soy	⅞ cup nuts or 1 cup meal or ½ cup butter 1 cup[2] ⅛ cup beans or grits or ¼ cup flour or 3 oz tofu	67	83	33

Quantities[1]	Combination (: = combined with)	Quantities[1]	NPU for the Combination[3]	Grams of Usable Protein	Calories Per Gram of Usable Protein
2½ cups bulgur or 3¼ cups flour	wheat : soy	¼ cup beans or grits or ½ cup flour or 6 oz tofu	73	67	31
	&				
	sesame	½ cup seeds or ⅔ cup meal or ¼ cup sesame butter or tahini			
1 cup meal or 6-7 tortillas	cornmeal : soy	⅙ cup beans or grits or ⅓ cup flour or 4 oz tofu	70	20	34
	&				
	milk	1 cup[2]			
1 cup meal or 6-7 tortillas	cornmeal : beans	¼ cup	63	14	41
1½ cups nuts or 2 cups meal or ⅞ cup butter	peanuts : soy	½ cup beans or grits or 1 cup flour or 12 oz tofu	69	117	33
	&				
	sesame	1¾ cups seed or 2⅓ cups meal or ⅞ cup sesame butter or tahini			

1¾ cups nuts or 2⅓ cups meal or 1 cup butter	peanuts : milk	1½ cups milk or ½ cup grated cheese or ½ cup ricotta cheese or 6 tbsp cottage cheese or 6 tbsp milk powder or ½ cup instant milk powder	67	84	31
¾ cup nuts or 1 cup meal or ½ cup butter	peanuts : sunflower seeds	1 cup seeds or 1¼ cup meal	64	.55	55
1¼ cups seeds or 1½ cups meal or ⅔ cup butter	sesame : milk	1 cup[2]	72	31	39
½ cup seeds or ¾ cup meal or ¼ cup sesame butter or tahini	sesame : beans	⅓ cup	64	19	35
½ cup	beans : milk	1 cup[2]	67	22	24
1 medium	potato : milk	1 cup[2]	67	9	36

[1] You may notice that some of the quantities (especially of soy products) differ from those listed in **Diet for a Small Planet.** I have changed these so that the ratios are internally consistent. For example: one-half cup of soybeans or grits will be equal to twice as much soy flour (one cup), regardless of which combination it occurs in; and you may use beans or grits or flour or tofu (in the amounts given) interchangeably.

[2] 1 cup milk = ⅓ grated cheese or ¼ cup cottage cheese or ⅓ cup ricotta or ¼ cup non-instant milk powder or ⅓ cup instant.

[3] These NPUs are estimated from the PER (Protein Efficiency Ratio) scores for each combination. PER is the ratio of weight-gain of experimental animals to the weight of protein consumed. See **Diet for a Small Planet,** Appendix D, for more details.

CHART IV—CALORIE/PROTEIN COMPARISONS

Listed here is the number of calories you have to con-sume in order to get *1 gram of usable protein* from se-lected foods. Foods having more than 60 calories per gram of protein are excluded.

Sources of Protein Listed in Increasing Order of Calories	No. of Calories per Gram of Usable Protein	Sources of Protein Listed in Increasing Order of Calories	No. of Calories per Gram of Usable Protein
1. Seafood*		Cottage cheese,	
Haddock	5	uncreamed	7
Cod	5	Creamed cottage	
Halibut	6	cheese	10
Shrimp	6	Nonfat milk and	
Squid	6	buttermilk	12
Lobster	6	Dried nonfat milk	
Rockfish	6	solids	12
Flounder or sole	6	Whole egg	14
Herring	8	Ricotta cheese	14
Clams	8	Parmesan cheese	16
Carp	8	Edam cheese	16
Swordfish	8	Plain yogurt from	
Tuna, bluefin	8	skim milk	18
Salmon, humpback	8	Swiss cheese	19
Bass, striped	8	Cheddar cheese	23
Mackerel, Pacific	9	Whole milk	23
Tuna, canned in oil	9	Camembert cheese	24
Shad	11	Blue mold cheese	24
Oysters	11	Roquefort cheese	26
Perch	13	Plain yogurt from	
Herring, Pacific,		whole milk	27
canned in oil	14	Yogurt sweetened,	
Sardines, Atlantic		w/fruit	30
canned in oil	22	**4. Fresh Vegetables**	
2. Nutritional Additives		Soybean sprouts	12
Egg white, dried	6	Mushrooms	14
Tiger's Milk	8	Broccoli	16
Brewer's yeast		Brussel sprouts	16
(nutritional yeast)	12	Kale	17
Baker's yeast	15	Spinach	18
Wheat germ	19	Asparagus	18
3. Dairy Products		Cauliflower	18
Dried egg white	6	Green limas	19
		Turnip greens	20

*Raw unless otherwise indicated.

Chard	20	protein)		40
Mustard greens	22	Oatmeal		41
Collards	24	Whole wheat bread		43
Mung bean sprouts	25	Buckwheat pancake		46
Peas	25	Pumpernickel		47
Okra	27	Rye bread and whole		
Artichoke	28	grain rye		48
Corn	37	Egg noodles, macaroni,		
Potato, white	60	and spaghetti		50
5. Legumes (Dry Seed)		Cracked wheat cereal		52
Tofu (soybean curd)	15	Bulgar, from hard red		
Soybeans	20	winter wheat		53
Mung beans	25	Cornbread with whole		
Broadbeans	28	ground meal		55
Split or whole peas	30	Millet		60
Cowpeas		Barley		60
(Blackeye peas)	33	Brown rice		69†
Limas	33	**8. Nuts and Seeds**		
Kidney beans (red)	39	Pumpkin and squash		
Common white beans	39	seeds		32
Garbanzos (chickpeas)	40	Pignolia nuts		36
Lentils	47	Sunflower seeds		40
6. Flour		Peanuts		49
Soybean flour,		Peanut butter		51
defatted	11	Cashews, roasted		55
Soybean flour, low fat	12	Whole sesame seeds		57
Soybean flour, full fat	18	Black walnuts		60
Gluten flour	23	Pistachio nuts		60
Rye flour, dark	34	Brazil nuts		88‡
Whole wheat flour	41	**9. For Comparison:**		
Buckwheat flour, dark	43	**Meat and Poultry**		
Barley flour	58	Chicken fryer, breast		7
Cornmeal, whole		Turkey, roasted		9
ground	80†	Lamb, lean only		10
7. Grains, Cereals, and		Porterhouse steak,		
Products		lean and marbled		14
Wheat germ	19	Hamburger		15
Wheat bran	24	Pork loin chop, lean		
Wheat, whole grain		and fat		18
(hard red spring		Lamb rib chop, lean,		
variety, w/most		marbled, and fat		32

†While cornmeal and brown rice exceed the stated limit, they are included because they are widely used as protein sources, and can be used in combinations that increase protein content and quality.

‡Brazil nuts also exceed the calorie limit but are included because of their very high content of sulfur—containing amino acids, a rare virtue among plant foods.

(From *Diet for a Small Planet*, pp.269-271)

Complementarity Simplified

You might wonder how I figured out the complements in each recipe. I made a small chart and tacked it right on the front of my refrigerator. (And every time someone comes into the kitchen for the first time they look curiously at the chart, then at me: "What's that?") While working on the recipes I used the chart and the most exact proportions possible for maximum usable protein.

I would like to suggest that a simple working knowledge of the basic complements, without actually knowing the precise proportions, can help to increase the protein in the dishes or meals that you make. For instance, if you make a bean loaf, what might complement those legumes? If you glance at the following chart you will see that legumes are complemented by seeds and whole grains, or, in certain cases, milk products. So without worrying about exact proportions you could make some brown rice, a nut-butter sauce, or a cheese sauce, or you could even serve a cottage cheese salad or salad dressing with the meal. It's really as simple as that. (For more precise proportions see Chart III.)

I am also including a list that was prepared by Frankie Lappé for use when she spoke to a group of Head Start people in the San Francisco area recently. This chart will give you more specific ideas about what you might add to various food categories for better protein. I have added a few suggestions of my own. See Appendix F.

CHART V—SUMMARY OF COMPLEMENTARITY

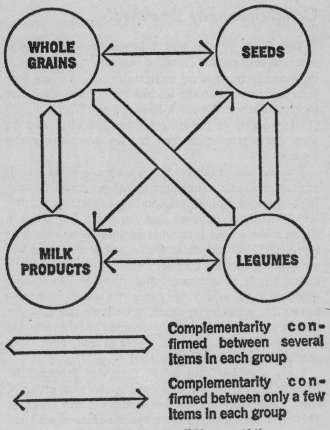

Complementarity confirmed between several items in each group

Complementarity confirmed between only a few items in each group

(After *Diet for a Small Planet*, p. 124)

II. Living with the Earth in Mind

A change to natural foods can be an experience of true liberation. Even though the food industry produces new plastic food products every day, there is nothing newer and more exciting than eating real foods that have simply grown up from the earth. Once we have learned to read labels and have discovered that most food products are largely sugar, modified food starch and flavorings, changing to natural foods is more like deciding to eat food instead of chemicals.

I once talked with my four-year-old neighbor about a flower that my husband Doug had picked on a fall afternoon. A sunburst of yellow, it was a giant puff with a perfect green stem and a mild scent like the memory of a meadow. "That isn't real," she said in her four-year-old voice, "and four-year-olds know." It was extremely difficult to explain how I knew that the flower was one that had grown in the earth. For each characteristic of the flower might have been manufactured in a factory; every aspect, except perhaps its death, could be duplicated by a machine.

I learned a heavy lesson. I had developed a sense for recognizing something that had grown naturally, but how was I to convey that sense to a child who is growing up in a world of plastics and synthetics?

To a small child, food is nearly anything that can be put in the mouth and swallowed, be it a crunchy sweet carrot pulled from the summer soil or a bottle of soda pop flavored, sweetened, carbonated, and of course preserved by chemicals. Does not a sausage grow on a sausage tree as does a peach on a peach tree? Some children will grow up never knowing why a carrot is different from soda pop, some will learn directly by not being able to plant soda pop in their gardens, and others will learn through their own ability to read and question what they have been eating all their lives.

What Is Natural Food?

The food I call "natural" is the food that resembles closely the state in which it grows (and I don't mean California). This means brown, not white rice; fresh, not canned vegetables. Ideally, I would have a cow or a goat and a year-round garden (Helen and Scott Nearing did it in Vermont) so I could grow everything that I need. Our garden now grows about nine months each year, so when I go to the supermarket and see the high prices for out-of-season produce it is easy to pass it by while thinking of the great abundance we had and will have soon again in our garden. We have lost our craving for peaches in the winter (even canned and frozen peaches are unappetizing in their adulterated forms), and all of the summer vegetables that are so beautiful in their time seem to lack something after being transported thousands of miles—to say the least. In the winter we rely on hearty dried foods like beans and rice, and winter soups which warm and fill you to the brim, heating the kitchen and steaming the windows while they cook on cold dark winter nights.

Using "natural" foods is a matter of practicality rather than fanaticism or purism. It is easy enough to begin with a dry bean if you're having beans for supper, but it's impractical to start with the soybean if what you need is some soy oil. I don't usually grind the wheat for flour, but we do often have fresh nut butters. We use canned tomatoes, but they are tomatoes that have come from our own garden surplus every fall.

24

We still have some choice about what we ingest for food. Each being has only one body, and he may choose to nourish that body with the foods that grow in the earth, or he may choose to have someone else harvest the earthy food, process it, add chemicals to it, mold it into a fancy shape, preserve it, put it into a plastic bag, put that plastic bag into a box, cover the box with more plastic, put a fancy price on it, call it new, tell us that it will taste good, and most incredibly, tell us that it is food that will sustain our bodies when we eat it!

Ecological Eating

As long as we are already inside a plastic bag in a plastic-covered box we can examine our eating habits from an ecological point of view. We have learned from *Diet for a Small Planet* that on an overall world basis we waste and waste again through the production of meat. But even after eliminating meat from the diet one can still make a lot of unnecessary garbage. Boxes, cans, plastic bags, and packaging for packaging—everything in your local supermarket comes wrapped. The food industry seems so hung up on the packaging business that even bananas and oranges, which nature carefully wrapped and protected eons ago, are also wrapped in plastic.

All of the garbage that we make as householders was once a living resource of the earth. Now, at least, there is some consciousness of the fact that the earth's resources are finite. However, let me give one example of the impracticality of the idea that we can just recycle everything. Our garbage has reached such proportions that recycling projects falter under the weight of the vast quantities of newspapers, cans, and bottles. In Berkeley, California, in the fall of 1970 a great recycling project was born. It seemed like a wonderful solution to some of the city's waste problems, and it would have involved many more people in recycling than were able to make the effort to get to the ecology center on their own. A group called "Volunteers of America" planned to pick up bottles and newspapers once a month from every address. Fantastic! Everyone was enthusiastic. One weekend we rode our bicycles around the city and were happily amazed at the piles of newspapers and bottles sitting on the curbs in anticipation of their collection the following Monday. Unfortunately, the program was abandoned after two months. The problem? Success. There was so much recyclable material that the Volunteers could not begin to handle the volume. So now some people continue to make the trip to the local recycling center, while others continue to send their garbage in the usual manner, unconcerned with its ultimate destination. Mountains of solid waste continue to grow, and even if recycling were working, it could not begin to cope with the continuous increase of waste in our society.

It seems obvious that we need to go backward—cut down on the amount of waste we produce—instead of putting so much energy into recycling. Let's see how natural foods enable us to take that step backward. First of all, making the choice of natural versus plastic food, we eliminate all of the packaging that is so essential to non-food (packaging needed for nothing more than to attract the eye of the shopper, since most non-foods would keep for years, box or no box). Because the natural food "craze" is not too big, there is very little packaged natural food, and those items that are packaged are usually prohibitively overpriced. In our community we are able to buy all of our staple foods in bulk either through our food "conspiracy"[1] or at local health food stores that do not operate for huge profits but are there to serve the people. We re-use bags, refill jars and cans as the need arises. You would be surprised how many times you can take one bag back to the store to have it refilled. You can eliminate packaging by keeping and reusing your own containers, and thus you have none of the type of trash (recyclable or not) that packaging creates.

Growing Your Own

One of the most important types of recycling, which can also be the most personally rewarding, is composting. Most of us have not lived close enough to nature to understand the great but subtle cycles that support life. Western man tends to ignore these cycles, and can rationalize logging or the vast use of pesticides without considering the long-term effects of his actions. In wil-

---

[1] The "Food Conspiracy" is a food-buying cooperative in Berkeley that claims to have about 1000 members in the community. We buy our food collectively from local farmers. It is then distributed to neighborhood groups and the neighbors distribute it to the families and individual members. These families and individuals are responsible for sharing the work involved in both their group organizations and in the group's commitment to the whole "conspiracy." Thus everybody can eat high-quality food (mostly organically grown items) at low prices. And in addition, by avoiding the middle man (i.e., grocery stores) we are working directly for the food that we need to survive instead of relying on the supermarket business to bring our food into the city.

derness areas where the forests have not recently been ravaged, the trees drop their leaves and branches down to the earth where they decompose and then supply the tree with nutrients needed for its own growth, or the growth of a small seedling.

In the city (which could easily be called a wilderness ravaged continuously by men) we found the soil to be hard clay. Who knows how long it had been since a tree had waved above it to drop some leaves? When we discovered, with the friends in our house, a tiny garden tucked between the row of garages and the unholy wall of a giant supermarket, we immediately began a compost pile. With the aid of friendly bacteria, many ambitious worms, the sun's energy, and our constant "feeding," the vegetable waste that we offer becomes rich fragrant soil asking to be returned to the exhausted earth. Even if we never planted any vegetables or flowers, it would be worth composting for the earth's sake. The area would be alive and ready to support growth.

But we did plant a garden and it bears delicious, nutritious vegetables for us. And for the fruit it gives us we must remember to make an offering in return. Each plant that grows removes nutrients from the soil. If we don't return those nutrients, our next crop (especially if it is the same vegetable) will have a deficiency. Chemical fertilizers don't make up the nutritional deficit either. In commercial farming in 1940, Kansas wheat had as much as 17% protein, but by 1951 (and this is more than twenty years ago already) no Kansas wheat had more than 14% protein.[1] If only we would all return our waste to the soil instead of dumping it into our nation's water supplies, we *could* have more nutritious food *and* less polluted lakes and streams.

---

[1] See *Diet for a Small Planet,* p. 18.

Compost, if worked with properly, will not smell out your neighbors. Besides, your neighbors should have a compost pile too. Why not start a community compost pile on your block and have a garden all together now? This can really be a delight if several backyards are connected: a giant garden, a big playground for all of the kids, a common community effort in working together, plus the reward of lots of delicious vegetables!

Complementary Camping

Basic complementary foods are ideal for camping. Since they are dry, they are lightweight and compact. We have had great success taking "complements" backpacking. Since there is very little vegetarian food available in freeze-dried form, we found it necessary to create our own protein combinations. We fill our backpacks with simple basic foods, and then to make our meals delicious we add extras—weightless items like spice mixtures prepared ahead (hot chili seasoning, Italian spices, curry, and a sweet spice mix made up of nutmeg, cinnamon, allspice, cardamom, ginger, et al.). We also add a few extravagant items that most backpackers wouldn't carry because of weight—honey, soy sauce, and bread (good whole-protein bread, of course).

Our first concern is to include a complement for every basic food in the exact proportions for maximum usable protein. For instance, if we are including 5 cups of raw brown rice, we mix in ½ cup of soy grits before we pack it up (see Chart III). We mix the right amount of milk powder (instant for camping) into the granola or familia, so the addition of hot or cold water is all that is needed for "instant" cereal.

Following is a fairly accurate list of what is needed for two average adults for ten days of complementary meals. Of course, you will have to adjust for your own appetite and the weight you want to carry. And if you are not going to backpack, this list should still help you to assemble the basics. Then you can add fresh vegetables, fruits, dairy products, and whatever you want (oil and popcorn)!

Ten days of food for two people will weigh 40 to 45 pounds!

5 cups raw brown rice mixed with ½ cup soy grits
2 cups bulgur or cracked wheat mixed with ⅓ cup soy grits
3 cups whole wheat noodles or macaroni (complement with grated cheese or milk powder)
6 cups dehydrated potato flakes mixed with salt and at least 6 tablespoons instant milk powder
3 cups of small beans (lentils, split peas, red, and mung beans cook quickly)
½ pound (or more) grated parmesan cheese—about 4 cups
3 pounds of hard cheese for sandwiches, snacks
dehydrated vegetables—as much as you want
3 loaves whole protein bread (see recipes on pp. 193-215) or 2 loaves of bread plus 1 package of rye crisp
1 cup of bean spread (see recipes pp. 55-64). You can also make this on the trail with the beans you're carrying.
1 cup peanut butter (or enriched peanut butter, p. 62)
20 cups of dry cereal (granola, familia—see recipes pp. 38-42) mixed with ⅓ cup instant milk powder for every cup of cereal. You may substitute instant oatmeal for part of the cereal.

3 to 4 pounds of dried fruit, all varieties—about 13 cups

10 cups of nuts of all kinds (mix sunflower seeds and peanuts in a ratio of 3 cups peanuts to 4 cups sunflower seeds)

1 huge recipe of super cookies (gorp cookies, or any whole-protein cookie—see recipes pp. 251-255)

hard candy for the trail

Condiments:

1 cup butter or margarine or ghee

1 cup to 12 ounces honey in a squeeze bottle

4 ounces of tamari soy sauce (tamari is more concentrated, so will go further), or substitute miso— more concentrated flavoring than tamari, but not as easy to use

½ to 1 cup sesame oil for sautéing wild onions, and for softening skin dried by the mountain sun and air

4 cups (approx.) instant milk powder

¼ cup each of mixed spices (hot chili, curry, Italian, and sweet) and salt

1 cup gomasio (sesame salt) made with roasted and ground sesame seeds mixed with salt to taste

teas

hot drink mixes—We take "postum" or "pero" and mix them with milk powder (instant) and raw sugar to taste. You can also do this with instant coffee or cocoa. OR take little containers of the drinks, a big one of milk powder, and use the honey you packed.

Extras: When we leave home there are always a few things in the refrigerator that won't keep till we return, so we find a place for things like hard-boiled eggs, a few carrots, and maybe a couple of oranges. These are a real treat the first days out.

Now you probably would like to know what to do with all of this food, both how to pack it up and how to cook it. We have a few packing tricks which free our camping days from time spent in transferring food from one broken plastic bag to another. Being fairly eco-conscious, I have a tendency to not throw out any container that might possibly contain food again. I save small yogurt cartons, containers from cottage cheese, cartons from pints of ice cream—anything that can be cleaned and has a tight-fitting lid. We use these to hold our food, along with plastic bags. You wouldn't want to put everything in a hard container because much pack space would be wasted. Although cardboard or plastic containers might add some weight, we find that the convenience is worth a few more ounces and eliminates a lot of wasted food. What do you do when the bottom of your pack has 5 cups of raw brown rice, a pound of crunchy granola, some hot chili spice, and dehydrated potatoes all mixed together? It would make an unusual meal (to say the least) if worse came to worst, but basically it's a big mess and a waste of food. Put both wet and dry things in secure containers—that is, wet things that would be messy if they got out (like bean spread, peanut butter, butter, honey), and dry things that must stay dry (like dehydrated potatoes, salt and spices, drink mixes, and other instant foods that react instantly to water).

Another packing trick is with bread. When the trip is planned we bake at least two loaves of bread in cans—one in a 48-ounce juice can and one in a 2-pound coffee can. The loaves are removed from the cans and cooled as usual. Once cooled, we put them back in the cans and put a plastic bag around each one. The trick is that the cans are our cooking pots. We use the 2-pound can for cooking big main dishes, and we try to use the smaller can for boiling water only. Doug usually cuts a coat hanger to measure one half the circumference of each can. He punches a hole in each side of the can, loops the hanger through, and there is a handle that folds completely out of the way. If you have a cover that fits the can, you can take it along to protect soaking fruit or grains.

Divide the food for the greatest ease in eating. One pack might contain all of the breakfast foods. One pocket could hold all of the condiments for dinner; another pocket might have spreads or bread. I won't specify exactly how the food should be divided because it depends on the types of packs, and on the weight that each tripper can carry.

Now that all of the food is packed, we can move on to the woods and spend our time experiencing the real life around us. Indulging completely in the pure pleasure of being alive, we seek only to satisfy our most basic needs. Some necessities that come from being civilized we carry on our backs, such as clothes, spoons, matches, and staple foods. The other things we will need are provided by nature—water, a bed of leaves, wild foods, and fuel for a fire. We have brought enough variety in food so that we have a large choice of what we'll eat, especially for our dinners. Daytime meals for us are usually irregular when we are hiking. We find that three or four stops on the trail for small snacks agree with us much more than eating a huge breakfast and lunch.

Breakfast can begin with some fresh fruit (the first few days) or soaked dried fruit, which is just as refreshing, either by itself or in granola. On cold mornings heat enough water to use in granola or instant oatmeal as well as for hot drinks. The final luxury is toast. Use a flat metal sheet or grate, toast one side, and while the second side toasts spread the first with butter or peanut butter, and honey.

Lunches and trail snacks might be any of the munchies that you've got in your pack. Usually we eat some cheese and rye crisp or bread, dried fruit or cookies, peanut butter and honey, or hard-boiled eggs (while they last) with gomasio. As long as you've included a variety of munchies, your lunches and snacks don't have to be dull.

Since dinner is usually the big meal and the one that is most structured and planned for, I have come up with five protein meals that will satisfy the stomach by filling you up, and provide enough variety so that you won't feel like you're eating the same thing every evening.

(1) For a hunger that needs to be satisfied immediately after a day on the trail: Boil a lot of water, add dehydrated vegetables if you have some (or fresh ones that you brought or found in the woods). Fill your cup with hot water and vegetables, add dehydrated *potatoes* to the consistency you like, and stir in butter, grated cheese, gomasio, salt or soy sauce. You might add milk powder and some hot chili spice. Round out the meal with some bread and bean spread or peanut butter, hot chocolate or postum, and a cookie or two.

(2) Another fairly quick meal is whole wheat *noodles* with butter, cheese (for complementing the wheat), plus one of the spices. We usually use about 1½ cups of dry noodles for the two of us. Hot chili spice or Italian spices are good. You can cook the noodles with some split peas or lentils or, if your bean spread has begun to ferment, you might stir it in. Of course you could include some fresh or dehydrated vegetables.

(3) When we stay in one spot for a day or more, we have very tender *rice and beans*. In the morning put about 1 cup of raw brown rice (already mixed with soy

grits) in the cooking can. (The lines on two-pound coffee cans are 2-cup marks, so you can measure pretty accurately.) Add a couple of handfuls of small beans and fill the can almost to the top with water. Put it where it will be warm during the day. Later, when you're ready to eat, the mixture should have increased in volume. Fire up the fire, set it on, and cook until the rice is tender. Add dehydrated vegetables, curry or Italian spice, salt, and water when necessary. Eat it with grated cheese and gomasio. The cheese will complement the gomasio and the beans you added. If you used split peas or lentils they will cook down to a delicious sauce that coats the rice. While you eat, continue to cook the mixture until it is very thick. Re-season it and pack it into a small container—you have a *sandwich spread* for tomorrow!

(4) *Sweet Spice Rice* is dinner that makes breakfast. Soak the rice all day if possible (as in #3). 1½ cups of raw brown rice should be enough for dinner and breakfast. Start cooking the rice, add 3 handfuls of raisins or other dried fruit, some mixed sweet spice to taste, and salt. When the rice is tender eat it with butter, honey, milk powder, and some walnuts or cashews. In the morning stir some hot milk and honey into the left-overs; heat it carefully for a hot, rich breakfast.

(5) *Bulgur wheat* will cook much faster than rice, so consider having it on days when you have cooking time but no soaking time (and you're too hungry to wait for unsoaked rice to cook.) Bulgur is good with Italian spice or hot chili spice or curry. Add beans, if you like, and vegetables. Eat the bulgur with soy sauce, cheese, and gomasio.

Half the meals have been prepared, and not one night has been the same. You can repeat the same five meals and add your own touches for the second half of the trip. When you are getting toward the tenth day, remember that it's quite possible to mix up whatever may be left into a big soup or stew. Since you have all of the complements with you, any combination will add up to high-quality protein. And do enjoy your trip.

III. The Recipes

Preface

This is a cookbook for daily living and eating, not a book to be used only when company comes or on special occasions. Many of the recipes require little preparation time; others take a good deal of time. I make no claim that meals will be as easy to prepare as meat-vegetables-and-potatoes (especially at first), but my purpose is not to show you how to throw a few things together for an "instant" meal.

If you are already complaining that you don't want to spend an extra minute in the kitchen, read no further. There is hardly a need for any cookbook when there are so many thousands of convenience foods at your supermarket. But let me say a word or two about this complaint, which I hear so frequently. Today, when most of the United States' population lives in cities, where there is rarely a patch of grass to rest one's soul or a tree to contemplate, food is perhaps the one thing left that enables us to interact directly with the earth. If we all took a little time to nourish our bodies in the best way possible (instead of in the quickest way), life could be long and healthy. If we choose to disregard the importance of what is in the food we eat, we may as well disregard the importance of having clean air to breathe. (But it should be obvious to all of us that most industries, including the food industry, consider profit before they consider air pollution and the internal pollution of our bodies.)

For me, cooking is using basic, simple and natural foods, putting them together into different appetizing forms (soups, loaves, salads), and seasoning them subtly to enhance their natural flavors. A table set with dishes of natural foods is not an empty extravaganza of rich, phony food, but a hearty feast of the earth providing all of the vitamins, minerals, and protein that our bodies need. (Those who eat mainly processed foods must obtain nutrients from various kinds of pills.)

If you have never experienced the gastronomical pleasures of eating whole grains or other natural foods, some of the dishes will be a surprise in the eating, unlike anything you have ever tasted before. The dishes vary from the exotic to downright plain, but the one quality that makes them all delicious is that they are made with unprocessed and otherwise unadulterated ingredients.

Once when I tried a variation on a recipe I discovered that it was just as delicious as the original. How could they be equally tasty with so many different ingredients? I discovered that if the basic ingredients are good natural foods, they will taste delicious no matter how you put them together (within reason)! With practice it becomes simple to create delicious basic (or fancy) meals with food from the earth.

'Tis The Gift To Be Simple

Simplicity can make a meal an elegant event. One of our favorites is hearty soup with fresh whole grain bread and natural cheese. A soup that is rich with vegetables, legumes, and grains will supply you with protein, vitamins, and a warm, full tummy!

Perhaps we were all brought up on meat, vegetables, and potatoes because no single food was satisfying by itself in both taste and nutrition. In the following recipes, many of the main dishes, soups, grain dishes, and vegetable dishes are totally satisfying to the palate and stomach and are also balanced nutritionally so they can be eaten as a one-dish meal. For the sake of variety and color I have also added menu suggestions that will fill out the meal with a minimum of preparation. If you spend a half hour making a nut loaf, there is no need to make an elaborate vegetable casserole to accompany it. Sautéed vegetables or a fresh raw salad will do the trick.

A Word To The Wise

Before you empty your kitchen of the familiar (and packaged) foods that you have always used, a word of warning. There is no easy way to make any kind of conversion, be it to a new religion, food, or way of life. All processes are more comfortable when they are worked out gradually. Changes must evolve slowly from within. When we find a better way of doing anything, changing from the old and comfortable (although "wrong") pattern is very difficult. Often a sudden shift will create the need for more "sacrifices" than we ever imagined. So don't throw away your sugar-frosted junkies until you can make good breakfast cereal without any fuss.

For those unfamiliar with natural food cookery, it would be best to try the recipes slowly, perhaps one each week at first. You need only buy the ingredients required for that particular recipe. And if you buy a little extra to store away, after trying several recipes you will have a good supply of natural foods. (The first time I went to a health food store I really went wild and bought a little of everything I saw. It was tremendous fun, but I didn't know what to do with half the food once I got it home!) Work with different types of foods to build up a group of several dishes that you can make well and feel comfortable serving. Then branch out and try the more exotic and time-consuming dishes.

To introduce your family to a new way of eating might cause problems at first. Instead of shocking them with many unfamiliar things, start by using the dishes as side dishes. Eventually they will become the center of interest! Start with familiar foods like soups, noodle and cheese dishes, and eggs. Feel free to adjust the recipes to your family's own tastes. If, for instance, some of your family doesn't like garlic or onions, you can eliminate them from the recipe, or you can substitute other vegetables, like celery or carrots. But don't change any of the protein ingredients—indicated by asterisks(*) in the recipes—as this could radically reduce the number of grams of usable protein in the recipe.

You may, however, substitute one whole grain for another (absolutely no white flour, please) or one type of bean for another without significantly changing the protein. And you won't ruin the recipe either. In cakes, quick breads, cookies and other dessert recipes, you may want to use more honey. Many children who are used to eating processed cookies made mostly from sugar may not like whole grain goodies right away. But if they are encouraged to chew well, the natural sweetness of whole grains soon becomes apparent.

Should Not All Food Be Health Food?

I hope you will find that natural food cookery can be as liberating as it is delicious. When we had our first natural food feast (prepared several years ago by my sister), it was an incredible learning experience. All of those weird grains, natural nuts and seeds were out of a new reality. Our supermarket shelves are overloaded with food *products* (and what are the implications of such a word applied to food?). But these products are either non-foods (which I call "plastic") or they are adulterated natural foods that have been processed and preserved to the point where they also deserve the adjective "plastic." Once natural foods become part of your daily meals, the supermarket will become inadequate and dull for your everyday shopping needs. Even if your supermarket is the most modern colossus giganticus, you are still being cheated out of dozens of foods. Health food stores are usually pretty small, but they can offer you one hundred times the excitement *and* good nutrition of your local superway.

All For Food and Food For All

For me, one of the most pleasing outcomes of using natural foods, and of the excitement that goes along with it, is that it truly sparked Doug's interest in cooking. Anyone who happens to be around our house at mealtime participates in the eating event. When everybody is hungry we decide together what we will eat. We gather in the kitchen, and then things start happening: someone washes vegetables, someone else chops; the pressure cooker hisses along gently while the rice and beans cook inside; the cheese is grated, and the salad dressing is made. There are many small chores that would consume a lot of one person's time, but by sharing the preparation nobody need be alone in the

kitchen, and each of us can add his personal touch to each dish. The meal is the outcome of a group effort, and it is usually a beautiful one at that (the meal *and* the group!).

Reading the Recipes

Be sure to see the section on Protein Complementarity so that the figures indicating *grams of usable protein* and *percent of average daily protein need* will be useful to you when you plan meals.

The boxes at the bottom of each recipe show the protein ingredients in terms of their complementarity—the relative amounts of grain and beans, for example, that combine to give maximum protein utilization in the recipe. Protein sources that are not complemented are also listed, so that you can see the whole protein picture for any particular dish.

I often indicate the size of a recipe by the number of portions. A *portion* is about what you would put in your bowl for your first, average-sized serving. If you share your meal with six friends, and seconds are anticipated, prepare a twelve-portion recipe, or double one with six portions.

If you're ready to start cooking, check the Glossary for unfamiliar foods, and check Chart III (High-Protein Combinations—Their Protein and Calories) to find substitutions for ingredients that are not available to you. Consult the appendices for basic cooking instructions and other ideas for setting up your kitchen to provide ease and comfort in cooking natural foods. EAT HEARTY!

What's for Breakfast?

It has been said over and over again that breakfast is the most important meal of the day. Whether you believe it or not, breakfast can be delicious and full of protein instead of full of empty calories and instant energy. If you are used to having a bowl of sugar-frosted junkies or even plain processed "cereal," you might find that true cereal grains, unadulterated and unprocessed, are much more delicious and satisfying. Whether you prefer hot or cold, cooked or uncooked, honeyed or unsweetened cereal, you will find at least one in the following section that you'll love with fresh fruit and milk.

If you aren't a cereal freak, you should have no trouble getting into some of the pancake and waffle recipes. Even though some are called pancakes and some waffles, they are interchangeable recipes. Use less liquid for pancakes, and make a thinner batter for waffles. Many of the waffle recipes are delicious desserts with ice cream or yogurt and fruit.

And if you don't like cereal, pancakes, or waffles, there's always that "perfect protein," egg, to fall back on, as well as dairy products that also have well-balanced proteins. I haven't included any egg recipes here because I feel that most cookbooks deal with them extensively. But let me suggest some other breakfast ideas for those who don't like to really eat in the morning. All of the high protein beverages make delicious liquid breakfasts. (You can pour them over cereal, too.) Or try having a bowl of yogurt and fruit with or without a little cereal sprinkled on top for flavor. And of course breakfast can always include sprout salads, fruit salads, coffee cake, quick breads, or whole grain toast. Let your imagination run free . . .

Cereals

All-Protein Crunchy Granola
about 12 cups

> 1 cup = approx. 8 grams of usable protein
> 16% to 19% of average daily protein need

Although it is delicious with milk, yogurt, and fruit, this granola requires no added milk protein to complement the grains. So eat it dry for snacks or camping.

½ to ¾ cup honey	*1 cup soy grits
½ cup oil	*1 cup wheat germ
1 tbsp vanilla	2 cups unsweetened
½ tsp salt	coconut, grated
*½ cup sesame seeds	*7 cups rolled oats

(1) In a large saucepan or dutch oven (cast iron works very well) heat the oil, honey, and vanilla until the mixture is thin.

(2) Turn off the heat and stir in the remaining ingredients in the order given. Make sure each ingredient is coated with the honey mixture (except for the coconut and rolled oats which you will just have to mix in).

(3) Put the dutch oven into your oven and turn the heat to 350°F. The cereal will begin to toast in about 15 minutes.

(4) Once it has begun to brown stir it every 5 to 10 minutes.

(5) I recommend that the cereal be toasted very

lightly, but toast it according to your own taste preference (or toast preference)! Be sure to stir it up from the bottom too.

(6)   Take the cereal out of the oven and let it cool before pouring into storage jars.

*

7	cups rolled oats : 1 tbsp soy grits
½	cup sesame seeds : about ⅓ cup soy grits
1	cup wheat germ

Familia
about 10 cups

1 cup = approx. 17 grams of usable protein
39% to 47% of average daily protein need

*2⅔	cups rolled oats
*2⅔	cups rolled wheat
*2	cups raw wheat germ
*¾	cup peanuts (raw or roasted), ground = about 1 cup meal
*1	cup sunflower seeds, raw or roasted
*¾	cup chopped peanuts, raw or roasted

1   cup (or more) raisins
1   cup unsulfured dried apricots or peaches chopped into bite-sized pieces, OR substitute other dried fruit. Familia is traditionally made with apples.

Stir in all of the ingredients together and store in a covered container. Serve with milk, yogurt, or buttermilk, golden honey or pure maple syrup.

Variations—

(1) *Fresh Fruit Familia:* In the spring and summer
     omit all of the dried fruits and use fresh grapes,
     peaches, strawberries or melon.

(2) *Sesame Familia:* Substitute 1 cup sesame seeds
     for sunflower seeds.

(3) *Traditional Familia:* is usually made with hazel-
     nuts and almonds, but for better protein I have
     substituted sunflower seeds and peanuts. You
     may add hazelnuts, almonds, or other nuts (cash-
     ews, walnuts) to the original recipe.

(4) *Camping Familia:* Add ⅓ cup instant milk pow-
     der for every cup of familia. Add hot or cold
     water and you have a bowl of cereal and milk!

Before you finish eating all of the familia check out the
familia cake recipe (p. 248).

* _____

2⅔   cups rolled oats, 2⅔ cups rolled wheat : ¾ cup
      peanuts : ¼ cup milk powder
  1   cup sunflower seeds : ¾ cup peanuts
  2   cups wheat germ

_____

Gramilia Cereal
about 10 cups

> 1 cup = approx. 13 grams of usable protein
> 30% to 36% of average daily protein need

*3 cups rolled oats
 1 cup unsweetened coconut
*1 cup sunflower seeds, toasted
*¾ cup roasted peanuts, chopped
*1 cup wheat germ

*2 cups rolled wheat
 1 cup chopped dates (or other dried fruit))
*1 cup chopped walnuts (or other nuts)

(1) Toast the oats in an oiled pan until lightly browned. Put them in a large bowl.
(2) Toast the coconut lightly, then mix with the oats.
(3) Stir in the seeds, peanuts, wheat germ, rolled wheat, dried fruit, and nuts.
(4) Serve the cereal with honey and *milk* to complement the oat and wheat proteins. For camping add a minimum of ⅔ cup instant milk powder. You would probably want to add about ⅓ cup instant for each cup of cereal, however.

*
_____

3 cups rolled oats : ¼ cup plus 2 tsp milk powder
1 cup sunflower seeds : ¾ cup peanuts
2 cups rolled wheat : 3 tbsp milk powder
1 cup wheat germ
1 cup walnuts

New Granola
about 12 cups

29% to 35% of average daily protein need
¼ cup milk plus 1 cup = approx. 13 grams of usable protein

*1   cup whole wheat
     flour
*1   cup rye flour
*1   cup yellow corn-
     meal
*1   cup soy flour
*½   cup wheat germ,
     toasted
 1   cup unsweetened
     coconut, toasted

*¼   cup sesame seeds,
     toasted
*1   cup sunflower
     seeds, toasted
oil
*2   cups rolled oats
*¾   cup roasted peanuts,
     coarsely chopped
 1   teaspoon salt
 1   cup honey
 ½   cup oil

(1)   Stir the flours together. Toast them over medium
      heat in a heavy cast iron frying pan or dutch
      oven. No oil is needed. Toast them until they are
      well browned, but not too dark. Watch carefully
      because once the flour gets hot it browns fast.
      Stir often.

(2)   Put the browned flours in a large mixing bowl and
      stir in the wheat germ, coconut, sesame, and sun-
      flower seeds. (If you have not already toasted
      these you can toast them in a dry pan one-at-a-
      time, then add to the flour.)

(3)   Now oil the pan and brown the oats until they are
      golden. Add these to the mixing bowl with the
      roasted peanuts. Stir everything together thor-
      oughly.

(4)   Heat the honey, oil, and salt in a small saucepan
      until the mixture is thin. Pour this over the cereal,
      blending carefully to spread it evenly.

(5) Let the cereal cool in the mixing bowl, where it will form large lumps. When cool, break it up and pour into storage jars.

(6) Serve this cereal with at least ¼ cup milk, buttermilk, or yogurt per serving. Add lots of fresh fruit. The milk is essential for complementing some of the grains (see below). If you want to take the cereal camping, add lots of instant milk powder; then when you're hungry, just add water.

*

¾	cup peanuts : 1 cup sunflower seeds
1	cup whole wheat flour, 1 cup rye flour, 2 cups rolled oats : ¾ cup plus 2 tbsp soy flour
½	cup cornmeal : 2 tbsp soy flour : 1 cup milk
¼	cup sesame seeds : ¼ cup milk
½	cup wheat germ
1¾	cups milk
½	cup cornmeal

Cinnamon Oatmeal
3 portions

> 1 portion = approx. 8 grams of usable protein
> 18% to 22% of average daily protein need

1¾	cups water	*2	tbsp soy grits
¼	tsp salt	*1⅓	cups rolled oats
1	tbsp cinnamon	*1	cup milk
¼	cup raisins (or more)		honey to taste

(1) Bring the water to a boil; add the salt, cinnamon, and raisins while it heats. When boiling, add the soy grits and rolled oats.

(2)   Lower the heat and cook the cereal, uncovered, until the water is absorbed and the oats are just tender. The mixture will become thick quite soon, but very little water is the trick to avoid slimy oatmeal. (If you prefer a gooey oatmeal, start with ¼ to ½ cup more water.)

(3)   Serve the cereal with ⅓ cup milk per portion. Add honey to taste.

Variation—Use ⅔ cup rolled wheat and ⅔ cup rolled oats. Add the wheat when the oats are nearly cooked.

*
───

1⅓   cups rolled oats : 2 tbsp soy grits
  1   cup milk

───

A Cold Morning for Hot Peanut Cereal
2 portions

1 portion = approx. 20 grams of usable protein
46% to 56% of average daily protein need

This cereal reminds me of peanut butter cookies. The raw peanut meal and raisins make it naturally sweet. Using all whole wheat flour, rather than cracked wheat, makes a very creamy cereal that is good for small children's breakfasts. Cracked wheat gives you a more coarsely textured cereal, so experiment with both to find the consistency your family likes best.

2½	cups water (or milk[1])	*¾	cup raw peanut meal
¼	tsp salt	*1½	tsp soy grits
*½	cup whole wheat flour OR cracked wheat OR combination making ½ cup	¼	cup raisins (more to taste)
		1-2	tbsp honey
		*½	cup milk[1]

(1) Start heating the water and salt. Stir in the flour, peanut meal, and grits using a wire whisk to stir the mixture smooth. Add the raisins and honey.

(2) While you are adding ingredients to the heated water the mixture will come to a boil. Turn the heat down quickly to avoid a boiled-over mess.

(3) Cook the mixture uncovered over medium-low heat until it thickens, about 10-15 minutes depending on how thick you like it. Serve with milk.

Variation—Peanut-Buckwheat Cereal: Substitute ½ cup buckwheat flour or flaked buckwheat for the whole wheat flour.

* _____

½ cup whole wheat flour : 2 tbsp peanut meal : 1½ tsp soy grits

⅔ cup peanut meal : ½ cup milk

_____

---

[1] When made with milk, this cereal is extremely rich and has even more protein than indicated above. We find it to be rich enough when made with water, with milk added at the table. Whatever combination of milk or water you choose, be sure to include at least ½ cup of milk. This ½ cup of milk complements most of the peanut meal (see above).

Wheat Sesame Cereal
2 portions

> 1 portion = approx. 7 grams of usable protein
> 17% to 20% of average daily protein need

*1	cup rolled wheat	*2 tbsp sesame seeds,
*1	tbsp soy grits	roasted and ground
¼	tsp salt	1½ cups water

(1) Bring the water to a boil; add the salt, soy grits, and rolled wheat. Lower the heat to a simmer and cook until the mixture is thick. (Thickening may happen very quickly with some types of rolled wheat.)

(2) Stir in the sesame seeds just before serving. Add honey and milk if you like.

Variation—Very Sesame Cereal: Add 5 or 10 tbsp more sesame seed before serving. Be sure to use ¼ cup of milk or yogurt for each 5 tbsp sesame. (For each 5 tbsp sesame and ¼ cup milk you add to a serving you will double the grams of usable protein in that serving!)

---
*

1   cup rolled wheat : 1 tbsp soy grits : 2 tbsp sesame seed

Pancakes and Waffles

Oatmeal Pancakes
16 pancakes

> 2 pancakes = approx. 5 grams of usable protein
> 11% to 14% of average daily protein need

These pancakes have an interesting texture, and they are hearty!

*½	cup whole wheat flour	1	tsp salt
*1½	cups rolled oats	*1	egg, beaten
1	tbsp baking powder	1	tbsp oil
		1	tbsp honey
		*1½	cups milk

(1) Stir the dry ingredients together in a large mixing bowl. Add the remaining ingredients and stir until well mixed.
(2) Fry on a hot oiled griddle, turning when the edges begin to get firm.

---

*

1 egg
½ cup whole wheat flour : ¼ cup milk
1½ cups rolled oats : ⅔ cup milk
about ½ cup milk

Orange Pancakes with Orange Sauce
4 portions

> 1 portion = approx. 19 grams of usable protein
> 44% to 53% of average daily protein need

This dish is a real beauty. When you slice it into wedges it looks like a four-layer cake with white filling, glazed with orange. With cottage cheese and a small amount of honey you have a perfect breakfast. With ricotta cheese and a larger amount of honey this dish is rich enough for dessert, and an elegant one at that! (And look at all the protein!)

*1	cup plus 2 tbsp whole wheat flour	*1	egg, beaten
*⅓	cup soy flour	3	tbsp honey
½	tsp salt	*¼	cup milk
2	tsp baking powder	¾	cup orange juice
2	tsp grated dry orange rind OR 1 tbsp grated fresh rind	3	tbsp oil OR melted butter
		*1	to 1½ cups cottage OR ricotta cheese

(1) Stir the dry ingredients together in the order given.

(2) In a separate bowl combine the egg, honey, milk, orange juice, and oil.

(3) Stir the wet ingredients into the dry—don't stir too much, just enough to moisten the dry ingredients well.

(4) Make four large pancakes on an oiled griddle. Use about ⅔ cup batter for each.

(5) Stack them up while spreading ⅓ to ½ cup cottage cheese between each one, ending with a pancake.

(6) For serving, cut the cake in wedges and pass Orange Sauce (below).

Orange Sauce:

1 tbsp cornstarch	1 cup orange juice
¼ tsp salt	¼ to ½ cup honey
2 tbsp freshly grated orange rind OR 1 tbsp dried rind	1 tbsp butter
	1 fresh orange, divided into sections

(1) Mix the cornstarch, salt, orange rind, orange juice, and honey in a small saucepan. Bring the mixture to a boil over medium heat, stirring constantly until thickened.

(2) Remove from the heat; stir in the butter until it melts. Add the orange sections. Serve warm with the pancakes.

* _____

1 cup plus 2 tbsp whole wheat flour : ⅓ cup soy flour
1 egg
¼ cup milk
1½ cups ricotta or cottage cheese

Sesame Waffles
7 waffles

> 1 waffle = approx. 5 grams of usable protein
> 12% to 14% of average daily protein need

Light waffles with a delightful sesame crunch!

*1 cup milk	*1 cup whole wheat flour
*1 egg, beaten	
½ tsp vanilla	2 tsp baking powder
2 tbsp honey	½ tsp salt
	*⅔ cup sesame seeds

(1) Beat the egg and milk together, then beat in the vanilla and honey.

(2) Stir in the whole wheat flour, baking powder, and salt.

(3) Fold in the sesame seeds and the batter is ready to be baked on a hot, oiled waffle iron.

* _____

1	egg
⅔	cup sesame seeds : ½ cup milk
1	cup whole wheat flour : ½ cup milk

Carob Yogurt Waffles
8 waffles

> 1 waffle = approx. 5 grams of usable protein
> 12% to 15% of average daily protein need

This recipe and its variation make rich, sweet waffles. You may serve them with butter and syrup, but for a delicious dessert serve them with ice cream—a real treat!

*1	cup yogurt	1	tsp baking soda
*1	cup milk	2	tsp baking powder
*2	eggs, beaten	*1⅔	cups whole wheat
2	tbsp honey		flour
3	tbsp soft butter	⅓	cup carob powder
½	tsp salt		

(1) If you have a blender, buzz all of the liquid ingredients in the order given. Otherwise, combine them in a mixing bowl.

(2) Stir the dry ingredients together in a large bowl, then add the liquid to them.

(3) Bake the waffles on a hot, oiled waffle iron.

Variation—Chocolate Spice Waffles:

      (1) Substitute ⅓ cup cocoa for carob powder.
      (2) Use ⅓ cup honey instead of 2 tbsp.
      (3) Add the following to the dry ingredients:
        ½ tsp cinnamon, ¼ tsp each nutmeg, allspice, and cloves.

*

 ⅚ cup milk : 1⅔ cups whole wheat flour
 1 cup yogurt
 ⅙ cup milk
 2 eggs

Peanut Butter Waffles
8 waffles

> 1 waffle = approx. 8 grams of usable protein
> 19% to 25% of average daily protein need

These waffles are crisp and light. Slightly sweet, they have just a subtle, but delicious taste of peanut butter.

*1   cup whole wheat flour
*¼   cup milk powder (⅓ cup instant)
½   tsp salt
2   tsp baking powder

*2   eggs, beaten
¼   cup honey
½   tsp vanilla
*½   cup peanut butter
1¼   cups water (or milk[1])

(1)   Stir together the flour, milk powder, salt, and baking powder.
(2)   In a separate bowl, beat the eggs, honey, vanilla, and peanut butter. Then mix in the water.
(3)   Add the liquid mixture to the dry and stir until the ingredients are smooth.
(4)   Bake on a hot, oiled waffle iron.

Variation—Peanut Butter Pancakes: Use the same recipe as above, but use only ¾ cup water (or milk[1]).

*————————————————————————————————

1   cup whole wheat flour : 2 tbsp peanut butter : 1 tbsp milk powder
6   tbsp peanut butter : 2¼ tbsp milk powder
2   eggs

————————————————————————————————

[1] If you choose to use milk, you will get slightly more usable protein and richer waffles or pancakes.

Sunflower Rolled Waffles
6 waffles

> .. 1 waffle = approx. 7 grams of usable protein
> 16% to 19% of average daily protein need

These waffles are hearty, but not particularly heavy. They are full of good texture and crunch.

*1	cup rolled oats	2	tbsp oil
*1	cup rolled wheat	2	tbsp honey
2	cups hot water	¼	tsp salt
*6	tbsp milk powder	*⅔	cup sunflower seeds
	(½ cup instant)	2	tsp baking powder
*1	egg, beaten		

(1) Put the oats and wheat into a small mixing bowl. Pour the hot water over them and stir. Let them sit and soften for a few minutes.

(2) Add the remaining ingredients in the order given, stirring carefully after each addition.

(3) To bake, spread about ½ cup of batter over a hot, oiled waffle iron. Use a wooden spoon to spread the batter almost to the edge (as this batter doesn't spread like thin waffle batters).

(4) Bake until very brown and crisp. Serve with yogurt, applesauce, and cinnamon, or syrup and butter.

* _____

2	cups rolled grain : 3 tbsp milk powder
⅔	cup sunflower seeds : 3 tbsp milk powder
1	egg

What's for Lunch?

Lunch at our house is a time for leftovers or quick sandwiches. Main-dish bean loaves make delicious sandwich fillings whether you spread or slice them. Salad lunches are refreshing treats, especially when you use your own garden's vegetables and add, for protein, nuts, seeds, and cheese, or a creamy yogurt or cottage cheese dressing.

Try some of the bean spreads with melted cheese, and if you don't want bread today dip raw vegetables into a Middle Eastern Garbanzo Spread.

On cold winter days lunch can be hot soup, but cold (even leftover) soup right out of the refrigerator is an unusual summer dish that most of us don't consider making when we plan summer meals.

There's always cheese, cold or toasted, and nut butters galore. Remember to complement butters with milk products of some kind . . . even if it's just to have a glass of milk with your peanut butter sandwich.

So let's have some lunch!

Sandwiches

Doug's Super Toasted Cheese Sandwiches
4 sandwiches

> 2 sandwiches = approx. 11 grams of usable protein
> 25% to 30% of average daily protein need

This sandwich evolved slowly through many lunches. It is a delicious, easy-to-prepare snack for many people—if you do it on an assembly line! Or prepare them before everyone is hungry, then broil them all at once when the word is food!

*4 slices whole grain bread, toasted	black or green olives, chopped
mustard or ketchup	*4 slices of cheese (that will cover the bread)
1 tomato, sliced thin	
1 dill pickle, sliced	chopped onion

(1) Spread each slice of toast with mustard or ketchup; layer on a tomato slice, pickle, chopped olives, and cover with cheese slices.

(2) Sprinkle the chopped onion over the cheese; broil until the cheese is melted and the onions are sizzling.

---

* _____

    4 slices whole grain bread : 4 slices cheese

Quick Rye Crisp Pizzas

Rye crisp (plain) is one of those packaged products that is still without preservatives, made simply enough with rye flour and water. One day when we were out of bread we discovered that a delicious and quick pizza-like sandwich could be made:

Break the *rye crisp* so that it will fit in your toaster oven, or leave whole for oven broiling.

Spread it evenly with *tomato sauce* from a can. Sprinkle the sauce with *garlic powder* and *oregano*.

Grate whatever *cheese* you have around and sprinkle it over the sauce. Top with chopped *onions,* then broil until the cheese melts and bubbles.

Eat!!

Garden Sandwich
4 sandwiches

> 1 sandwich = approx. 9 grams of usable protein
> 20% to 24% of average daily protein need

Take these sandwiches out to the garden and eat them in the sun. They will stay warm to the last bite. Have a fresh vegetable salad right from the garden, too!

*4 slices whole grain bread	1 sliced tomato
*½ cup Soy-Sesame-Peanut spread (see below)	*4 thick slices of cheese to cover the bread

(1) Spread 2 tablespoons of S.S.P. spread on each slice of whole grain bread. Cover with tomato slices, and top with cheese.

(2) Broil until the cheese melts.

Soy-Sesame-Peanut Spread[1]
For 2 cups:

½ cup roasted soy flour	⅓ cup (heaping) peanut butter
	½ cup sesame butter

(1) Blend the ingredients together, adding water if necessary.

(2) Season with onion and garlic powder.

* _____

½ cup Soy-Sesame-Peanut spread
4 slices whole grain bread : 4 slices cheese

_____

[1] From *Diet for a Small Planet*, p. 229.

Spreads

Middle Eastern Garbanzo Spread
2 cups

¼ cup = approx. 4 grams of usable protein
10% to 12% of average daily protein need

*⅔ cup dry garbanzo beans, cooked very tender

1 large onion, minced and sautéed in sesame oil with 1–2 cloves garlic, crushed or minced

juice of two lemons

1 tbsp soy sauce

½ tsp salt

*¼ cup tahini or sesame butter

*½ cup whole sesame seeds, roasted and ground (¾ cup roasted sesame meal)

(1) Puree the garbanzo beans with a small amount of their cooking water. Put about ½ cup of the puree back into the blender with the sautéed onion and garlic; buzz until smooth, then add the mixture to the rest of the garbanzo puree.

(2) Add the remaining ingredients and combine thoroughly.

(3) Chill the mixture and serve as a dip with taco chips or raw vegetables; or spread it on bread or crackers.

Variations—Garbanzo Vegetable Sauce: Thin the spread with more lemon juice, heat it gently and serve it over hot vegetables or casseroles.

Thick Garbanzo Spread: Add 1 to 2 cups of ricotta cheese to the spread (or substitute pureed cottage cheese). This will expand as well as thicken it. Adjust the seasoning.

* _____

⅓ cup garbanzos : ½ cup sesame seeds
⅓ cup garbanzos : ¼ cup sesame butter

_____

Pizza Spread
6 cups

½ cup = approx. 8 grams of usable protein
19% to 23% of average daily protein need

This spread makes a good party appetizer as well as a sandwich spread. It freezes well too, so make a big recipe and store it away.

*1 pound cheddar cheese   finely chopped and sautéed mushrooms
*3 hard-boiled eggs   1 medium onion
1 small can of chopped black olives OR 2–3 cups   salt
    chili powder
    oregano

(1) If you have a food grinder: grind the cheese, eggs, and onion. If you don't have a food grinder: grate the cheese, chop the eggs and onion. Blend in the olives, salt, and chili powder to taste.

(2) Spread on whole wheat sour dough french bread (p. 170), sprinkle with oregano, broil until bubbly, about 2 or 3 minutes.

* _____

3 eggs
1 pound cheddar cheese

_____

Blue Ricotta Spread
about 1 cup

> 2 tbsp = approx. 4 grams of usable protein
> 9% to 11% of average daily protein need

Blue cheese is awfully strong to eat alone as a spread, but the mild flavor of ricotta mellows it perfectly.

*½ cup blue or roque-   temperature
    fort cheese,   *¾ cup ricotta cheese
    softened to room

(1)   Blend the cheeses together with a knife.
(2)   Spread on whole grain bread, and eat as is; or
      broil briefly to make it soft and aromatic.

* _____

¾   cup ricotta
½   cup blue cheese

_____

Peanut Paté
6 cups

> ¼ cup = approx. 5 grams of usable protein
> 12% to 14% of average daily protein need

We have taken Peanut Paté backpacking. It will ferment after 4 to 5 days, but it's still delicious and tangy.

*⅔ cup dry soybeans,   2   tbsp soy sauce
    cooked very tender   1   tsp salt
*1½ cups raw peanuts,   *1¾ cups sesame OR
    cooked very tender   sunflower seeds,
1½ medium onions   ground (about 2⅓
1   clove garlic   cups meal)

(1)   Grind the cooked soybeans and peanuts in a food

grinder, OR puree them in a blender, OR mash them with a fork.

(2) Buzz in a blender the onions, garlic, and soy sauce, OR grate the onion and mince the garlic.

(3) Combine the onion mixture with the beans; add the salt and sesame or sunflower meal.

(4) Let the mixture sit for 24 hours so the flavors can mingle. If you let it sit at room temperature you will have a spread with a bit of a bite! After it sits you may freeze all or part of the paté.

---

* _____

1½ cups peanuts : ½ cup soybeans : 1¾ cups sesame seeds
⅙ cup soybeans

Sunflower-Peanut Butter
about 1¼ cups

> ¼ cup = approx. 11 grams of usable protein
> 25% to 30% of average daily protein need

This recipe could be very complicated for a simple nut butter. What is important is the proportion of sunflower seeds to peanuts. If you substitute butter for nuts, or meal for sunflower seeds, just be sure the proportions are correct. You may also use either raw or roasted nuts, seeds, meals, or butters in any combination.

*1 cup sunflower seeds OR 1¼ cups sunflower seed meal OR ½ cup sunflower seed butter, raw or roasted

*¾ cup peanuts, OR 1 cup peanut meal, OR ½ cup peanut butter, raw or roasted

(1) For whole seeds and nuts: grind them together in

your blender, adding ¼ to ½ cup oil to start them into butter. Add salt to taste.

(2)   For meals: stir the meals (and salt) together. Add oil to turn them into butter.

(3)   For butters: simply combine the two butters, adding salt if desired.

(4)   *Combinations:* A delicious and crunchy butter could be made by reserving about ⅓ to ½ cup of whole sunflower seeds. Add these whole seeds (raw or toasted) to the finished butter.

*

1   cup sunflower seeds : ¾ cup peanuts

Ricotta and Peanut Spread
about 2½ cups

2 tbsp = approx. 5 grams of usable protein
11% to 14% of average daily protein need

This is a light peanut buttery spread that gives you a new texture and a slightly different taste for peanut butter sandwiches!

*1   cup peanut butter,   *1¼   cups ricotta cheese
      either crunchy or   1-2   tbsp honey
      plain

(1)   Stir the peanut butter and ricotta together until they're fluffy.

(2)   Stir in the honey.

Variations—

Spiced Ricotta and Peanut Spread: Add cinnamon and nutmeg to the recipe.

Savory Ricotta and Peanut Spread: Omit the honey. Season with garlic and onion (powders or fresh). Add a little salt and a pinch of oregano or thyme.

---

* _____

> 1 cup peanut butter : ½ cup ricotta
> ¾ cup ricotta

_____

Enriched Peanut Butter
about 1 cup

> 2 tbsp = approx. 11 grams of usable protein
> 24% to 29% of average daily protein need

Use this spread in place of regular peanut butter for sandwiches. Try stuffing celery stalks with it for snacks. Complemented peanut butter has a usable protein increase of 20%.

*1 cup peanut butter	2 to 3 tbsp soft butter
*⅓ cup milk powder	OR oil
(½ cup instant)	(3 tbsp honey— optional)

(1) Add a few drops of water to the milk powder and stir it into a smooth paste.
(2) Blend it into the peanut butter with a knife, then blend in the butter or oil (and honey).

* _____

> 1 cup peanut butter : ⅓ cup milk powder

_____

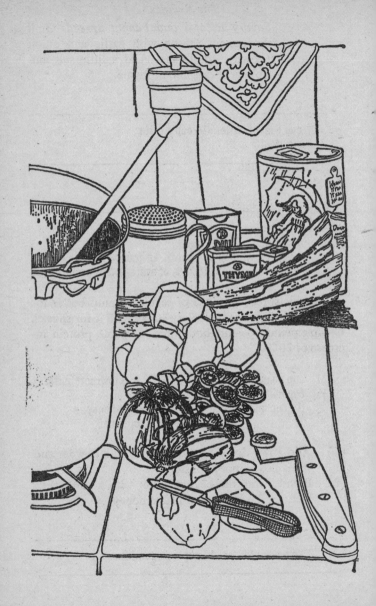

Meals in One Pot (Soups and a Stew)

When winter comes, soups and stews warm our insides most. I love the steamy kitchen windows on cold dark nights, the smells of soup and freshly baked bread. Yeast breads, hot from the oven, are so scrumptious with soup. But it's quicker and just as delicious to make quick breads or muffins.

Can you make soup that's much better than what comes condensed in a can or dried in an envelope? A few adventures with the following soups will convince you of their superiority in taste, freshness, and high-quality protein. There are no convenience soups available that combine whole grains, beans, or noodles to make high-quality protein. In fact, most prepared soups use white noodles and white rice that fill you up with calories and starch, but no protein.

When you make your old favorites, add any protein combination. After you have made a few of the following soups, you will know how easy it is to increase the protein in your own recipes.

Have soup for lunch or dinner with delicious bread.

Barley and Yogurt Soup
about 2½ quarts

> 1 cup = approx. 6 grams of usable protein
> 13% to 16% of average daily protein need

This is a very rich soup that gets thicker and thicker as it cools. You might use left-over soup as a vegetable sauce seasoned with cayenne or curry. Everyone at our house thought the soup was very elegant. A small serving wouldn't be too rich for a first course, but with a big salad and a couple of bowls-full, your meal is complete.

*1½	cups raw barley, cooked	2	tbsp or more chopped onion
1	quart cold water	2	tbsp butter
*2	cups yogurt	2	to 3 tsp salt
*4	eggs	2	tbsp chopped fresh green herbs, such as parsley, coriander or chives
2	tbsp whole wheat flour		

(1) Stir the yogurt into the quart of cold water in a large mixing bowl. Set aside.

(2) Beat the eggs in a large saucepan or soup pot and whisk the flour into them gradually; then whisk in the yogurt mixture.

(3) Put the pot over a high flame; don't let it boil, but keep it simmering until it thickens slightly. Stir or whisk often.

(4) Stir in the cooked barley, onions, butter, and salt. Sprinkle with the fresh herbs just before serving.

* _____

2 cups yogurt : 1½ cups barley
4 eggs

_____

Black Bean Soup
3 quarts

> 1 cup = approx. 4 grams of usable protein
> 9% to 11% of average daily protein need

Accompany this soup with whole wheat sourdough french bread for a hearty meal.

*1   cup dry black
     beans, cooked
¼   cup oil
1   cup chopped
     onions
1   cup chopped
     celery
2   cloves garlic,
     crushed OR
     minced
*⅔   cup raw brown rice

5-6 cups stock
⅛   tsp cayenne
1   bay leaf
½   tsp thyme
½   tsp dry mustard
1-2 tsps salt
2   peppercorns
2   whole cloves
*6   tbsp milk powder
     (½ cup instant)

(1) Drain the beans when they are tender and mash
     them slightly with a fork. (The bean stock would
     be excellent stock for the soup, so don't throw it
     away.)

(2) Heat the oil in a large soup pot or pressure cooker
     that holds at least 4 quarts. Sauté the onions, cel-
     ery, garlic, and rice until the vegetables are soft
     but not browned.

(3) Stir in one cup of stock; and while continuing to
     cook over low heat, add the herbs and spices.
     You might want to put the bay leaf, peppercorn,
     and cloves in a teaball or a square of cheesecloth.

(4) Add the remaining stock and the black beans.

(5) Cover the pot and pressure cook for 10 minutes
     OR simmer 2 to 3 hours.

(6) Blend the milk powder with about ½ cup of the
     soup and add the mixture back to the pot. Ready
     for serving . . .

Variation—Add a can of tomatoes and their stock for a
            thinner soup. Adjust the seasoning.

* _____

¾   cup black beans : 6 tbsp milk powder
¼   cup black beans : ⅔ cup brown rice

Luscious Potato Soup
about 2½ quarts

> 1 cup = approx. 5 grams of usable protein
> 12% to 15% of average daily protein need

This soup is extremely hearty. It precludes the need for much beside toast or crackers to make a complete meal. Serve some beer for a true peasant feast!

¼	cup oil	1	quart stock
2	cups chopped onions	2	tsps salt
1	cup diced carrots	1	tsp marjoram
1	cup chopped celery	1	tsp dill seeds
*6	medium potatoes, diced	½	tsp paprika
		1	tsp caraway seed
		*1½	cups milk powder (2 cups instant)

(1) Heat the oil in a pressure cooker or large soup pot; sauté the onions, carrots, celery, and potatoes until the onions are transparent.

(2) Pour in the stock, salt, and spices (not the milk powder), bring to a boil, cover and pressure cook 20 minutes, OR simmer about 1 hour until the potatoes are very tender, but won't fall apart.

(3) Dissolve the milk powder in 1½ to 2 cups of the soup liquid. You might do this in the blender to avoid lumps. Return the mixture to the pot and simmer about 1 minute. Serve hot with toast.

Variation—Thin Potato Soup: Instead of using milk powder, add 6 cups of milk and adjust the seasoning.

* _____

6   potatoes : 1½ cups milk powder

_____

Curried Garbanzo Soup
4 portions

1 portion = approx. 6 grams of usable protein
13% to 15% of average daily protein need

This soup is a fine example of how a rich stock can make a simple soup flavorful and unusual. If you have a mild stock, you may want to add other seasonings. Carrots and celery add a touch of sweetness to a pungent base.

*½   cup dry garbanzos, cooked tender
 4   cups stock
 1   tsp curry powder
*¼   cup milk powder (⅓ cup instant)
 1   large carrot, sliced small
 1   stalk celery, chopped
salt and pepper to taste

(1) Heat the stock, then remove a small amount of it for pureeing the garbanzos. Buzz the beans in a blender, then add them to the pot.

(2) Sprinkle in the curry, and add the milk powder. (You might blend the milk powder in the blender as long as it's already been used.)

(3) Bring the soup to a boil; add the celery and carrots. Simmer the soup until the vegetables are tender but not mushy. Serve hot, or try it cold if there is some left over.

*
½   cup garbanzos : ¼ cup milk powder

Creamy Mushroom Soup
about 3 quarts

1 cup = approx. 5 grams of usable protein
12% to 15% of average daily protein need

1½	cups chopped on-ions	5	cups hot stock
		2	tsp salt
*3	cups chopped mushroom stems	¼	tsp paprika
7	tbsp butter	*4	cups sliced mushroom caps
3	tbsp oil		
1	cup hot water (or stock)	¼	cup or more chopped parsley
		¼	cup dry white wine
*3	medium potatoes, about 4 cups, diced small	*1½	cups milk powder (2 cups instant)

(1) Melt three tablespoons of the butter and 2 table-spoons of the oil in a large soup pot. Sauté the onions and mushroom stems for about 15 min-utes, until the onions are transparent and begin to brown. Stir in the 1 cup of stock and simmer for 10 minutes. Put the mixture into a blender and buzz until it's completely smooth. Set the puree aside.

(2) Melt 2 tablespoons of butter and the remaining ta-blespoon of oil in the same soup pot. Add the po-tatoes and sauté them over low heat, stirring for about 7 minutes until they become translucent. Stir in the mushroom-onion puree and five cups of stock. Bring the mixture to a boil, lower the heat, cover, and simmer for 15 minutes, stirring occasionally until the mushrooms are tender.

(3) In a small frying pan sauté the sliced mushroom caps in the remaining 2 tablespoons of butter un-til they are soft.

(4) Stir the salt and paprika into the soup pot along with the sautéed cap slices, and the wine.

(5) Simmer the soup while you mix the milk powder with a small amount of water to make a paste. Add this to the soup and simmer a few more minutes while you check the seasoning. Now it's ready to serve.

* _____

```
3   potatoes : ¾ cup milk powder
¾   cup milk powder
7   cups mushrooms
```

Hot Cheese Soup
about 1½ quarts

> 1 cup = approx. 21 grams of usable protein
> 49% to 59% of average daily protein need

This soup is decidedly spicy. If you are not fond of chilies, omit them and the soup will be mild. It's a filling soup, but it sparks the appetite, so it's an ideal first course.

2	tbsp butter	5	cups stock (or stock and wine)
¼	cup minced onion		
¼	cup finely chopped carrots	*½	cup sesame tahini OR sesame butter
¼	cup finely chopped celery	*½	pound cheddar (or other soft cheese), grated—about 2 cups
¼	cup finely chopped red or green sweet pepper		
		*6	tbsp milk powder (½ cup instant)
2	tbsp minced hot green chili pepper	1	tsp salt
*¼	cup whole wheat flour	*1¼	cups toasted sunflower seeds

(1) Melt the butter in a large soup pot; sauté the onion, carrots, celery, green pepper, and hot pepper until all the vegetables are soft, but not brown.

(2) Stir in the whole wheat flour and heat for 1 minute; add the stock and bring the mixture to a boil.

(3) Use a whisk to blend in the tahini (which will look curdled). Lower the heat and simmer for five minutes.

(4) Add the cheese by handfuls, whisking until each one has melted completely. Carefully whisk in the milk powder (or use a blender to buzz it with 1 cup of the soup).

(5) Add the salt, and just before serving stir in the sunflower seeds.

*_____

1½ tablespoons milk powder	: 1¾ cups grated cheese
¼ cup whole wheat flour	: 1½ teaspoons milk powder
½ cup tahini	: ¼ cup grated cheese
1¼ cups sunflower seeds	: ¼ cup milk powder

_____

Peanut Soup
1½ quarts

1 cup = 16 grams of usable protein
37% to 45% of average daily protein need

A bowl of this soup for lunch and you have nearly half your daily protein accounted for. Your kids should like the peanutty taste, too.

3 tbsp butter	½ tsp salt
½ cup chopped onions	*1 cup of smooth
½ cup chopped celery	peanut butter
2 tbsp whole wheat flour	2 tsp lemon juice
1 quart stock	*¾ cup milk
¼ tsp celery seed	*1 cup toasted sunflower seeds

(1) Melt the butter in a soup pot or dutch oven; sauté the onions and celery until they are soft. Stir in the whole wheat flour and cook for about 1 minute. Add the stock, celery seed, and salt.

(2) Bring the mixture to a boil, lower the heat, and simmer about 25 minutes.

(3) To incorporate the peanut butter, EITHER add it to the hot soup ¼ cup at a time while mashing it until it melts, OR use your blender: put about 2 cups of soup in the blender; add the peanut butter a little at a time and blend until smooth. If you have only crunchy peanut butter around, this process will make it smooth.

(4) When the peanut butter has been returned to the pot, add the lemon juice, then the milk, and heat again. (If you like a thinner soup, add more milk and adjust the seasoning.) Serve the soup immediately, sprinkling 2 to 3 tablespoons of the toasted sunflower seeds over each cupful.

*
_____

1   cup sunflower seeds : ½ cup peanut butter
¾   cup milk : ½ cup peanut butter

_____

Sour and Hot Soup
4 portions

> 1 portion = approx. 7 grams of usable protein
> 15% to 19% of average daily protein need

This soup requires a large portion of rice to complement the tofu. If you prefer a soupier soup, serve the grain on the side with fresh steamed vegetables.

*1¼ cups raw brown rice, cooked

*1 cup sliced mushrooms

*9 cubic inches of tofu—about 3 ounces, grated

½ cup sliced water chestnuts

4 cups stock

1 tbsp tamari soy sauce

2 tbsp white vinegar

1 tsp salt

¼ tsp pepper

2 tbsp cornstarch mixed with . . .

3 tbsp cold stock

*1 egg, beaten

2 tsp sesame oil

1 scallion OR several chives, chopped

(1) To grate the tofu, use the coarse side of a cheese grater; grate the tofu as you would grate cheddar cheese.

(2) Bring the stock, soy sauce, and vinegar to a boil; stir in the tofu, mushrooms, water chestnuts, salt, and pepper.

(3) Bring to a second boil; then pour in the cornstarch mixture. Stir until the soup thickens slightly.

(4) Simmer the soup as you slowly pour in the beaten egg, stirring constantly for egg drops. Stir in the sesame oil.

(5) To serve: dish up some of the grain into the soup bowls, pour a serving of soup over the grain, sprinkle with scallions; and you're ready to serve.

*

3 ounces tofu : 1¼ cups raw brown rice
1 cup sliced mushrooms
1 egg

Soybean Stew
6 portions

1 portion = approx. 8 grams of usable protein
18% to 22% of average daily protein need

Serve the stew over rounds of whole grain toast with a salad on the side. If you have a pressure cooker, the stew can be on the table an hour after you first think of it!

*1 cup dry soybeans, cooked
1 8-ounce can tomato sauce
⅓ cup chopped onions
1 clove garlic, crushed or minced
1 stalk celery, chopped
stock from the soybeans

½ tsp cumin, ground
½ tsp salt
pinch each of: cinnamon, cloves, nutmeg, allspice
½ cup chopped green pepper
*⅔ cup grated parmesan cheese

(1) Combine all ingredients in a cast iron dutch oven EXCEPT for the cheese, stock, and green pepper.
(2) Cook the stew for about ½ hour over low heat, adding stock if the mixture becomes dry.
(3) Remove from the heat and stir in the green pepper and grated cheese. The residual heat will melt the cheese and warm the pepper. Ready to serve.

* _____

1 cup soybeans : ⅔ cup grated cheese

_____

Peanut, Tofu and Sesame Soup
about 2 quarts

> 1 cup = approx. 7 grams of usable protein
> 17% to 20% of average daily protein need

We loved this soup for lunch with potato salad, whole grain bread, and fresh carrot juice.

*¾ cup raw peanuts, cooked
*6 ounces tofu, cut in ½" cubes
¼ cup chopped celery
¾ cup chopped onions
½ to 1 cup chopped mushrooms
4 cups stock, from cooking the peanuts

2 cups canned tomatoes with some juice
*⅞ cup sesame seeds, ground and roasted
1 tbsp miso (soybean paste)
2 tsp salt
¼ tsp dried chili peppers
1 bay leaf (remove when soup is cooked)

(1) Spread the cooked peanuts on a large cutting board and chop them coarsely. Set aside.
(2) Using a small amount of oil, sauté the tofu cubes with the celery, onions, and mushrooms. The tofu should brown lightly and the onions should be golden.
(3) Combine the sautéed vegetables with the chopped peanuts in a large soup pot or saucepan. Stir in the peanut stock, tomatoes, and the roasted sesame seeds.
(4) Bring the soup to a simmer. Then dissolve the miso in a small amount of the broth and return it to the pot.

(5) Season with salt, chili peppers, and bay leaf. Simmer covered 20-25 minutes OR pressure cook for 3 minutes.

* _____

¾ cup peanuts : 6 oz. tofu : ⅞ cup sesame seed

_____

Exotic Barley Stew
2½ quarts

> 1 cup = approx. 2 grams of usable protein
> 4% to 5% of average daily protein need

Add a dab of yogurt to each serving to cool the stew and give it a bit of tang. Serve with fresh whole grain bread and salad for a fulfilling meal.

*1⅓ cups raw barley, cooked	¼ cup chopped fresh parsley
*½ cup dry beans, cooked	6 cups stock
3 tbsp oil	*3 tbsp miso
1 large onion, chopped (about 1½ cups)	1 tsp salt
	2 tsp dill seed, ground
3 cups fresh green beans, chopped into ½" pieces	3-4 large fresh tomatoes, chopped (or substitute canned tomatoes)
2 tsp chopped fresh mint	

(1) Heat the oil in a large soup pot or dutch oven. Start sautéing the onion, then add the green beans and continue sautéing until the onions are very soft and the green beans are tender but still crisp.

(2)   Stir in the mint, parsley, stock, miso, salt, and dill
       seed. Be sure to dissolve the miso in a small
       amount of hot stock or water first so it won't sit
       in a lump.

(3)   When the mixture has begun to simmer, add the
       tomatoes, cooked barley, and beans. (Try using
       small red beans for nice color contrast in the
       soup.)

(4)   Simmer the soup, covered, for about ½ hour, stir-
       ring occasionally.

Variation—for more of a soup, add 2-4 cups more
              stock; adjust the seasoning.

*

1⅓   cups barley : ½ cup beans
3   tbsp miso

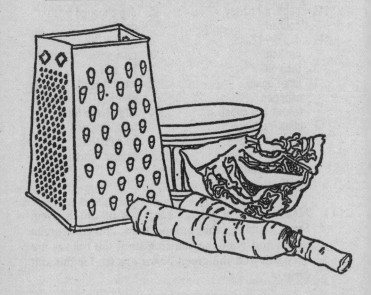

Cashew and Carrot Soup
about 2½ quarts

> 1 cup = approx. 4 grams of usable protein
> 9% to 11% of average daily protein need

You can serve this soup either hot or cold. Its sweetness comes naturally from the carrots, apples, raisins, cashews, and tomato paste.

1	tbsp butter	6	cups stock
¼	cup oil	2	tsp salt
1½	cups chopped onion	*⅓	cup raw brown rice
4	cups grated carrots (packed tight for measuring)	1	cup raisins
		*1	cup raw cashew pieces OR chopped whole cashews
3	ounces tomato paste	(1-3	tsp honey—optional)
1	cup of chopped apples	*2½	cups dairy products (see the last step)

(1) Melt the butter and oil in a soup pot or pressure cooker; sauté the chopped onions for 1 minute, stir in the carrots and sauté until the onions are soft and transparent. They will be orange rather than brown!

(2) Stir in the tomato paste, apple, stock, and salt. Bring the mixture to a boil and stir in the brown rice.

(3) Cover and pressure cook for 15 minutes, OR cook regularly for about 45 minutes, until the soup is a beautiful orange and the carrots are tender, but not mushy.

(4) (Optional step—remove one cup of soup from the pot; put it in the blender and buzz until smooth; return it to the pot.)

(5) Add the raisins and cashews (and optional honey), bring to a boil again, and simmer until the raisins are plump—about 5 minutes.

(6) You may now EITHER:
add 2½ cups of milk and heat through,
> OR: serve as is but add ¼ cup of yogurt to each bowl of soup,
> OR: serve the soup cold, adding ¼ cup yogurt or buttermilk,
> OR: serve the soup cold after the 2½ cups of milk have been added.

*
_____

⅓ cup rice : about ½ cup milk
2 cups milk
1 cup raw cashews

_____

Oatmeal Soup
about 2 quarts

> 1 cup = approx. 2 grams of usable protein
> 5% to 6% of average daily protein need

This soup is unusual, and somewhat sweet. It is easy to assemble for the first course of any meal.

*1 cup rolled oats
oil and/or butter
1 onion, sliced
3 cloves garlic, crushed or minced
2 large tomatoes, chopped
7 cups stock
*1 cup milk
salt and pepper

(1) In a soup pot or cast iron dutch oven brown the rolled oats over low heat, stirring frequently. It is not necessary to use oil for this.

(2) Take the oats out of the pan and set them aside. They should be toasty dark brown.

(3) Add a little oil or butter to the pot; sauté the onion and garlic until the onion is transparent. Stir in the tomatoes, stock, and browned oats. Bring the soup to a boil, lower the heat and simmer it for about 5 minutes.

(4) Season it with salt and pepper or soy sauce to taste. Stir in the milk and serve.

* _____

   1 cup rolled oats : 1 cup milk

_____

Cabbage Soup for a Meal
about 2½ quarts

> 1 cup = approx. 7 grams of usable protein
> 17% to 20% of average daily protein need

A complete meal with bread and cheese . . .

¼ cup oil	½ to 1 cup tomato sauce
1½ cups chopped onions	¼ to ½ cup chopped fresh parsley
2 tsp minced garlic	1 bay leaf
1 cup chopped carrots	salt to taste
1 cup chopped celery	1 tsp thyme
*2½ cups diced potatoes	*½ cup dry soybeans, cooked
7 to 8 cups of cabbage, shredded and chopped into ¾ inch pieces— about 2 pounds	*½ cup raw whole wheat berries, cooked
	*¾ cup raw brown rice, cooked
8 cups stock	3-4 chopped tomatoes
	*2½ cups yogurt

(1) Heat the oil in a large soup pot or dutch oven; sauté the onions, garlic, carrots, celery, and potatoes for about 10 minutes, until the onions are soft and transparent and the potatoes are translucent.

(2) Add a little more oil and stir in the cabbage; sauté until the cabbage is soft and its volume is reduced.

(3) Stir in the stock, all of the seasonings, plus the soybeans, wheat, and rice. Bring the mixture to a boil, lower the heat, cover, and simmer about ½ hour.

(4) Just before serving, stir in the chopped tomatoes. Top each cup of soup with ¼ cup of yogurt (or use 2 tablespoons of grated cheese or cottage cheese).

*
¾	cup raw brown rice : ½ cup wheat berries : ½ cup soybeans
2½	cups potatoes : 2½ cups yogurt

Corn and Bean Chowder
about 1½ quarts

1 cup = approx. 6 grams of usable protein
15% to 18% of average daily protein need

This is not a thick chowder, but it's still hearty.

¼	cup oil	*6	tbsp milk powder (½ cup instant)
2	cups sliced onions		
2	tsp minced garlic	*½	cup dry black OR kidney beans, cooked just tender, and drained
*4	cups corn, either fresh or frozen		
4	cups stock		
¼	tsp nutmeg	½	tsp salt

(1) Heat the oil in a large soup pot or cast iron dutch oven. Stir in the onions and garlic; sauté them until the onions are very soft, but not browned.

(2) Add 3 cups of the corn, the stock, and nutmeg; bring the mixture to a boil, then simmer until the corn is tender. If you use fresh garden corn, you'll hardly have to simmer it at all.

(3) Meanwhile, puree the remaining cup of corn in a blender with some of the stock. You may also blend the milk powder at the same time, or just whisk it into the soup.

(4) Add the puree to the soup pot with the drained beans and salt. Bring the soup almost to boiling, lower the heat, and simmer for a few minutes. Check the seasoning and serve (with a pat of butter on top of each serving, if you like).

Variation—Thick Corn and Bean Chowder: Add up to 1 cup of milk powder and 1 or 2 cooked potatoes to the soup.

*
_____

½   cup beans : ¼ cup milk powder
2   tbsp milk powder
4   cups corn

_____

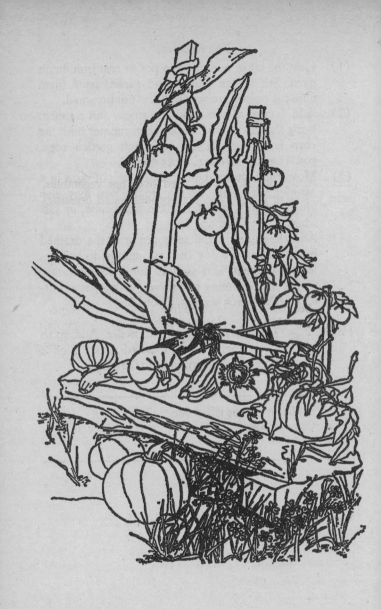

Raw Repast

In the summertime a salad can be your whole meal. Leftover grains can be dressed and tossed with chopped vegetables, or a simple green vegetable salad becomes a protein-rich meal with the addition of croutons from whole grain bread, cheese cubes, and nuts or seeds.

Besides several bean and grain salads, I have included sauces which can be used over hot vegetables, bean loaves or grains, and high-protein salad dressings for plain vegetable salads.

Don't forget to eat salad in the winter. Although there aren't as many fresh vegetables available, it's still important to eat some raw foods for roughage and for vitamins and minerals.

Young children often won't eat salads. I have found that it's because they don't like foods all mixed together. Offer them whole recognizable vegetables like carrots, celery sticks, avocado quarters, raw mushrooms, cauliflower, or broccoli. They might enjoy dipping them in some dressing, too.

Salads

Paul's Ambrosia
6 portions

> 1 portion = approx. 8 grams of usable protein
> 19% to 22% of average daily protein need

This fruit salad is delicious for breakfast without honey and with just a light sprinkling of spices. Serve it for lunch with more spice, and for dessert add some honey and you have a delectable dish that should satisfy everyone's sweet tooth!

*⅓ cup cottage cheese
*⅓ cup ricotta cheese
*½ cup yogurt
1½ to 2 tsp cinnamon
¼ to ½ tsp ginger
⅛ to ¼ tsp cloves
¼ to ½ tsp cardamom
½ to 1 tsp nutmeg
(honey—optional)
*½ cup of cheese cubes
(diced into ¼-inch
pieces)
1 apple, diced into
½-inch pieces

1 orange, diced into
½-inch pieces
1 cup of melon,
diced into 1-inch
cubes. Use cante-
loupe, honeydew or
persian melon.
1 pear, diced into
½-inch pieces
1½ to 2 bananas,
sliced
*¼ cup brewer's yeast
*⅓ cup wheat germ

(1) Stir the cottage cheese, ricotta, and yogurt together in a small bowl. Stir in all of the spices. If
I am going to serve the Ambrosia for dessert I use
the larger amounts of spices. (Add the optional
honey to the dressing now, too.)

(2) Prepare the cheese and fruits and toss them gently
in a serving bowl. Pour the cheese and yogurt
mixture over; sprinkle with brewer's yeast and
wheat germ. Toss again.

(3) Refrigerate the salad until you're ready to serve.

* _____

½ cup of cheese cubes
⅓ cup cottage cheese
⅓ cup ricotta
½ cup yogurt
¼ cup brewer's yeast
⅓ cup wheat germ

Cumin Cucumber Salad
4 portions

> 1 portion = approx. 5 grams of usable protein
> 11% to 13% of average daily protein need

Far more interesting than the usual cucumber, sour cream, and parsley, this spicy salad was inspired by a recipe from India.

1 medium-sized cucumber	1 tsp cumin seeds
1 small onion, chopped fine (¼ to ⅓ cup)	*½ cup cottage cheese
	*½ cup yogurt
1 to 1½ tsp salt	a few sprigs of parsley, chopped
1 tomato, chopped into 16ths	

(1) Quarter the cucumber lengthwise, then hold the quarters together and slice it into half-inch chunks. Place in a small bowl.

(2) Add the onion, salt, and tomato to the bowl with the cucumber and toss gently.

(3) Toast the cumin seeds in a small dry frying pan over medium heat only until they are brittle, not browned. It should take about 1 minute.

(4) Place the cottage cheese and yogurt in your blender, add the toasted cumin, and buzz until the mixture is smooth.

(5) Pour the dressing over the salad vegetables, toss gently, and refrigerate for an hour, if possible, before serving.

*_____

½ cup cottage cheese
½ cup yogurt

_____

Curried Rice Salad
about 12 cups

> 1 cup = approx. 10 grams of usable protein
> 22% to 27% of average daily protein need

We fixed this for a neighborhood potluck and everyone wanted to know what the kernels of wheat were! They give the salad an interesting texture, so I don't recommend any substitution. You might want to add toasted sunflower seeds or sesame seeds, for there is quite a bit of extra cheese that would complement them.

*1 cup whole wheat kernels (or berries), cooked	4 stalks celery, chopped
*2 cups raw brown rice, cooked	**Dressing:**
*1 cup dry soybeans, cooked	¼ cup oil
2 tsp salt	1 tbsp (or more) curry powder
*1⅓ cups grated parmesan cheese (or cheddar)	⅓ cup apple cider vinegar
2 onions, coarsely chopped	2 tbsp lemon juice
	2 tbsp honey
	¾ to 1 cup raisins

(1) Please keep the soybeans, wheat, and rice separated for cooking. Wheat and soybeans take a bit longer than rice to get tender, so you might cook them first in the pressure cooker. Put the wheat in small containers with water, and put the soybeans in the water that surrounds the containers. You could then cook the rice by the regular method, or if you have time, do it in the pressure cooker when the wheat and beans are done.

(2) When the wheat is done, stir into it ½ teaspoon of the salt and ⅔ cup of the grated cheese. Stir until the cheese melts, then chill until very cold. I speeded up the process by chilling the mixture in the freezer.

(3) After the soybeans have been cooked, drain and chill them also.

(4) Stir the remaining ⅔ cup of grated cheese into the hot cooked rice with 1½ teaspoons of salt. Chill the rice as you did the wheat, above.

(5) Prepare the dressing: In a small saucepan heat the oil, stir in the curry powder and sizzle it for about 1 minute; stir in the vinegar, lemon juice, honey, and raisins. Simmer until the raisins puff up—about 7 minutes.

(6) Chop the vegetables, and if the grains and soybeans are chilled, the salad is ready to assemble. Toss each grain gently to separate the kernels (now coated with cheese). In a big bowl toss together the grains, soybeans, and chopped vegetables. Pour the dressing over all and toss again. Chill again until you're ready to serve on a bed of fresh greens.

---

*

1	cup rice : ½ cup wheat : ½ cup soybeans
½	cup wheat : ⅛ cup soybeans
⅜	cup soybeans : ¼ cup grated cheese
1	cup rice : ⅓ cup grated cheese
¾	cup grated parmesan cheese

Cool Slaw
4 portions

> 1 portion = approx. 12 grams of usable protein
> 29% to 34% of average daily protein need

Unusual banana-flavored dressing you should like . . .

1 cup grated carrots	*⅔ cup sunflower seeds, raw or roasted
2 cups shredded cabbage	½ cup raisins
*½ cup peanuts, raw or roasted	½ cup diced apple

(1) Toss all the ingredients together with this dressing:

½ banana	*½ cup ricotta cheese
*⅓ cup buttermilk	¼ cup apple juice

(2) Process the dressing in a blender until it's very
smooth. Its creaminess is a delightful contrast to
the textures of the vegetables, nuts, and seeds.

*_____

½ cup peanuts : ⅔ cup sunflower seeds
⅓ cup buttermilk
½ cup ricotta cheese

_____

Kidney Bean Salad
6 portions

> 1 portion = approx. 7 grams of usable protein
> 17% to 21% of average daily protein need

Serve this salad on a bed of greens. It's refreshing in
the summer and is also a good accompaniment to a hot
meal in any season.

*1	cup dry kidney beans, cooked and drained	⅛	teaspoon paprika
		¼	tsp salt
		1	tsp honey
1	green pepper, chopped (about ¾ cup)	1	tsp worcestershire sauce
		1	tbsp tomato catsup
½	cup chopped onions OR scallions		dash hot sauce
		2	tbsp chopped fresh parsley
1	teaspoon crushed or minced garlic	*1	cup yogurt whisked with . . .
½	cup olive oil		
¼	cup wine vinegar	*¼	cup milk powder

(1) Combine the cooked beans, green pepper, scallions, and garlic.

(2) Make a dressing of the olive oil, wine vinegar, and the remaining ingredients EXCEPT yogurt and milk powder.

(3) Pour the dressing over the bean mixture and toss gently. Refrigerate this marinade at least one hour.

(4) Just before serving, stir in the yogurt-milk powder mixture.

Variation—Cucumber–Kidney Bean Salad: Add 1 chopped cucumber plus ½ to 1 cup chopped celery to the salad before marinating.

---

*

1 cup kidney beans : 1 cup yogurt and ¼ cup milk powder

Recipes for a Small Planet

Gado Gado
6 portions

> 1 portion = approx. 38 grams of usable protein
> 88% to 105% of average daily protein need

This traditional Javanese dish contains an incredible amount of protein per portion. As a side dish, it would still have lots of protein, even if it were serving 12!

Sauce:

1 cup finely chopped onions	1 tsp tabasco sauce OR 1 tbsp finely chopped fresh hot chilis
6 cloves garlic, crushed or minced	
3 tbsp oil	juice and rind of one lemon
1 cup boiling water	
*2 cups crunchy peanut butter	1 tbsp grated fresh ginger root
2 tbsp honey	2 crushed bay leaves salt to taste
	*3 cups milk

(1) Sauté the onions and garlic in the oil until lightly browned.

(2) Stir in the boiling water, peanut butter and remaining ingredients EXCEPT milk.

(3) Cook the sauce over medium heat until it is very hot and the peanut butter has melted and blended in.

(4) Gradually stir in the milk; cook for a few more minutes.

(5) Serve the sauce, hot or cold, over raw or cooked vegetables. This traditional Javanese dish is served with:

2 cups bean sprouts
raw spinach leaves
sliced cucumber
finely shredded lettuce
1 pound raw or
blanched green
beans

*6 hard-boiled eggs,
quartered
*1 pound tofu, cubed
and sautéed

Arrange the vegetables on a platter; season with salt, pepper, and lemon juice. Serve the sauce separately for pouring over the vegetables.

* _____

2 cups peanut butter : 3 cups milk
6 hard-boiled eggs
16 ounces tofu

_____

Potato Salad
10 portions

> 1 portion = approx. 10 grams of usable protein
> 22% to 27% of average daily protein need

—delicious and refreshing on a summer day.

*12 average potatoes,
steamed until just
tender
*6 eggs, hard boiled
¼ cup lemon juice
¼ cup apple cider
vinegar
(¼ cup oil—optional)
1½ cups chopped on-
ions
1½ to 2 cups chopped
celery

Dressing:
*1 cup yogurt
*1 cup milk powder
(1⅓ cup instant)
2 tbsp honey
1 tsp dill seeds,
ground
2 tsp salt

(1) When the potatoes are cool enough to handle, cut

them into bite-sized chunks without removing the skins. Place them in a large bowl and pour over them the lemon juice and cider vinegar (and optional oil).

(2) Chunk the eggs and add them to the bowl. And add the onions and celery.

(3) Prepare the dressing by whisking the milk powder into the yogurt ¼ cup at a time. Stir in the honey, dill seeds, and salt.

(4) Pour the dressing over the vegetables in the bowl, tossing gently.

(5) Refrigerate the salad, overnight if possible, but at least for a few hours before serving so the flavors have a chance to mingle.

* _____

4 potatoes : 1 cup milk powder
1 potato : 1 cup yogurt
6 eggs
7 potatoes

Egg Salad
7-8 portions

1 portion = approx. 8 grams usable protein
17% to 21% of average daily protein need

Fine for a summer salad or sandwiches, this interesting egg salad will keep well when refrigerated.

*5 eggs, hard boiled	*½ cup sesame seeds, ground and toasted
⅓ cup finely chopped carrot	
⅓ cup finely chopped celery	**Dressing:**
	*½ cup ricotta cheese
⅓ cup finely chopped onion	*¼ cup yogurt
	¼ cup mayonnaise
*½ cup toasted sunflower seeds	salt
	paprika

(1) Prepare the vegetables and combine them with the sunflower and sesame seeds in a mixing bowl.
(2) Smooth the ricotta with a fork and then blend in the yogurt and mayonnaise. Season with salt and paprika to taste.
(3) Combine the dressing with the vegetables. Refrigerate for several hours, if possible, and serve on lettuce or on whole grain bread.

* ───────────────────────────────

5 eggs
½ cup sunflower seeds : about ¼ cup ricotta
½ cup sesame seeds : about ¼ cup ricotta
¼ cup yogurt

Soy-Peanut Marinade
4 portions

> 1 portion = approx. 19 grams of usable protein
> 45% to 54% of average daily protein need

Refreshing on a summer day . . .

*1	cup raw peanuts, cooked	½	tsp salt
*½	cup soybeans, cooked	¼	tsp dry mustard
¼	cup honey	¼	tsp dry tarragon
¼	cup apple cider vinegar	1-2	tbsp chopped parsley
2	tbsp sesame oil	½	onion, sliced into thin rings
*¼	cup sesame tahini OR sesame butter	*⅔	cup sesame seeds, toasted

(1) After the beans are cooked, drain them well.
(2) Combine the honey, vinegar, oil, tahini, salt, herbs, and spices EXCEPT sesame.
(3) Toss the dressing into the cooked peanuts and beans; add the onion rings, cover, and chill several hours or overnight.
(4) Just before serving stir in the sesame seeds and transfer the marinade to a bowl lined with greens.

---

*

1　cup peanuts : ½ cup soybeans : ¼ cup tahini and ⅔ cup sesame seeds

Three-Bean Salad
8 portions

> 1 portion = approx. 8 grams of usable protein
> 19% to 23% of average daily protein need

A tangy and creamy salad. Serve it very cold in a bed of greens.

*½ cup dry garbanzo beans
*½ cup dry kidney beans
*½ cup dry black beans
*1 cup yogurt
2-4 tbsp lemon juice
*½ cup milk powder (⅔ cup instant)

2 tbsp honey
½ tsp salt
¼ tsp curry powder
1 tsp fresh basil OR ½ tsp dried leaves
2-3 tbsp chopped fresh chives
3 tbsp chopped fresh parsley

(1) Cook the beans separately, if possible, to maintain their individual colors. Cook them until tender but still firm. Drain them well.

(2) Put the yogurt into a small mixing bowl. Stir it with a whisk until it is creamy-smooth. Stir the lemon juice and milk powder together to form a smooth paste; whisk this mixture into the yogurt. Blend in the honey and herbs.

(3) Pour the dressing over the beans. Toss gently, cover, and refrigerate several hours or overnight before serving.

*
½ cup garbanzo beans : ¼ cup milk powder
½ cup kidney beans : 1 cup yogurt
½ cup black beans : ¼ cup milk powder

Salad Collage

The protein in this salad
depends entirely on you.

shredded cabbage
torn lettuce
raisins
grated fresh coconut
cheese cubes
peanuts[1]
sunflower seeds[1]

leftover cooked but cold
    vegetables, includ-
    ing potatoes[2]
whole grain croutons[3]
chopped fresh pineapple
Dressing:
  1 part mayonnaise
  2 parts yogurt

(1)   Mix the dressing in the bottom of a large bowl.
      Try to judge the amount by the size salad you in-
      tend to make.

(2)   Add the remaining ingredients and toss to coat
      them all.

---

[1] Be sure to use the peanuts and sunflower seeds in a ratio
of 4 to 3.

[2] The cheese you use will complement potatoes.

[3] To make whole grain croutons: Cut thick slices of whole
grain or whole protein bread; cut the slices into cubes. Sauté
the cubes in butter until they're crisp and fragrant.

Salad Dressings

Herbed Cottage Cheese Dressing
about 2 cups

2 cups = approx. 37 grams of usable protein
¼ cup = 11% to 13% of average daily protein need

You can really use any fresh herbs for this dressing.

⅔	cup fresh parsley	¼	cup apple cider
1	tbsp fresh rose-		vinegar
	mary leaves	*½	to 1 cup milk
½	tsp salt	*1	cup cottage cheese
¼	cup oil		

(1) Buzz all ingredients in the blender until smooth. The amount of milk you use will determine the thickness of the dressing.

(2) Try substituting any of these fresh herbs: basil, chives, dill, coriander, mint, thyme, oregano, tarragon, or summer savory.

*————————————————————————

1 cup cottage cheese
½ to 1 cup milk

————————————————————————

Cottage Cheese Dressing
1½ cups

1½ cups = approx. 24 grams of usable protein
¼ cup = 9% to 11% of average daily protein need

Serve this dressing over hot cooked vegetables or raw vegetable salads.

*½ cup buttermilk   4 small radishes
*½ cup cottage cheese   1 tbsp poppy seeds
¼ cup wine vinegar   2-3 green onions OR
*2 tbsp brewer's yeast   chives
1 tsp tamari soy sauce

Process all ingredients in the blender until smooth.

* _____

½ cup buttermilk
½ cup cottage cheese
2 tbsp brewer's yeast

_____

Green Goddess Dressing
about 1 cup

1 cup = approx. 7 grams of usable protein
¼ cup = 4% to 5% of average daily protein need

A cool dressing for summer salads—not too rich.

1 tsp vinegar   2 sprigs fresh
1 large clove garlic   parsley
4 whole green onions   1 tsp dried tarragon
OR 10 large fresh   3 tbsp mayonnaise
chives   *1 cup buttermilk

(1) Blend all ingredients (except ¾ cup of the buttermilk) in a blender until smooth.
(2) Stir in the remaining buttermilk. This makes the
dressing somewhat thicker than if all the buttermilk is blended.

* _____

1 cup buttermilk

_____

Easy Roquefort Dressing
about 1 cup

> 1 cup = approx. 17 grams usable protein
> ¼ cup = 10% to 12% of average daily protein need

*6 tbsp yogurt	*3 tbsp crumbled
3 tbsp mayonnaise	roquefort cheese
*3 tbsp cottage cheese	

Blend all ingredients in a blender until smooth. Use this dressing on any type of salad. It is especially nice on plain lettuce leaves.

* _____

6 tbsp yogurt
3 tbsp cottage cheese
3 tbsp roquefort

Easy Yogurt Dressing
2 cups

> 2 cups = approx. 11 grams of usable protein
> ¼ cup = 3% to 4% of average daily protein need

*1½ cups yogurt	½ tsp onion powder[1]
2 tsp tamari soy sauce	1 tsp celery salt
½ tsp garlic powder[1]	

Stir all of the ingredients together in a small bowl. Serve on tossed greens or other fresh vegetables.

* _____

1½ cups yogurt

---

[1] You may use fresh minced onion and garlic, if desired.

Easy Cole Slaw Dressing
about 1 cup

> 1 cup = approx. 24 grams of usable protein
> ¼ cup = 14% to 17% of average daily protein need

Use this dressing on cabbage or carrot salad. Add some peanuts, sunflower seeds, and raisins for a delicious treat!

*⅓	cup yogurt	1	tbsp honey
*⅔	cup cottage cheese	1	tsp vinegar

Whip all ingredients in a blender until they're smooth and creamy.

---

*

⅓ cup yogurt
⅔ cup cottage cheese

Dilled Yogurt Dressing
about 2 cups

> 2 cups = approx. 7 grams of usable protein
> ¼ cup = 2% of average daily protein need

This sharp dressing will perk up any vegetable dish or salad.

*1	cup yogurt	¼	tsp dry mustard
2	tbsp vinegar	¼	tsp minced garlic
½	small onion		OR garlic powder
½	tsp salt		(pepper—optional)
½	tsp dill seeds		

Process all the ingredients in a blender until the onion is completely pureed.

* _____

1   cup yogurt

_____

Mock Thousand Island Dressing
about 1½ cups

> 1½ cups = approx. 13 grams of usable protein
> ¼ cup = 5% to 6% of average daily protein need

By substituting yogurt for mayonnaise, not only do we increase the protein of Thousand Island Dressing, but we also drastically reduce the calories. 1 cup of whole milk yogurt has about 160 calories, while a cup of mayonnaise has about 1750 calories or 11 times more than the yogurt!!

*1 cup yogurt	2 tbsp chopped scallions OR chives
6 tbsp catsup OR chili sauce	2 tbsp chopped green olives
1 clove garlic, minced	1 tsp prepared mustard
2 tbsp chopped pickle	1 tsp paprika
*1 chopped hard-boiled egg	1 tbsp Worcestershire Sauce

(1) Combine all ingredients in the order given.
(2) Keep refrigerated, and eat with eggs and tomatoes or plain lettuce.

* _____

1   cup yogurt
1   egg

_____

Sauces

Bean Sauce
about 2 cups

> 2 cups = approx. 21 grams of usable protein[1]
> ¼ cup = 6% to 7% of average daily protein need

Serve this savory sauce over vegetables and rice.[1]

½ cup stock	½ tsp salt
*⅓ cup pinto beans, cooked	½ tsp dried tarragon leaves
1 onion, quartered	¼ tsp turmeric
1 stalk celery, quartered	1 tsp honey

(1) Puree the beans with the ½ cup of stock in a blender.
(2) Add the quartered onion, and celery; buzz again until the vegetables have been blended smooth.
(3) Pour the mixture into a small saucepan, add the spices, and cook for about 10 minutes, until there is no taste of raw onion.

* _____

⅓ cup beans: 1 cup raw brown rice

_____

[1] The usable protein indicated results only when all the sauce is complemented by 1 cup of raw brown rice.

Dairy Rich Sauce
1½ cups

> 1½ cups = approx. 29 grams of usable protein
> ¼ cup = 17% to 20% of average daily protein need

Serve this sauce hot over vegetables, or chill it and you have a delicious salad dressing.

*½ cup ricotta cheese
*½ cup buttermilk
*½ cup tofu
½ medium avocado

1 tsp fennel OR caraway seeds
(½ tsp salt—optional)
*¼-½ cup grated parmesan cheese

(1) Buzz in a blender the ricotta, buttermilk, tofu, avocado, and fennel seeds. Buzz until the seeds are completely ground.
(2) Taste and decide if you want salt.
(3) Place the mixture in a small saucepan, heat over a low flame; add the parmesan cheese and heat until it has completely melted.

* _____

½ cup ricotta
½ cup buttermilk
¼-½ cup parmesan cheese
½ cup tofu

Mushroom and Onion Sauce
about 4½ cups

> 4½ cups = approx. 55 grams of usable protein
> ¼ cup = 7% to 9% of average daily protein need

This sauce was such a hit that I caught a friend heaping it on her plate and eating it straight!

2	tbsp butter	*3	cups milk (hot if possible)
2	tbsp oil		
1	cup finely chopped onions	1	tsp salt (more to taste)
*2	cups mushroom slices	¼	tsp cayenne pepper (less to taste)
*¼	cup whole wheat flour	*1	cup ricotta cheese

(1) Heat the butter and oil together in a 2-quart saucepan. Sauté the onions and mushrooms until the onions are transparent.

(2) Gradually stir in the whole wheat flour, stirring constantly so that it coats the vegetables. Cook this mixture over gentle heat for about one minute, stirring all the while.

(3) Add the milk, one cup at a time. Simmer the mixture until it has thickened slightly. Add the salt and cayenne while you simmer.

(4) Stir up the ricotta until it is separated and soft. You can even put it in the blender if you're up to it, but it isn't necessary. Add the cheese to the sauce and use a whisk to break up any lumps. The sauce is ready when it's all hot.

---

*

    1 cup ricotta
    3 cups milk minus 2 tbsp
    2 tbsp milk : ¼ cup whole wheat flour
    2 cups mushrooms

Split Pea Caraway Sauce
about 2 cups

                    1 cup = approx. 14 grams of usable protein
                    33% to 39% of average daily protein need

2 portions with ¾ cup raw brown rice:

> 1 portion = approx. 20 grams of usable protein
> 46% to 54% of average daily protein need

4 portions with 1¾ cups raw brown rice:

> 1 portion = approx. 14 grams of usable protein
> 31% to 38% of average daily protein need

6 portions with 3 cups raw brown rice:

> 1 portion = approx. 11 grams of usable protein
> 26% to 31% of average daily protein need

This most versatile sauce, which is complementary protein by itself, can complement up to 3 cups of raw brown rice. Use it alone as a vegetable sauce, or pour it over your cooked rice. Either way you are getting good quality protein.

*½ cup split peas, cooked until smooth (about 1 cup puree)	½ tsp salt
	1 tbsp caraway seeds, crushed
*1 cup milk	*3 tbsp brewer's yeast

(1) Combine the milk and split pea puree in a small saucepan.

(2) Cook over low heat, adding the salt and caraway seeds, until the sauce is smooth.

(3) Remove from heat and stir in the brewer's yeast, which will thicken the sauce.

*———————————————————————

The combinations for the increasing cups of rice are increasingly complex. The following proportions occur when the sauce complements 1¾ cups raw brown rice.

3 tablespoons brewer's yeast : ¾ cup rice
¼ cup split peas : ½ cup milk
¼ cup split peas : ⅔ cup rice
½ cup milk : ⅓ cup rice

What's for Dinner?

This section on main dishes is quite long because it includes several types of main dishes which might or might not fit into other categories. For instance, I could not include a section that included grains alone because for full protein complementarity, grains must be eaten with beans, seeds, or dairy products. I have labeled each section according to the predominant characteristic of the dishes in it—the form (loaves and casseroles), the type of food mainly used (vegetables, noodles and potatoes), or the cooking process (top-of-the-stove grains or main dishes).

Since all of these sections contain high-protein recipes, I felt they could all fit into a main-dish group. Many of our meals consist of one vegetable dish or one grain dish with a green salad or steamed vegetable. Many of these dishes have one third or more of the daily protein need, which means that you don't need to have a vegetable entree and a grain casserole at the same meal.

Enjoy enjoy . . .

Loaves and Casseroles

Instead of making loaves in loaf pans, try patting them into ring forms, cake pans, or casseroles of interesting shapes. For serving several people, put the loaf mixture into a large flat baking dish, reduce the baking time, and, for serving, slice into squares for eating out-of-hand. You can serve at any temperature, too.

Remember, loaves and casseroles are delicious cold, sliced as they are, or spread onto bread for sandwiches.

Reheat loaves and casseroles by covering them so they won't dry out and placing in a hot oven.

Complementary Pie
8 portions

> 1 portion = approx. 8 grams of usable protein
> 19% to 21% of average daily protein need

This is a good main course when accompanied by a tossed salad. It's creamy and somewhat rich, but ever-so-hard to stop eating!

*¾ cup raw brown rice (OR barley), cooked	*2 eggs, beaten
	*1 cup milk
	*1 cup grated cheddar cheese
*½ cup dry beans, cooked (use large colorful beans like kidneys or black)	1 tsp salt
	1 tsp crushed dried tarragon
1 tbsp butter	½ tsp worcestershire sauce
2 cups sliced onions	

(1) While the beans and rice are cooking, sauté the sliced onions in the butter until they are very soft and just begin to turn golden. Set them aside.

(2) Beat the milk into the eggs; stir in the grated cheese, salt, tarragon, and worcestershire sauce. Then fold in the sautéed onions, cooked beans, and cooked rice.

(3) Turn the mixture into an oiled 10-inch pie plate.

(4) Bake at 325°F for 25 to 30 minutes, until the custard has set and the edges are browned. Let stand for 10 minutes before serving, then slice into wedges.

Variation—Complementary Pie with a Crust: Prepare any whole wheat pie crust for a more elegant pie. There is plenty of extra cheese to complement the wheat. Use a larger pie pan, press the crust in, pour in the custard, and bake as above.

*

⅔ cup grated cheese
¾ cup raw brown rice : 1 cup milk
½ cup beans : ⅓ cup grated cheese
2 eggs

Baked Cottage Cheese Squares
8 portions

> 1 portion = approx. 14 grams of usable protein
> 32% to 38% of average daily protein need

This creamy rich dish, delicately flavored with rosemary, might be accompanied by a green salad and some dark bread.

*1 cup raw brown rice, cooked
*½ cup dry small red beans, cooked (or substitute other beans)
*3 eggs
*1 cup milk
*2 cups cottage cheese

2 tsp salt
3 tbsp chopped fresh parsley
1 tbsp chopped fresh rosemary
½ cup grated raw carrot
2 tbsp butter
¼ cup minced onion

While the rice and beans are cooking—
(1) Beat the eggs; beat in the milk, cottage cheese, salt, herbs, and grated carrot.

(2) Melt the butter in a small frying pan and sauté the onion until it is very soft, but not brown. Stir the onions into the cottage cheese and egg mixture.

(3) Drain the cooked beans and stir them into the cottage cheese mixture along with the rice.

(4) Turn the whole mixture into an oiled 7" x 11" pan. Bake at 375°F with a pan of hot water on the lower oven shelf for about 25 minutes. When it is done, a knife inserted in the center will come out clean, and the top will have a thin light-brown crust.

(5) Cool the casserole for about 10 minutes, cut into squares and serve. You may also chill it completely and serve cold.

*

3	eggs
¾	cup raw brown rice : 1 cup milk
¼	cup raw brown rice : 2 tbsp cottage cheese
½	cup beans : 6 tbsp cottage cheese
1½	cups cottage cheese

Roasted Wheat and Celery Au Gratin
6 portions

1 portion = approx. 8 grams of usable protein
19% to 23% of average daily protein need

2 cups chopped celery	1½ cups water
¼ cup chopped chives or scallions	*1 cup grated cheese (try some hot pepper, smoked cheddar, and parmesan)
½ tsp celery seed	
½ tsp salt	
*1 cup raw bulgur wheat	*1 cup whole grain bread crumbs
¼ cup oil	butter
*1½ cups milk	

(1) In a flameproof casserole sauté the celery, chives, celery seed, salt, and bulgur in the oil until the celery becomes soft.

(2) Stir the milk and water together and add them to the sautéed mixture. Simmer partially covered for about 15 minutes, until most of the liquid has been absorbed.

(3) Stir in ¾ cup of the grated cheese. Sprinkle the remaining ¼ cup over the top, followed by the bread crumbs. Dot with butter.

(4) Bake at 325°F for 10 to 15 minutes, until the casserole is sizzling and firm.

Variation—Bean and Celery Au Gratin:

(1) Follow the recipe above through (1) and (2).

(2) For (3), along with the grated cheese, stir in ½ to 1 cup (dry measure) of cooked small beans. Check the seasoning.

(3) Top with cheese, bread crumbs and butter, and bake as above.

---

*

¾	cup bulgur : ½ cup milk
¼	cup bulgur : about 3 tbsp milk
½	cup bread crumbs : ¼ cup milk
½	cup bread crumbs : ⅙ cup grated cheese
⅙	cup grated cheese and 1 tbsp milk
⅔	cup grated cheese

Autumn Black Beans
4 small portions

> 1 portion = approx. 7 grams of usable protein
> 16% to 20% of average daily protein need

A subtle sweet and sour dish, this "pudding" goes
well with yams baked with orange juice and dried fruit,
and a salad of chopped celery and sprouts dressed with
oil and vinegar.

*½	cup dry black beans, cooked tender	½	tsp dry mustard
		1	tbsp molasses
		1	tbsp honey
*⅔	cup raw bulgur wheat, cooked	*¾	cup yogurt
			raw wheat germ
½	tsp salt		

(1) After the black beans are cooked, drain them and
place in a small mixing bowl.

(2) Add the salt, mustard, molasses, and honey. Stir
in the yogurt and then the cooked bulgur. Blend
carefully to break up any lumps of cooked wheat.

(3) Pour the mixture into a small oiled baking dish,
sprinkle with wheat germ, and bake at 350°F for
20-25 minutes, until the pudding is firm.

Variation—Bulgur With Black Bean Sauce: Instead of
stirring the bulgur into the beans,
keep it separate and serve the beans
and yogurt over it. Sprinkle each
portion with wheat germ. This variation is a quicker dish than the
original, as there is no baking time.

* _____

⅛ cup black beans : ⅔ cup bulgur
6 tbsp black beans : ¾ cup yogurt

Lasagna
8 portions

> 1 portion = approx. 18 grams of usable protein
> 41% to 50% of average daily protein need

A filling dish like lasagna needs only the company of a tossed salad. But perhaps you would like to indulge in hot whole wheat sourdough french bread with garlic butter!

8 ounces lasagna noodles, cooked tender	2-3 tsp salt
	*½-¾ pound sliced mushrooms, sautéed in olive oil
2 medium onions, chopped	
4 cloves garlic, minced	*¾ cup dry small red beans, cooked tender
3 tbsp olive oil	
2 cups tomato sauce, canned tomatoes, or thinned paste	*¾ pound mozzarella cheese, thinly sliced
2 tsp dried oregano	*2 cups ricotta or cottage cheese
1 tsp dried basil	*½ cup freshly grated parmesan cheese
¼ cup chopped fresh parsley	

(1) Rinse the cooked noodles in cold water so they won't stick together. Set them aside.

(2) Sauté the onions and garlic in the olive oil until they are soft and transparent, but not browned. Stir in the tomato, oregano, basil, parsley, and salt. Cook the sauce about ½ hour, simmering it and stirring often until it has thickened. Stir in the sautéed mushrooms and cooked beans.

(3) To assemble the lasagna: place a layer of the noodles on the bottom of a shallow baking dish,

put ⅓ of the tomato sauce over the noodles, spread a layer of ricotta or cottage cheese over the sauce, then a layer of mozzarella cheese, then sprinkle ⅓ of the parmesan cheese over all. Repeat the layers twice more, ending with parmesan.

(4)   Bake the lasagna in a 375°F oven for 20 minutes.

*

½	to ¾ pound mushrooms
¾	cup beans : ½ cup parmesan cheese
1	cup ricotta cheese
1	cup cottage cheese
¾	pound mozzarella cheese

Chiles Rellenos en Casserole
8 portions

1 portion = approx. 12 grams of usable protein
27% to 33% of average daily protein need

A dish that will warm your insides.

*2¼	cups raw brown rice, cooked	1	tsp oregano
		1	tsp salt
*½	cup soybeans, cooked	½	tsp garlic powder OR minced garlic
1	7-ounce can whole green chilis OR 10-12 fresh chilis	2	tbsp chives or scallions
*½	pound monterey jack cheese	(2-3	medium-sized zucchini squash, sliced—optional)
1	cup drained canned tomatoes	*½	cup sesame meal (raw or roasted)

(1)   Oil a large deep casserole; place ½ of the cooked rice on the bottom; set aside.

(2)   If you are using fresh chilis, blanch them or hold

them over an open gas flame until the skin crackles and burns all around; peel the skins off. Slit the fresh or canned chilis lengthwise and remove all of the seeds and cut off the stem ends.

(3) Slice the jack cheese so you have chunks that will fit into the chilis; stuff all of the peppers and nestle them into the rice in the casserole. Cover with the remaining rice. (Top the rice with the zucchini slices.)

(4) Puree the tomatoes, soybeans, oregano, salt, garlic, and onions in your blender; pour this mixture over the second layer of rice (or zucchini, if you are using it).

(5) Sprinkle the sesame meal on top of the sauce; bake the casserole, uncovered, at 350°F for 25-30 minutes.

* _____

2¼ cups raw brown rice : about 4½ ounces cheese
½ cup beans : 1¼ ounces cheese
½ cup sesame meal : about ½ ounce cheese
about 1¾ ounces cheese

_____

Savory Rye Casserole
4 portions

> 1 portion = approx. 10 grams of usable protein
> 23% to 28% of average daily protein need

This unusual casserole combines the strong flavor of whole rye with the delicate flavors of the herbs and vegetables. Add salad and a leafy green vegetable for a light meal.

*1	cup raw whole rye, cooked tender	½	tsp dill seeds, ground
*6	tbsp dry split peas, cooked	¼	tsp sage
1	stalk celery, chopped	½	tsp salt
		2	tbsp tamari soy sauce
1	cup tomatoes, chopped fresh or canned	*1	egg, beaten
		*½	cup grated cheese

(1) Combine all of the ingredients EXCEPT the grated cheese.

(2) Turn the mixture into an oiled casserole.

(3) Bake at 350°F for 45 minutes, until firm, sprinkling the grated cheese over the top during the last 10 minutes of baking.

Variation—Rye Rice and Kidney Casserole: Use ½ cup raw brown rice and ½ cup raw whole rye instead of all rye. Substitute kidney beans for the split peas.

*_____

1 cup rye : 6 tbsp split peas
1 egg
½ cup grated cheese

_____

Herbed Soybean Bulgur Casserole
8 portions

1 portion = approx. 7 grams of usable protein
16% to 19% of average daily protein need

Serve this casserole with a big salad and some freshly picked and steamed garden greens.

*½	cup dry soybeans, cooked	½	cup chopped green pepper
*1½	cups raw bulgur, cooked	*2	tbsp. milk powder
		*2	tbsp brewer's yeast
1	cup chopped celery	1½	tsp salt
1	6-ounce can tomato paste	⅓	cup chopped fresh parsley
10	fluid ounces stock or water	1	tsp sage
		½	tsp oregano
*1	egg	1	tbsp tamari soy sauce

(1) Put into your blender ½ cup of the cooked soybeans, ½ cup of the chopped celery, the tomato paste, stock, and egg; buzz until smooth.

(2) Turn the mixture into a large bowl. Stir in the remaining soybeans, the bulgur, the remaining celery, and all of the other ingredients. Combine everything thoroughly.

(3) Turn the mixture into an oiled casserole and bake at 350°F for 45 minutes, until the top is crusty. You may top with grated cheese for the last few minutes of baking.

For leftovers: shape into patties and brown lightly in hot oil.

---
*

¼	cup soybeans : 1½ cups bulgur
¼	cup soybeans : 2 tbsp milk powder
2	tbsp brewer's yeast
1	egg

Savory Bean Loaf with Tomato Cheese Sauce
8 portions

> 1 portion = approx. 13 grams of usable protein
> 30% to 36% of average daily protein need

Serve this loaf with baked winter squash, a green salad, and fresh bread. Bake it in a ring form or round casserole for a change from the loaf syndrome.

1	onion, chopped	1	tsp summer savory, dried
*1½	cups dry beans, cooked and chopped (pinto, lima, black, or garbanzo)	*3	tbsp brewer's yeast
		*¼	cup sesame tahini OR sesame butter
1-2	carrots, grated (about 1 cup)	*⅔	cup sesame seeds, roasted and ground (about 1 cup meal)
*2	eggs, beaten		
1	tsp salt		

(1) Sauté the onions in a small amount of oil until golden.

(2) Use a big bowl to combine all of the remaining ingredients with the sautéed onions. The mixture will be dry and heavy, but this loaf is destined to be solid.

(3) Oil a casserole or loaf pan and put the mixture in. Pat it down gently.

(4) Place it in a 350°F oven and bake about 1 hour. During the last 10 minutes of baking, pour ½ cup of this sauce over:

Tomato Cheese Sauce

2	tbsp butter	1	tsp salt
2	tbsp whole wheat flour	1	tsp oregano
*2	cups milk	*⅓	cup grated parmesan cheese
3	ounces tomato paste		

(1) Melt the butter in a small saucepan; stir in the flour and cook over low heat for about 1 minute.

(2) Stir in 1 cup of the milk and cook until thick.

(3) Stir in the second cup of milk, the tomato paste, salt, and oregano. Cook over low heat for 5 minutes; then stir in the parmesan cheese.

(4) Pour about ½ cup of sauce over the loaf during the last 10 minutes of baking. Serve the rest at the table for pouring over individual portions.

---

*

1	cup sesame seeds : ⅔ cup beans
⅓	cup grated parmesan cheese : ½ cup beans
¾	cup milk : ⅓ cup beans
1¼	cups milk
2	eggs
3	tbsp brewer's yeast

Savory Nut Cake
6 portions

> 1 portion = approx. 13 grams of usable protein
> 30% to 37% of average daily protein need

This "cake" is delicious both hot and cold. Slice it for sandwiches or spread the leftovers on whole grain toast.

*½ cup raw cashews	*¼ cup wheat germ
½ cup raw almonds	½ cup chopped fresh
*½ cup raw peanuts	parsley
*⅔ cup sunflower seeds	½ tsp sage
*2 eggs	½ tsp thyme
2 onions, quartered	½ tsp salt
*½ cup raw brown rice,	*2 tbsp brewer's yeast
cooked	*⅓ cup grated cheese

(1) In your blender coarsely grind the nuts (not the sunflower seeds) ½ cup at a time. Put the coarse meal in a small bowl and stir in the sunflower seeds.

(2) Put the 2 eggs in the blender, drop in the onion quarters and buzz until smooth. Stir this mixture into the mixed nut meals.

(3) Stir the remaining ingredients EXCEPT the grated cheese into the egg-meal mixture and blend it carefully with a wooden spoon.

(4) Pat the mixture into a well-oiled cake plate. Bake the cake at 350°F for 25 minutes. Sprinkle with grated cheese during the last 10 minutes of baking. Slice the cake into wedges and serve.

Variation—Savory Nut Patties: Shape the Mixture into patties instead of putting it into the

cake plate. Fry each patty on a hot
oiled griddle. Add a slice of cheese
and let it melt before taking the patty
off the griddle.

* _____

½ cup cashews
½ cup peanuts : ⅔ cup sunflower seeds
2 eggs
½ cup raw brown rice : 2 tbsp brewer's yeast
⅓ cup grated cheese
¼ cup wheat germ

_____

Garbanzo and Cheese Loaf
6 portions

> 1 portion = approx. 11 grams of usable protein
> 25% to 30% of average daily protein need

The texture is light and crunchy. Try this loaf tomorrow for a sandwich spread.

*½ cup dry garbanzo
beans, cooked tender and drained
*1 cup whole grain
bread crumbs
1 cup pineapple
juice
1 cup chopped onion
½ cup chopped celery
3 tbsp oil

¼ cup chopped parsley
*1 egg, beaten
*1 tbsp miso
1 tsp salt
a few dashes hot
sauce
2 pinches cayenne
*1 cup grated cheese
(try hot pepper
and swiss)

(1) Combine the bread crumbs and pineapple juice
and let them soak while you prepare the vegetables.

(2) Either chop the garbanzos coarsely or grind them

in a food grinder using the coarse blade. Don't puree them in a blender, because you want them to maintain their nutty texture.

(3) Combine the garbanzos, the crumb mixture, and all the remaining ingredients in the order given. Make sure you dissolve the miso in a small amount of hot water so it doesn't stay in a lump.

(4) Turn the mixture into an oiled loaf pan or small casserole. Bake at 350°F about 40 minutes, until the edges are nicely browned.

*

½ cup garbanzos : ⅓ cup grated cheese
1 cup whole grain crumbs : ⅓ cup grated cheese
⅓ cup grated cheese
1 egg
1 tbsp miso

Top-of-the-Stove Main Dishes

These are some of my favorite recipes. You can assemble them while the grains that they will be served over are cooking. They are quicker than loaves and casseroles because there is no oven time involved. Many of the recipes, such as the Nut and Seed Patties, are excellent and quick enough dishes for lunchtime hunger. And the leftovers make delicious sandwich fillings, especially leftover Fesenjon.

Fesenjon—Spiced Ground Beans
8 portions

> 1 portion = approx. 16 grams of usable protein
> 38% to 45% of average daily protein need

This is an adaptation of a Persian dish made with ground lamb and walnuts. Its sweet spiciness is unusual and delicious.

*1	cup dry soybeans, cooked	2	tsp allspice
*1¼	cups raw peanuts, cooked	2	tbsp cinnamon
2	large onions, chopped (about 3 cups)	1	tsp powdered ginger
1	tbsp curry powder	1	tsp ground nutmeg
⅓	cup oil	*⅞	cup sesame seeds, roasted and ground
1½	cups tomato catsup	*1½	cups raw brown rice, cooked and then mixed with—
1	cup stock—more if needed		
1	tbsp plus 1 tsp salt	*1⅓	cups raw bulgur, cooked OR 1 cup whole wheat berries, cooked

(1)   You may cook the soybeans and peanuts together; then grind them in a food grinder using the small

blade, or chop all of the cooked beans fine.

(2) In a 4-quart dutch oven sauté the onions and curry powder in the oil until the onions are very soft. Stir in the catsup, stock, salt, and spices.

(3) Add the ground beans and stock. If too dry, add more stock. The mixture should have the consistency of (excuse me) a meat sauce you might make for spaghetti. Cover the mixture and simmer it at least 15 minutes, adding stock if necessary.

(4) Stir in the sesame meal, and the fesenjon is ready to serve over the rice and wheat. Include a salad and yellow vegetable for a delicious meal.

---

*

⅔ cup soybeans : ½ cup peanuts : 1⅓ cups bulgur : 1½ cups raw brown rice

⅓ cup soybeans : ¾ cup peanuts : ⅞ cup sesame seeds

Split Pea Rarebit
5 portions

> 1 portion = approx. 11 grams of usable protein
> 26% to 31% of average daily protein need

*½ cup split peas (or other small bean), cooked just tender	1 recipe cheese sauce (below)
1 small onion, chopped and sautéed in oil	*1½ cups raw brown rice, cooked

(1) Stir the cooked peas, sautéed onions, and cheese sauce (below) together. You may add ½ cup beer to make a more authentic rarebit, if you wish.

(2) Serve the rarebit over the cooked rice. Traditionally, rarebit is served over toast, but rice here increases the protein, by being complemented by the cheese.

Cheese Sauce:

¼ cup oil	¼ tsp dry mustard
¼ cup whole wheat flour	½ tsp worcestershire sauce
1½ cups water	pinch of dried chili peppers
½ tsp salt	
1 tbsp tomato paste	*1 cup grated cheddar cheese
dash of nutmeg	

(1) Heat the oil and stir in the whole wheat flour. Cook for about 2 minutes over a low flame.

(2) Stir in the water and simmer until the mixture is thick, adding the salt, tomato paste, nutmeg, mustard, worcestershire, and chili peppers.

(3) Gradually add the grated cheese and stir until it is melted. It is ready to mix with the split peas and onions.

* _____

½   cup split peas : ⅓ cup grated cheese
⅔   cup grated cheese : 1½ cups raw brown rice

_____

Nut Seed Tacos
8 large tacos

1 taco = approx. 9 grams of usable protein
21% to 26% of average daily protein need

An easy dish for feeding several without much fuss. Let everyone assemble their own taco once you've made the filling.

8 flour tortillas, the 8″ size

*¾ cup raw peanuts, cooked

*1 cup sunflower seeds: cook ⅔ cup with the peanuts and roast ⅓ cup

1 6-ounce can to-mato paste

1 tsp cumin seeds

½ tsp dried crushed chili peppers

pinch cayenne

2-3 cloves garlic

*10 tbsp roasted sesame seeds

tomato slices

chopped green onions

chopped parsley

chopped lettuce tossed with wine vinegar

*⅓ cup (or more) grated cheese

(1) Put the cooked peanuts and sunflower seeds into a blender with the tomato paste, cumin seeds, chili peppers, cayenne, and garlic; buzz until smooth, adding stock if the mixture is too thick to puree completely.

(2) Turn the puree into a small saucepan and cook over low heat until it's very thick. Stir in the roasted sunflower and sesame seeds.

(3) Brown the tortillas lightly on both sides. Fold in half while they're still hot.

(4) Put the tortillas, filling, and remaining ingredients on the table in separate plates or bowls.

*_____

¾ cup peanuts : 1 cup sunflower seeds

10 tbsp sesame seeds : ⅙ cup grated cheese

⅙ cup grated cheese

Egg Rolls
12 rolls

2 rolls = approx. 6 grams of usable protein
14% to 17% of average daily protein need

These egg rolls make an excellent first course, or when eaten right with the cooked rice, a whole meal. Just be sure, if you eat them without rice, that you include rice in the meal to complement the soybeans.

1 package egg roll wrappers, or substitute 1 recipe of cheese blintz pancakes (p. 174)	1 cup finely chopped mushrooms
sesame oil	1 green pepper, finely chopped
1 cup finely chopped celery	½ cup finely chopped water chestnuts
1 small onion, finely chopped	1 cup fresh bean or seed sprouts
1-2 cloves garlic, minced	*¼ cup dry soybeans, cooked and pureed with a small amount of stock
1 cup finely shredded cabbage	3 tbsp soy sauce
	*2½ cups raw brown rice, cooked

(1) In a wok or frying pan sauté the vegetables in sesame oil in the order given. After the onion has started sautéing, add the remaining vegetables quickly so that the total time with the heat on is about 5 minutes. As soon as you add the bean sprouts to the pan, turn off the heat.

(2) Stir the pureed soybeans and soy sauce together. Then stir this mixture into the vegetables.

(3) The whole mixture may be chilled several hours,

but I have made very successful egg rolls with warm filling.

(4) To prepare the rolls: Place about ¼ cup filling in the center of each pancake or egg roll wrapper; fold the corners over envelope-style and seal with a flour-water paste.

(5) Heat a large frying pan with oil in the bottom. Fry the rolls until they are crisp and brown, turning only once. You may deep fry the rolls if you are into deep frying, but I like them better cooked only in a little oil. Drain on paper bags or towels.

(6) Keep the rolls hot in a 250°F oven up to an hour. Or reheat them at 450°F for about 10 minutes.

(7) Serve 2 egg rolls with about 1 cup of cooked rice and any of the following:

mustard		
horseradish	½	cup pineapple juice
soy sauce	2	tbsp honey
sweet and sour sauce	1	tsp soy sauce
OR	¼	cup cider vinegar

	dry mustard
hot sauce	soy sauce
	cider vinegar
	honey

*

2½   cups raw brown rice : ¼ cup soybeans

Bean Stroganov
6 portions

1 portion = approx. 12 grams of usable protein
28% to 34% of average daily protein need

The flavor of stroganov doesn't really require beef. Try this recipe and you'll agree.

1½	cups sliced onions	2	tsp worcestershire sauce
*3	cups chopped mushrooms	2	tsp dry mustard
¼	cup oil and butter	a few	gratings fresh nutmeg
¼	cup whole wheat flour	*1	cup dry soybeans, cooked
¾	cup stock	*1½	cups yogurt
¼	cup sherry	*1½	cups raw bulgur wheat, cooked
1½-2	tsp salt		

(1) Heat 2 tablespoons of oil and 2 tablespoons of butter (or any combination you prefer) in a large cast iron frying pan. Sauté the onions and mushrooms until they are soft.

(2) Stir in the whole wheat flour and cook for about 2 minutes until the flour has browned lightly and has coated all of the vegetables.

(3) Stir in the stock, sherry, salt, worcestershire, mustard, and nutmeg; cook until the mixture is thick. It will be very thick until the other ingredients are added.

(4) Stir in the cooked soybeans and cook over low heat until they are heated through. Remove from the heat and stir in the yogurt. You should have a luscious creamy mixture now.

(5) Serve the stroganov over the cooked bulgur while it's hot.

---

*	
1½	cups yogurt : ¾ cup soybeans
¼	cup soybeans : 1½ cups bulgur wheat
3	cups mushrooms

Nut and Seed Patties
5 patties

> 1 patty = approx. 8 grams of usable protein
> 18% to 21% of average daily protein need

These patties are crunchy on the outside and soft inside. Try them cold for lunch with bread, ketchup, or yogurt.

½ cup chopped onions	¼ cup chopped fresh parsley
*⅔ cup finely chopped mushrooms	*⅓ cup grated cheese
*⅓ cup sunflower seeds, ground (½ cup meal)	*⅓ cup sesame butter OR tahini
*¼ cup peanuts, ground (⅓ cup meal)	2 tbsp lemon juice
	1 tbsp soy sauce
	wheat germ
	oil for frying

(1) Stir all ingredients together (EXCEPT wheat germ) in a small bowl. You might add other seasonings, like garlic, oregano, or other herbs.

(2) Shape into patties, coat with raw wheat germ, and fry in hot oil until nicely browned on each side. Don't overcook them. They should be hot and crunchy when you eat them.

---

*

⅓ cup sunflower seeds : ¼ cup peanuts
⅓ cup tahini : ⅙ cup grated cheese
⅔ cup mushrooms
⅙ cup grated cheese

Vegetable Entrees

When you have certain vegetables in your garden or your refrigerator, it's nice to be able to make something delicious with them that's a good main course at the same time. Many of these dishes are just that, but if you are serving several people they can be delicious side dishes as well. Note that many of the recipes provide one third or more of your daily protein need, so they certainly would qualify as main dishes.

Crusted Cauliflower
6 portions

> 1 portion = approx. 9 grams of usable protein
> 21% to 25% of average daily protein need

Although this casserole contains no eggs, it has a soufflé-like texture. The grain and cheese crust is an interesting contrast to the smoothness of the cauliflower. You will find this to be an unusual and delightful way to eat cauliflower.

3	cups steamed cauli-flower	*½	cup wheat germ
½	cup stock	¼	tsp ground nutmeg
*½	cup grated cheese	*½	cup raw brown rice
*½	cup chopped peanuts, raw or roasted		(OR whole wheat OR whole oats), cooked
*3	tbsp brewer's yeast		grated cheese
*¼	cup soy flour		nutmeg

(1) Buzz the cauliflower and ½ cup stock in the blender until it's very smooth. You should have about 2 cups of puree.

(2)   Stir the grated cheese, peanuts, brewer's yeast, soy
      flour, wheat germ, and nutmeg into the puree;
      turn the mixture into an oiled 2-quart casserole.

(3)   Fluff the cooked grain with a fork; carefully sprin-
      kle it over the puree. Top with more grated
      cheese and another dash of nutmeg.

(4)   Bake the casserole at 350°F for 20 to 25 minutes.

* _____

½   cup raw brown rice : 2 tbsp brewer's yeast
½   cup peanuts : 2 tbsp grated cheese
¼   cup soy flour : 1/12 cup grated cheese
½   cup wheat germ
about 5 tbsp grated cheese

_____

Cheesey Chard (or Spinach)
4 portions

> 1 portion = approx. 4 grams of usable protein
> 10% to 12% of average daily protein need

You might serve this colorful dish with a bean loaf
and a bowl of soup. It's quickly assembled if you have
some leftover rice available.

*¾ cup raw brown rice, cooked (about 1½ cups of cooked rice)	1 large bunch chard, spinach, OR any leafy green. Chop stems and leaves separately.
*⅓ cup (or more) grated cheese	2 onions, chopped
oil	1 clove garlic, minced or crushed
	soy sauce to taste

(1)   In a wok or large frying pan sauté the chard
      stems, onions, and garlic until the onions are
      transparent.

(2) Stir in the cooked rice and put the chopped chard leaves on top. Cover the pan and cook over low heat until the chard leaves are wilted. Then you can stir the leaves into the rice mixture underneath.

(3) Add the grated cheese and soy sauce; stir until the cheese melts and holds the mixture together somewhat. Serve at once.

Variation—Bean Cheesey Chard

1 portion = approx. 10 grams of usable protein: 23% to 27% of average daily protein need.

To make a heartier dish, stir in ½ cup of dry kidney beans, cooked, when you stir in the rice. Use ⅔ cup grated cheese in all.

* ─────────────────────────────

¾ cup raw brown rice : ⅓ cup grated cheese
for the variation, add ½ cup beans : ⅓ cup grated cheese

─────────────────────────────

Creamed Spinach
2 to 3 portions

1 portion = approx. 9 grams of usable protein
21% to 25% of average daily protein need

2 tbsp oil	*1 egg, beaten
*¼ cup whole wheat flour	3-4 cups chopped fresh spinach
*1 cup milk, hot	*3 tbsp freshly grated parmesan cheese
1 tsp salt	*¼ cup yogurt
½ to 1 tsp nutmeg (freshly grated if possible)	

(1) Heat the oil in a 1½ to 2 quart saucepan. Stir in

the flour and cook over very low heat 1-2 minutes to remove the raw taste.

(2) Stir in the hot milk, salt, and nutmeg. Cook until the sauce thickens, stirring often.

(3) Add ¼ cup of the hot sauce to the beaten egg, then add the egg mixture back to the saucepan. Stir briskly to avoid curdling.

(4) After the sauce has cooked for about 1 minute with the egg in it, stir in all of the spinach.

(5) Cover tightly and simmer over low heat for five minutes, until the spinach just wilts. Remove from heat.

(6) Stir in the parmesan and yogurt, and you are ready to serve. We had the spinach over dark caraway rye toast, and it was delicious.

*

¼ cup whole wheat flour : 2 tbsp milk
⅞ cup milk
3 tbsp parmesan cheese
1 egg
¼ cup yogurt

Spicy Sweet Potatoes
6 portions

> 1 portion = approx. 10 grams of usable protein
> 23% to 27% of average daily protein need

This dish is an interesting variation on the usual yam casseroles served at Thanksgiving time. You will find this to be a delight any day of the year, more delicious and higher in protein than most yam dishes. As a dish in its own right, serve it with slices of apple or other fresh fruit.

2	cups cooked and mashed cold yams OR sweet potatoes	*½	cup ricotta cheese
		1½	tsp cinnamon
		¾	tsp nutmeg
*1	cup milk, warm	¾	tsp allspice
*3	eggs, beaten	½	tsp cloves
*1¼	cups toasted sunflower seeds	(2	tbsp honey—optional)

(1) Beat the milk and eggs together; stir them into the mashed yams and blend thoroughly.

(2) Mash up the ricotta cheese so it isn't in one lump; stir the spices and sunflower seeds into it. Then add the mixture to the yams, and blend well. (Stir in the honey.)

(3) Turn the mixture into an oiled casserole. Bake at 350°F for about 25 minutes.

* ———————————————————————————

    3 eggs
1¼ cups sunflower seeds : 1 cup milk
    ½ cup ricotta cheese

Swiss String Beans
8 portions

> 1 portion = approx. 9 grams of usable protein
> 21% to 25% of average daily protein need

I love the gooey-crunchy crust of this casserole. There is plenty of extra grated cheese to complement some rice or bulgur wheat that you might serve with it. And serve a raw carrot salad for color and crunch.

4 cups string beans, about 1 pound, chopped into ¾ inch pieces

½ cup minced onions

2 tbsp whole wheat flour

½ tsp salt

*1 cup yogurt

1 heaping tsp honey

*2 cups grated swiss cheese

*1¼ cups sesame seeds, toasted and ground (about 1½ cups meal)

butter

(1) Steam the string beans for about 3 minutes in a small amount of water. They should just begin to get tender. Drain them immediately (and put the stock into your refrigerator stock pot).

(2) Combine the beans, minced onions, whole wheat flour, and salt. Stir well so that the flour coats the vegetables. Stir in the yogurt and honey.

(3) Turn the mixture into an oiled 2-quart casserole. The deeper and narrower the casserole, the gooier will be the topping crust. The only thing I don't recommend is a shallow baking dish.

(4) Cover the bean mixture with the grated cheese; then spread the sesame meal over the cheese and dot with butter.

(5) Bake at 325°F for about 25-30 minutes.

---
*

1 cup yogurt : 1¼ cups sesame seeds

2 cups grated swiss cheese

Garbanzo Stuffed Cabbage
12 rolls

> 1 roll = approx. 5 grams of usable protein
> 10% to 13% of average daily protein need

If you eat 3 or 4 cabbage rolls, they are a filling main course. You might want to serve them individually as appetizers, or as a side course with a cheese or potato soup.

12 outer cabbage leaves, steamed until tender for rolling, but not too soft	½ tsp oregano
	1 tbsp soy sauce
	*2 tbsp brewer's yeast
	⅓ cup chopped celery
	⅔ cup chopped mushrooms
Stuffing:	*¼ cup soy grits, soaked in ¼ cup stock
*¾ cup raw brown rice, cooked	*⅓ cup grated cheese
*½ cup dry garbanzo beans, cooked tender	**Topping:**
*½ cup yogurt	1 small can of tomatoes OR several fresh tomatoes
2 tbsp chopped fresh parsley	*⅓ cup grated cheese oregano
2 tbsp chopped fresh chives	
¼ tsp crushed or ground celery seeds	

(1)   Buzz the cooked garbanzos and yogurt in a blender until the mixture is smooth. Pour the mixture into a mixing bowl; stir in the rice, parsley, chives, and all the remaining stuffing ingredients.

(2)   Place 2 tablespoons of the stuffing in the middle

of each cabbage leaf. Roll or fold the leaves and place them on the bottom of a pressure cooker, casserole, or dutch oven.

(3)   Arrange the canned or chopped fresh tomatoes on top and in between the cabbage rolls. Pour in a small amount of the tomato liquid or water; sprinkle with grated cheese and oregano.

(4)   You may cook the cabbage rolls by any of these 3 methods:

(a)   Pressure cook at 15 pounds pressure for 8 to 10 minutes.

(b)   Bake covered in a 350°F oven for about 30 minutes, adding tomato liquid or water during the baking if necessary.

(c)   Simmer covered over low heat for 30 minutes, adding liquid as necessary.

* _____

¾   cup raw brown rice : ⅓ cup grated cheese
¼   cup soy grits : ½ cup yogurt
½   cup garbanzos : ⅓ cup grated cheese
2   tbsp brewer's yeast

_____

Sweet and Sour Cabbage
8 portions

1 portion = approx. 7 grams of usable protein
17% to 20% of average daily protein need

This dish has the tang of sweet and sour, but is especially unusual because of the caraway flavor. It might be a side dish at a big feast, but it is delicious enough all by itself for a one-course meal.

½	head of a large cabbage, shredded	¼	cup oil
		¼	cup honey
2	medium onions, chopped	1	tbsp caraway seeds, crushed
	juice of 2 lemons	½	cup raisins
(4	apples, diced—about 2 cups—optional)	⅛	tsp allspice
		*1	cup cottage cheese
¼	cup apple cider vinegar	*1½	cups raw bulgur wheat
		*1	cup yogurt

(1) Combine all ingredients EXCEPT yogurt.
(2) Place in an oiled casserole and bake covered at 350°F for about 30 minutes, until the bulgur is tender. Place a dab of yogurt on each portion.

Note: When I first mixed up the ingredients for the cabbage dish, several of us started eating it raw. Try it raw and add the cooked bulgur or other cooked grain for a wonderful salad.

* _____

1½ cups bulgur : ¼ cup cottage cheese
¾ cup cottage cheese
1 cup yogurt

_____

Eggplant Elegant
6 portions

1 portion = approx. 14 grams of usable protein
32% to 39% of average daily protein need

This dish was delicious and filling with a salad alongside. We put tomato sauce on top of the leftovers and reheated them the next day. They were still delicious! If you wish a big meal, there is plenty of extra cheese to complement rice too.

Sauce:

1	onion, chopped	2-3	cups canned tomatoes
2	cloves garlic, chopped	2-3	tsp oregano
¼	pound mushrooms, chopped	1	tsp basil
1	can tomato paste	1	tsp honey

(1) Sauté the onion, garlic, and mushrooms in a small amount of oil in a 2-quart saucepan.

(2) Stir in the tomato paste and remaining ingredients. Add a little water if necessary.

(3) Simmer the sauce while you prepare the rest of the dish.

Batter:
- *1 cup whole wheat flour
- ¼ tsp salt
- *4 eggs, beaten
- water

Eggplant:
- *½ pound cheese
- oil for frying
- 1 medium eggplant

(1) Stir together the flour and salt. Add the beaten eggs to the flour and mix lightly, adding enough water to make a very thick batter. You want the batter to coat the eggplant without sliding off.

(2) Peel the eggplant and slice it into ½-inch rounds.

(3) Dip each slice into the batter, then fry in hot oil until golden.

(4) Arrange the batter-fried slices on a baking sheet.

(5) You may use sliced mozzarella or jack cheese, or grated parmesan mixed with jack or mozzarella. Put a slice of cheese or grated cheese on each round of eggplant.

(6) Place the baking dish (with the eggplant slices topped with cheese) into a 350°F oven for about

10 minutes, until the cheese is melted and the eggplant is very hot.

(7)   Serve at once topped with the tomato sauce.

* ───────────────────────────────

    4 eggs
    1 cup whole wheat flour : less than 1 ounce cheese
    about 7 ounces cheese

─────────────────────────────────

Mushroom Curry
8 portions

> 1 portion = approx. 7 grams of usable protein
> 15% to 19% of average daily protein need

A delicious one-dish meal, or add a salad for a simple feast.

2-3 tbsp butter	salt
*½ pound fresh	paprika
mushrooms—chop	*2⅔ cups yogurt
the stems and	*2 cups raw brown
leave the caps	rice, cooked and
whole	hot OR 1½ cups
1 onion, minced	raw bulgur wheat,
1 tbsp curry powder	cooked and hot
2 apples, chopped	
fine (chop one of	
the apples just be-	
fore serving)	

(1)   Sauté the mushroom caps in butter for about 5 minutes, until they just absorb the butter and get slightly brown. Set them aside in a small bowl.

(2)   Add more butter to the pan and sauté the onion and curry powder until the onion is almost transparent. Add one chopped apple and the

mushroom stems; continue sautéing until the onion is transparent. Don't let the apple get too mushy. Remove from the heat and stir in paprika, salt to taste, and the yogurt.

(3) To assemble the dish: Place the cooked grain in a 2 or 2½ quart casserole. Spread the mushroom-yogurt sauce evenly over the grain. Then arrange the mushroom caps on the top. Sprinkle with more paprika.

(4) Bake the casserole at 350°F until the sauce is firm. Sprinkle the freshly chopped apple over the top just before serving.

Variations: Instead of a casserole dish, use a shallow 7″ x 11″ baking dish. Arrange the ingredients as in (3), and bake until the sauce is firm.

Quick Mushroom Curry: Stir the sautéed mushroom caps into the yogurt sauce and either combine the sauce with the cooked grain OR serve the mushrooms and sauce over the cooked grain. You may also stir the uncooked chopped apple in with the caps.

*
_____

2   cups raw brown rice : 2⅔ cups yogurt
½   pound mushrooms

_____

Mushrooms in Parmesan Sauce for Toast
4 portions

1 portion = approx. 10 grams of usable protein
22% to 27% of average daily protein need

This might be an elegant first course for a big meal, or an appetizing side dish. For two people it makes a simple, high-protein meal.

1   cup stock or wine
¼   cup chili sauce or
    tomato catsup
¼   tsp grated fresh
    ginger root
¼   cup minced onions
    butter or sesame oil

*2   cups sliced
    mushrooms
*¾   cup freshly grated
    parmesan cheese
*4   slices whole grain
    toast

(1)   Heat the stock, chili sauce, ginger, and onions in a small saucepan; simmer for about 5 minutes.

(2)   Meanwhile, melt some butter in a small frying pan; sauté the mushrooms for about 5 minutes.

(3)   Stir the sauce into the mushroom mixture and cook for about 2 minutes. Remove the pan from the heat, and just before serving, stir in the grated cheese.

(4)   You may quarter or halve the pieces of toast. Spoon the mushrooms and sauce over, and serve at once.

*
_____

4   slices whole grain bread: ¼ cup parmesan cheese
½   cup parmesan cheese
2   cups sliced mushrooms

_____

Eggplant Bake
4 portions

> 1 portion = approx. 21 grams of usable protein
> 47% to 56% of average daily protein need

If you have some leftover cooked rice, this dish will take only 15 minutes to prepare for the oven. It's a light dish, because the eggplant is not fried.

*1½	cups raw brown rice, cooked	2	tsp fresh chopped basil (or 1 tsp dried)
1	eggplant, peeled and sliced into 1-inch rounds	½	tsp dried oregano
1	can (6 ounces) tomato paste	½	tsp onion powder
*1	cup cottage cheese	½	tsp garlic powder stock or water
*1	cup yogurt	*1	cup grated cheese
		*1	cup whole grain bread crumbs butter

(1) Oil a shallow baking dish and spread the cooked rice over the bottom. Lay the eggplant slices over the rice.

(2) Prepare the sauce by combining the tomato paste, cottage cheese, yogurt, herbs, and powders; add enough stock to make the sauce easy to pour.

(3) Pour the sauce over the eggplant slices, cover with grated cheese, top with bread crumbs, and dot with butter.

(4) Bake the casserole at 350°F for about 30 minutes, until the eggplant is tender and the top is crisp.

*
_____

1½	cups raw brown rice : 1 cup yogurt and ⅓ cup grated cheese
1	cup bread crumbs : about ⅓ cup grated cheese
⅓	cup grated cheese
1	cup cottage cheese

_____

Summer Squash Deluxe
8 portions

> 1 portion = approx. 7 grams of usable protein
> 16% to 19% of average daily protein need

You might use zucchini, yellow crooked neck, or pale green scalloped summer squash, or mix all three types for this beautiful casserole.

*1½ cups raw brown rice, cooked with—	*⅓ cup grated cheese
1 tsp salt and ...	½ tsp salt
1 tsp paprika	*1 egg, beaten
	¼ cup chopped fresh chives OR scallions
5 cups summer squash, sliced into bite-sized pieces	*⅓ cup toasted sesame seeds
*2 cups yogurt	whole protein bread crumbs
¼ cup sesame oil	butter

(1) Cook the rice with salt and paprika in a pressure cooker or by the regular cooking method.

(2) Prepare the squash and set it aside.

(3) Stir the yogurt, sesame oil, grated cheese, and salt together in a small saucepan; heat over a low flame until the cheese melts. Remove from heat and stir in the beaten egg and the chives. The sauce should not be so hot that it will curdle the egg.

(4) To assemble the dish: Stir the cooked rice and sesame seeds together and spread on the bottom of a 7″ x 11″ shallow baking dish. Arrange the squash pieces over the rice, pour the yogurt sauce over, top with a thick layer of bread crumbs, and dot generously with butter.

(5) Bake the casserole at 375°F until the crumbs are browned and the squash is tender but still firm.

*

1½ cups raw brown rice : 2 cups yogurt	
1 egg	
2 tbsp grated cheese : ⅓ cup sesame seeds	
⅓ cup less 2 tbsp grated cheese	

Sesame Tomatoes on Rice
6 portions

> 1 portion = approx. 7 grams of usable protein
> 17% to 20% of average daily protein need

A colorful dish with the surprise of sesame. Add to it
a green salad or steamed green vegetables for a beautiful
meal.

¼ cup sesame oil	1-2 tsp salt
1½ cups chopped on-	*2 eggs, beaten
ions	12 to 15 half-inch-
*2 cups raw brown	thick tomato slices,
rice	from firm red or
3½ cups water (for	green tomatoes
pressure cooker)	sprigs of fresh
OR 4 cups	oregano
1 tsp salt	sprigs of fresh
1 tsp dried oregano	parsley
*⅔ cup sesame seeds,	chunks of fresh
ground (about 1	tomato
cup meal)	

(1)   Heat the oil in the bottom of your pressure cooker
       OR in a regular saucepan for cooking rice.

(2)   Sauté the chopped onions until they are golden,
       add the raw rice, and continue to sauté until the
       whole mixture is golden. Add the 3½ cups water
       (or 4 cups for regular cooking), salt, and ore-
       gano. Stir, cover, and cook until the rice is tender.

(3)   While the rice cooks, stir the sesame meal and salt
       together in a flat dish or pie plate. Oil a large
       frying pan and turn the heat high.

(4)   Dip the tomato slices in the beaten egg, then into
       the sesame meal, coating both sides well. Fry the

slices quickly in hot oil to brown the meal and heat them through. You don't want the tomatoes to get mushy, so keep the heat high. As soon as they are brown, remove them from the pan.

(5) Arrange the rice on a platter or shallow bowl. Place the sesame-browned tomatoes over the rice. Top with fresh tomato chunks, sprigs of oregano and parsley. Serve while it's hot.

*

2 cups raw brown rice : ⅔ cup sesame seeds
2 eggs

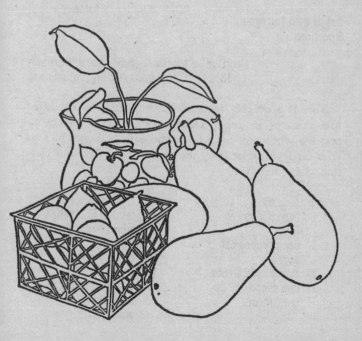

Top-of-the-Stove Grains

These dishes are prepared with either cooked or raw grains on your stove top. We like to have sautéed vegetables or a big salad with grains. Try reheating them for lunch or leftover dinners: heat some oil in a wok or frying pan and sauté the grain dishes quickly over high heat. Grain dishes aren't as high in protein as many of the vegetable entrees, main-dish casseroles, or dishes made with a lot of beans or cheese (they only provide about 10 to 20 percent of your daily protein need), so eat two portions or make sure your salad has some high-protein cottage cheese or yogurt dressing.

Bulgur cum Tarragon
6 portions

> 1 portion = approx. 5 grams of usable protein
> 13% to 15% of average daily protein need

This is a quickly assembled dish, ready to eat after five minutes in the pressure cooker. It's perfect to prepare when you have odds and ends of vegetables in your refrigerator or from the garden. Feel free to substitute what you have.

3-4	tbsp oil	1	clove garlic, minced or crushed
1	cup chopped onions	*1½	cups raw bulgur wheat
1	cup chopped celery	*¼	cup soy grits
1	cup sliced carrots	½	tsp salt
1	cup sliced mushrooms	2	tsp dried tarragon
		3	cups stock or water, hot

(1) Sauté the vegetables in the oil in your pressure cooker until the onions soften and the volume of the vegetables has decreased.

(2) Stir in the bulgur and soy grits, salt and tarragon; continue sautéing, adding more oil if necessary, until the mixture is fragrant with tarragon and the bulgur is well coated with oil and sizzling.

(3) Add the 3 cups of stock and bring the mixture to a boil. Stir several times, cover, and pressure cook 5 minutes at 15 pounds. Without a pressure cooker, cover and simmer about 20 minutes or until all of the water has been absorbed. (You may want to add a little more liquid at this time for a more tender grain.)

*

1½ cups bulgur wheat : ¼ cup soy grits

Very Brown Rice
8 portions

1 portion = approx. 6 grams of usable protein
13% to 16% of average daily protein need

Have a tomato and cottage cheese salad and steamed broccoli with this savory rice.

¼ cup oil
*2 cups raw brown rice
2 tbsp butter, divided into small chunks
4½ OR 5½-6 cups water, for pressure cooking or regular cooking, respectively

*¾ cup dry mixed small beans, such as mung, split peas, red, or lentils (soaked for regular cooking)
2 tsp salt

(1) Heat the oil in a large saucepan or pressure cooker.

(2) Add the rice and sauté it for 5-7 minutes, until it crackles and browns lightly.

(3) Stir in the chunks of butter until they melt; then add the water and mixed beans.

(4) Pressure cook for 15 minutes. For regular cooking, cook until the rice and beans are tender, adding more water if necessary.

(5) Stir in the salt and serve.

* ──────────────────────────────────────

2 cups raw brown rice : ¾ cup mixed beans

──────────────────────────────────────

Vegetable Rice Curry
8 portions

1 portion = approx. 8 grams of usable protein
19% to 23% of average daily protein need

Curry dishes go well with something sweet on the side. Make a cabbage slaw with "Easy Cole Slaw Dressing" (p. 112), adding some sliced pitted dates and chopped walnuts, for a perfect accompaniment to curry.

¼ cup olive oil
1 cup chopped onions or scallions
3 tbsp curry powder (more or less depending on your taste and your powder)
*2 cups raw brown rice
*3 tbsp soy grits
4 OR 5 cups water
1 tsp salt

*⅔ cup sunflower seeds
½ cup raw peanuts, chopped
½ cup oil
½ cup chopped green or sweet red pepper
2 cups chopped fresh tomatoes
1 medium summer squash (zucchini or crooked neck), chopped

(1) In a pressure cooker or large saucepan heat the olive oil; sauté the onions, curry, and raw rice until the onions are very soft. Add the soy grits and sauté a few minutes more.

(2) Add 4 cups of water for pressure cooking, 5 cups for regular cooking. Stir in the salt, sunflower seeds, and raw peanuts. Cover and pressure cook 20 minutes, or regular cook until all of the liquid is absorbed and the rice is tender.

(3) Turn the heat to low and add the ½ cup of oil and all of the chopped vegetables. Toss them with the rice and heat until they are all hot. Serve at once.

*

2	cups raw brown rice : 3 tbsp soy grits
⅔	cup sunflower seeds : ½ cup peanuts

Vegetable Barley
6 portions

1 portion = approx. 4 grams of usable protein
8% to 10% of average daily protein need

Colorfully full of vegetables, this dish is especially quick to prepare if you have some leftover barley (or brown rice).

*1¼	cups raw barley, cooked with ...	¾	cup chopped green pepper
*2	tbsp soy grits and ...	*1½	cups chopped mushrooms
2	tsp salt	2	tsp ground coriander
¼	cup oil		
2	cups sliced carrots	2	tsp ground dill seeds
1	large onion, sliced		
2	stalks celery, chopped		

(1) While the barley cooks, heat the oil in a large frying pan or wok. Sauté the vegetables in the order given, adding each one as the one before gets hot and starts to sizzle. The total cooking time should be about 10 minutes. The carrots should be crisp, the onions lightly browned, the celery and green pepper crisp, and the mushrooms browned.

(2) Stir in the dill and coriander, then the cooked barley. Brown the barley slightly with the cooked vegetables and serve at once.

* _____

1¼   cups barley : 2 tbsp soy grits
1½   cups mushrooms

_____

Bulgur and Garbanzos
6 portions

> 1 portion = approx. 8 grams of usable protein
> 17% to 21% of average daily protein need

This quick dish goes beautifully with steamed summer squash and butter. Quick bread or muffins and a salad round out the meal.

*1¼	cups raw bulgur wheat	1	tsp dill seeds
3	tbsp oil	1	tbsp tamari soy sauce
2½	cups stock	*¾	cup garbanzo beans, cooked tender
1	bay leaf (remove before serving)	oil	
		*1	cup yogurt

(1) Sauté the bulgur in the oil for about 5 minutes until it sizzles and is slightly brown. Add more oil if it sticks to the pan.

(2) Add the stock, bay leaf, dill seeds, and soy sauce to the bulgur. Bring to a boil, lower the heat, cover and simmer until all of the stock is absorbed.

(3) While the bulgur is cooking, sauté the garbanzos in an oiled frying pan for about 10 minutes. Add oil as needed. The garbanzos won't get crisp like nuts, but they should brown on the outside.

(4) When the bulgur is cooked, stir in the garbanzos and 1 cup of yogurt. Let the mixture stand for a few minutes to allow the grains to absorb the yogurt. Then serve.

*

1¼ cups bulgur : ¼ cup garbanzos
1 cup yogurt : ½ cup garbanzos

Risi e Bisi
6 portions

1 portion = approx. 9 grams of usable protein
21% to 26% of average daily protein need

Traditionally, this dish is made with all fresh peas. However, for complete protein it would require far too many fresh peas for the amount of rice we are including, so I have substituted split peas to make this colorful dish more nutritious.

½ cup chopped onion
*1⅓ cups raw brown rice
2⅔ cups hot stock or water
1 cup fresh shelled green peas

*½ cup dry split peas, cooked until just tender
2 tbsp butter
*1 cup grated parmesan cheese
soy sauce or salt to taste

(1) Use a small amount of oil to sauté the onions and rice in 3-quart pan or casserole. Stir constantly, adding more oil as necessary, until the onions are transparent.

(2) Stir in the hot stock, bring to a boil, lower the heat, cover, and simmer the mixture until the rice is tender and almost all of the liquid is absorbed.

(3) Stir in the fresh peas and cook about 1 minute until they are warm. Don't overcook them.

(4) Add the cooked split peas, butter, and grated parmesan cheese. Blend the mixture gently, adding salt or soy sauce. Serve immediately while the rice is hot and creamy.

*

1⅓ cups raw brown rice : ½ cup dry split peas
1 cup grated parmesan cheese

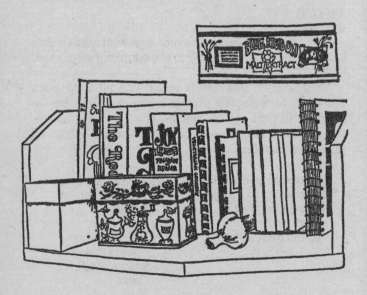

Alpine Rice
6 portions

> 1 portion = approx. 8 grams of usable protein
> 17% to 21% of average daily protein need

Accompany this quick rice dish with a bean loaf and green salad for a tasty feast.

*1½ cups raw brown rice, cooked and hot	*⅓ cup grated swiss cheese
2 tbsp butter	*⅓ cup roasted sesame seeds, ground (about ½ cup meal)
*⅓ cup grated parmesan cheese	*½ cup hot milk

(1) Toss together the hot rice, butter, cheeses, and sesame meal, mixing until the cheese melts and coats the rice evenly.

(2) Pour the hot milk over and toss again. Serve at once.

* _____

1½ cups raw brown rice : ⅔ cup grated cheese
½ cup sesame meal : ⅓ cup milk
a few extra tbsp milk

_____

Egg and Cheese Dishes

Many of these dishes could be anything from an appetizer to a main dish to a snack. However you use it, a dish rich with cheese always brings a note of elegance to your table. Do use natural cheeses, and try some of the more exotic flavors. Some types that I find abominable when raw are absolutely delicious when they are melted in or on hot dishes. There should never be any need to buy processed cheeses; they contain not only chemical preservatives, but also emulsifiers and stabilizers, which give them their characteristic plastic quality.

For the best results, use specific cheeses when they are called for in the recipes, but use whatever you have on hand when a recipe just calls for cheese or grated cheese.

Cheese is like solid milk (⅓ cup grated has about the same amount of protein as 1 cup of milk). Some types, especially low-fat cheeses, keep very well without refrigeration.

We always take cheese on our camping trips. We buy fresh parmesan, grate it, and put it in a plastic bag for sprinkling on fireside dinners. You might think that fresh parmesan is expensive, but for a box of grated parmesan at the local supermarket (with preservatives added, of course) the price can range from $1.68 to $2.08 per pound of grated cheese.

Cheese can do marvelous things for food. It can make a plain potato elegant. It can add a finishing touch to a casserole while adding a significant amount of protein. It can be munched or melted, or crunched with apples. It goes with all types of foods: bread, vegetables, fruits, whole grains, eggs, noodles, potatoes, even desserts. Can you discover some new ways to use it?

I haven't included any breakfast egg dishes (specifically), because I feel that most cookbooks deal with this perfect protein extensively enough. Use the egg dishes included here for quick dinners, or snacks.

The freshest eggs make the best egg dishes. If you've ever eaten an organically "grown" egg, you've already tasted the difference. (Organically grown eggs are produced—not manufactured—from chickens that are fed organically grown feed without the addition of hormones or antibiotics to force them to lay. Usually they are not confined to a minimum of space, as manufacturing chickens commonly are.)

Remember, eggs are the most perfect protein available for us humans, and you can eat them any time of day.

Cheese Fondue (with Whole Wheat Sourdough French Bread)
6 portions

1 portion = approx. 24 grams of usable protein
56% to 68% of average daily protein need

*1 pound swiss emmenthaler cheese OR ½ pound emmenthaler and ½ pound gruyere cheese, grated
1 clove garlic
2 cups dry white wine
3 tbsp kirsch
1 tbsp cornstarch
nutmeg
paprika
apple chunks
*1 recipe whole wheat sourdough french bread (see below)

(1) Rub the garlic over a heavy saucepan (and also rub it over your fondue dish for serving).
(2) Pour in the wine and heat until it has foamy bubbles all over the surface. This is best done quickly over high heat. Don't let the wine boil.
(3) Add the grated cheese a handful at a time, stirring constantly. Keep the heat high so that the cheese melts quickly, but never let the mixture boil.

(4)   When all of the cheese has been added, pour in
       the kirsch, which has had the tablespoon of corn-
       starch mixed in. Continue to stir, and the fondue
       will thicken slightly. Add nutmeg and paprika to
       taste.

(5)   Transfer the fondue to a fondue dish or chafing
       dish with a small flame below to keep it warm.

(6)   To serve, have everyone spear the bread from the
       soft side through the opposite crust (see the bread
       recipe for how to cube the bread). Dip the bread
       into the fondue. Dip apple chunks, or dip apple
       and bread together. We also like to dip raw vege-
       tables like cauliflower, asparagus, broccoli, or po-
       tatoes (these are also good cooked). Serve the
       fondue with green salad and your favorite wine.

Whole Wheat Sourdough French Bread
2 oblong loaves OR 1 large round loaf

Ostensibly for the fondue, this bread is delicious any
time. Since it isn't complete protein by itself, be sure to
eat it with cheese, bean spread, or a glass of milk.

1½	cups warm water	*4	cups whole wheat flour
1	tbsp baking yeast		
1	cup sourdough starter (see p. 216)	½	tsp baking soda
		*2	cups whole wheat flour
2	tsp honey		
2	tsp salt		

(1)   In a large bowl stir together the water, yeast,
       starter, honey, salt, and 4 cups of whole wheat
       flour. Stir for about 5 minutes until the dough
       feels elastic. Cover and let rise until double
       (about 1½ to 2 hours).

(2)   Mix the baking soda with 1 of the remaining cups of whole wheat flour and add it to the dough. Knead the dough for about 10 minutes, using the other cup of whole wheat flour if it is needed. The dough should be very elastic and satiny.

(3)   Let rise again until double (about 1 hour). Punch down, add more flour if necessary, and knead a few times.

(4)   Shape the dough into 2 oblong loaves (for fondue) or 1 round loaf. Place on a lightly oiled cookie sheet, cover, and let rise until double— 45-60 minutes.

(5)   Slash with a knife or razor blade, brush with water. To slash the bread, cut four lines into the top of the loaves about one-half inch deep.

(6)   Bake at 400°F, with a pan of hot water on the lower shelf of the oven, for about 45 minutes until well browned.

(7)   For fondue, cut the bread into 1-inch cubes after it has cooled. Be sure each cube has some crust. You can store the cubes (or loaves) in plastic (not PVC) bags for a day or more.

* _____

6   cups whole wheat flour : 1 cup grated cheese
3   cups grated cheese

_____

Tomato Quiche
8 portions

> 1 portion = approx. 9 grams of usable protein
> 22% to 26% of average daily protein need

This quiche is somewhat spicier than the traditional quiche. It makes an attractive main dish or, when sliced small, an elegant appetizer. Its flavor stands up even when it's served cold.

2 tbsp butter	*1 cup grated swiss cheese
1 cup finely chopped onion	
	2 large tomatoes, peeled and sliced ¾ inch thick
1 cup tomatoes, peeled and chopped	
pinch of thyme	*1 10″ pie crust (made from ½ the recipe for Wholesome Whole Wheat Pie Crust in the dessert section) OR any whole wheat pie crust.
dash salt	
*3 eggs, beaten	
*1 cup milk	
½ tsp salt	
*½ cup freshly grated parmesan cheese	

(1) Melt the butter in a small frying pan and sauté the onions until they are transparent and very soft. Add the thyme, salt, and chopped tomatoes; cover the mixture and simmer for 5 minutes.

(2) Uncover the pan and mash the tomatoes; cook uncovered until the mixture is dry and thick. When done the tomatoes should be completely mashed into the onions. Set aside to cool.

(3) Beat the eggs, milk, and salt together; stir in the grated cheese and cooled tomato mixture.

(4) Line the bottom of the pie crust with the sliced tomatoes; pour the cheese mixture over.

(5) Bake the quiche at 350°F for 25 to 30 minutes, until a knife inserted in the center comes out clean.

(6) You may serve it at any temperature—from piping hot to cold.

*

1	cup swiss cheese
1	Wholesome Whole Wheat Pie Crust
3	eggs
1	cup milk
½	cup parmesan cheese

Mushrooms Supreme
6 portions

> 1 portion = approx. 13 grams of usable protein
> 31% to 37% of average daily protein need

Although this may seem to be a very rich dish, it is delightfully light, like a soufflé, but doesn't require special preparation. It's elegant as a main dish or for Sunday brunch, and it goes beautifully beside a bean loaf or vegetable casserole.

*2 cups chopped mushrooms	*½ cup whole wheat flour
¼ cup chopped onions	½ tsp salt
¼ cup butter	a few grindings pepper
1 tbsp oil	⅛ tsp nutmeg
*1 tbsp whole wheat flour	*4 eggs, at room temperature
*2¼ cups cold milk	*1½ cups grated cheese
¼ tsp salt	

(1) Sauté the mushrooms and onions in 1 tablespoon of the butter and the 1 tablespoon oil until they are browned—about 5 minutes.

(2) Sprinkle in the 1 tablespoon of whole wheat flour and stir over low heat for about 1 minute to coat the vegetables, and to remove the raw taste of flour.

(3) Add ¼ cup of milk and stir until the mixture is thick. Stir in the ¼ teaspoon salt and set aside.

(4) Place the ½ cup of whole wheat flour in a 2-quart saucepan; beat in the remaining 2 cups of milk with a wire whisk.

(5) Place the mixture over medium heat and stir constantly until it thickens and then boils. Remove from the heat and beat in the remaining 3 tablespoons of butter, the seasonings, and the eggs—

one by one. Finally, stir in 1 cup of the grated cheese.

(6) Place ½ of the mixture (about 1¾ cups) in a well oiled casserole, spread the mushroom mixture over, then cover with the remaining cheese mixture. Sprinkle with the remaining ½ cup of grated cheese.

(7) Bake in the upper third of a 400°F oven for 25 minutes. Serve at once.

Variation: You may refrigerate the cheese mixture and the mushroom mixture separately. Assemble them as in (6), but add 10 to 15 minutes to the baking time.

*　————————————————————

2	cups mushrooms
½	cup plus 1 tbsp whole wheat flour : ¼ cup plus ½ tbsp milk
2	cups milk
4	eggs
1½	cups grated cheese

————————————————————

Cheese Blintzes
12 blintzes

2 blintzes = approx. 15 grams of usable protein
34% to 40% of average daily protein need

Pancakes:

*¾	cup whole wheat pastry flour	⅓	cup water
½	tsp salt	½	tsp vanilla OR grated orange rind OR grated lemon rind
1	tsp baking powder		
*2	eggs, beaten		
*⅔	cup milk or buttermilk	2	tbsp honey

(1) Stir the dry ingredients together. Combine the liquid ingredients in a separate bowl.

(2) Make a well in the dry ingredients and pour the liquid in all at once. Stir gently about 7 times until most of the lumps are gone. Don't beat the batter.

(3) Heat a small curved omelette pan or a small skillet. Oil it lightly.

(4) To cook the pancakes, put 3 to 4 tablespoons of batter in the pan. Tip the pan so that the batter spreads evenly over the bottom. Cook on one side until the top is dry. Place on a moist towel, cooked side up, while you make the rest. Do not stack the cakes. They will only be spread around the kitchen as long as it takes you to make them all.

Filling:

*2¼	cups cottage OR ricotta cheese	orange rind OR grated lemon rind
*2	egg yolks	(Match your filling
1½	tsp soft butter	flavor to your cake
1½	tsp vanilla OR grated	flavor.)

(1) Stir all ingredients together.

(2) To assemble the blintzes: place 2 tablespoons of filling in the center of the cooked side of each pancake; fold the pancakes over the filling like an envelope.

(3) You may place the blintzes seam-side-down in a closely covered dish and chill until needed.

(4) To cook: oil a large skillet and fry the blintzes on both sides until they are golden. Handle them carefully while you do this so as not to puncture the pancake.

(5)   If you plan to double or triple the recipe in order to serve several people, keep the blintzes warm in a covered dish in a low oven.

(6)   Serve with cinnamon, yogurt, and apples or applesauce, or top with a fruit sauce or jam, for a rich and elegant dessert.

*—————————————————————————————

    2   eggs
    ¾   cup whole wheat flour : about ⅓ cup milk
    ⅓   cup milk
    2¼ cups ricotta or cottage cheese
    2   egg yolks

—————————————————————————————

Egg Tacos
4 tacos

> 1 taco = approx. 17 grams of usable protein
> 34% to 45% of average daily protein need

Another quick dinner, these tacos also are good if you're into exciting midnight snacks.

*6	eggs	½	cup chopped onion
*½	cup milk	2-3	tsp chili powder
*2	tbsp soy grits	½	tsp salt
2	tbsp oil	1	tsp cumin, ground
2	to 3 tsp fresh chopped hot green chilis OR ¼ to ½ tsp crushed dried chilis	*4	corn tortillas, fried quickly in hot oil and folded in half
		*1	cup grated cheese
		1-2	sliced tomatoes

(1)   Beat the eggs with the milk; stir in the soy grits and let the mixture sit.

(2)   Sauté the fresh chilis and onions in the oil until the onions begin to brown. If you are using dried

chilis, stir them into the egg mixture along with the chili powder, salt, and ground cumin.

(3) When the onions are golden, add the eggs and then scramble them until they are somewhat dry. Their color will be unusual, but they should be delightfully spicy!

(4) Serve the eggs, fried tacos, tomatoes, and cheese separately, and assemble the tacos as you are ready to eat them:

(5) Place a generous amount of egg in the shell, cover with cheese, top with tomato, and then eat!

* _____

6 eggs
4 tortillas : ½ cup milk : 2 tbsp soy grits
1 cup grated cheese

Creamy Cottage Eggs
2 portions

1 portion = approx. 20 grams of usable protein
45% to 56% of average daily protein need

These eggs are an interesting change from the usual scrambled eggs, and they are extremely rich in protein.

*4 eggs, beaten   1 tsp butter
*½ cup cottage cheese   salt and red pepper
1 tsp oil   to taste

(1) Beat the cottage cheese into the eggs ¼ cup at a time, so that it is well broken up and mixed in with the eggs.

(2) Brush an egg or omelette pan with the oil, then add the butter and melt it over low heat.

(3) Turn the egg mixture into the pan and cook as for

scrambled eggs. The cottage cheese should melt and the mixture will be very creamy. Take care not to overcook the eggs or you will end up with chewy eggs in a puddle of water.

(4) Add salt and cayenne to taste; serve with rounds of whole grain toast.

* _____

4 eggs
½ cup cottage cheese

_____

Simple Supper Eggs
2 portions

1 portion = approx. 14 grams usable protein
31% to 38% of average daily protein need

Although these eggs might seem similar to many of the other recipes, they can be put together to make a special-looking dish. We love them with toasted whole grain bread or rolls and a glass of beer (egg in your beer?) ... delicious!

*4 eggs, beaten
*6 tbsp milk
sliced onion
sliced tomato

2 tbsp chopped ripe olives (or green ones if you prefer)
10 sprigs parsley, chopped
tamari soy sauce

(1) Beat the milk into the eggs; scramble the eggs until they are just a little *less* done than the way you like them. It is simplest to cook the eggs in a pan that you can bring to the table.

(2) Place the tomato slices on top of the almost-cooked eggs, surround them with onion rings, and

sprinkle with ripe olives. Cover and steam for about 1 minute, until the vegetables are heated through and the eggs are cooked to your liking. Sprinkle with parsley and soy sauce. Serve at once.

---

*

4   eggs
6   tbsp milk

Vegetable Scramble
2 portions

> 1 portion = approx. 14 grams of usable protein
> 32% to 39% of average daily protein need

This is one of our favorite quick suppers. Eggs alone might not make a full meal, but with the vegetables and some whole grain bread or toast it will fill you up.

*4	eggs, beaten	extra butter
*¼	cup milk	1 tomato cut in
3	tbsp butter	eighths
*½	cup chopped	1 tbsp tamari soy
	mushrooms	sauce
½	cup chopped onions	

(1) Beat the milk into the eggs and set aside.
(2) Melt the butter in a small omelette or egg pan. Sauté the mushrooms and onions for about 5 minutes.
(3) Add more butter to the pan at this time if it is dry. Pour in the egg mixture and stir. Cook like plain scrambled eggs. When the desired consistency is reached, stir in the tomato sections and soy sauce. Serve at once.

Variations—
Cheese Scramble: add about ½ cup grated cheese to the egg-milk mixture. Cook as above.
Pepper Scramble: Sauté ½ cup chopped green peppers (or sweet red peppers) with the mushrooms and onions.

---
*

4 eggs
¼ cup milk
½ cup chopped mushrooms

Noodles and Potatoes

Creamy noodle or potato dishes can be delectable main courses or elegant side courses with other dishes. Most can be prepared ahead of time, then popped into the oven in time for dinner or lunch. Be sure to use whole wheat or whole wheat and soy noodles for maximum protein quality in the following recipes. You may also substitute buckwheat noodles, if they are available to you. We often get fresh whole wheat and whole wheat soy noodles from our food conspiracy. These fresh noodles are so delicious you can eat them without cooking them!

Noodle Surprise
4 portions

> 1 portion = approx. 23 grams of usable protein
> 53% to 64% of average daily protein need

The surprise is the crunch of sunflower seeds in a creamy sauce. And more than half of your daily protein just for eating it!

*2 cups whole wheat macaroni OR other whole grain noodles	*1 generous cup grated cheese (reserve some for the top)
1 medium onion, chopped	*2 eggs, beaten
6 large mushrooms, chopped	*2/3 cup yogurt
*2/3 cup sunflower seeds	2 pinches cayenne
3 tbsp oil	1 tsp salt
	1/2 tsp worcestershire sauce
	whole grain bread crumbs

(1) Cook the noodles until tender; drain.

(2) Sauté the onion, mushrooms, and sunflower seeds in the oil until the vegetables are soft, and the seeds crisp.

(3) Combine the drained noodles with the sautéed vegetables. Stir in the cheese, eggs, yogurt, and seasonings.

(4) Turn into an oiled casserole, top with bread crumbs and reserved grated cheese.

(5) Bake at 350°F for 30 minutes, until the casserole is firm.

* _____

2	cups whole wheat noodles : ⅔ cup grated cheese
⅔	cup sunflower seeds : ⅙ cup grated cheese
2	eggs
⅙	cup grated cheese
⅔	cup yogurt

Noodle Omelet
8 portions

1 portion = approx. 15 grams of usable protein
34% to 40% of average daily protein need

An easily prepared supper dish and one that you can vary with different vegetables, spices, and herbs.

1	cup chopped onions	*1	cup grated cheese (smoked cheddar is delicious)
⅔	cup green peppers, sliced into 1-inch strips	*8	eggs, beaten
2	tbsp butter	*2¼	cups whole wheat noodles, cooked
1	tbsp oil	1	tsp salt

(1) Melt 1 tablespoon of the butter and 1 tablespoon oil together in a 10- to 12-inch frying pan. Sauté the onion and green pepper until the onion begins to brown. Stir in the second tablespoon butter and keep the pan warm over very low heat.

(2) Stir together the cheese, eggs, cooked noodles, and salt. Pour the mixture over the sautéed vegetables, cover, and cook WITHOUT STIRRING over medium-low heat for 15 to 20 minutes. You may sprinkle extra grated cheese over the top during the last few minutes of cooking.

(3) When done the casserole will be slightly puffed, browned around the edges, and firm to the touch. Serve.

Variations—(a) Add chopped mushrooms to the sautéing vegetables.

(b) Try parmesan or swiss cheese instead of smoked cheddar.

(c) Separate the eggs. Stir in the yolks as in (2). Beat the egg whites until stiff and fold in. Cook 10 to 15 minutes until puffed and dry.

* _____

2¼ cups whole wheat noodles : ⅔ cup plus 4 tsp grated cheese

4 tbsp and 1 tsp grated cheese

8 eggs

Macaroni and Beans
4 portions

> 1 portion = approx. 18 grams of usable protein
> 42% to 50% of average daily protein need

This dish is an interesting and spicy blend. No one would ever guess that there were soybeans in it! It's a quickie, too.

*1½ cups dry whole wheat macaroni, cooked until tender	(1 cup chopped mushrooms—optional)
*½ cup dry soy beans, cooked until soft, then pureed with a small amount of stock	½-¾ cups stock
	2 tsp oregano
	*1 cup yogurt
	*½ cup sesame seeds, ground and roasted
1 cup chopped onions	(parmesan cheese—optional)
1-2 cloves crushed or minced garlic	

(1) While the macaroni is cooking, sauté the onions, garlic, (and mushrooms) in a small amount of oil until the onions are soft. Pour in ½ cup stock and add the oregano. Simmer the mixture 5-10 minutes until the oregano is very fragrant and has softened completely. Add more stock if the mixture becomes too dry. Turn the onion sauté into a saucepan (2½ quarts should be big enough).

(2) Stir the pureed soybeans into the sauté, then add the macaroni. Simmer the mixture until it is at serving temperature.

(3) Remove it from the heat and stir in the yogurt, which will make it creamy.

(4) You may next EITHER stir in the sesame seed meal OR turn the prepared dish onto a serving platter and sprinkle the sesame meal over all. (Stir in or sprinkle the parmesan cheese as well— your choice!)

Variation: In reference to (4) above—if you are interested in making the dish a little more elegant, and your oven happens to be on: sprinkle first the sesame meal, then the parmesan cheese, dot with butter, and heat in the oven until the dish is bubbly.

*_____

| 1½ | cups macaroni (whole wheat) : ¼ cup soybeans :
½ cup sesame seeds |
| ¼ | cup soybeans : ½ cup yogurt |
| ½ | cup yogurt |

Two Spaghetti Dinners in One
5-6 portions for each dinner

1 portion = approx. 13 grams of usable protein
31% to 37% of average daily protein need

The preparation for these meals is fairly simple; and while today's dinner is taken from the stove top, the meal for tomorrow will be baked in the oven. Of course, you can make all of one or the other if you want to serve several people.

Sauce:

¼ cup (olive) oil	2 tsp oregano (dried)
2 cups chopped onions	½ tsp dried basil
2-3 cloves garlic, crushed or minced	½ cup fresh chopped parsley
1 cup chopped celery	2 cups drained canned tomatoes (or fresh)
½-1 cup chopped mushrooms	1 cup of the drained juice
1 bay leaf	

(1) Heat the oil in your pressure cooker or in a saucepan. Sauté the onions, garlic, celery, and mushrooms until the onions are very soft.

(2) Stir in the bay leaf, oregano, basil, parsley, tomatoes, and juice. Cover and pressure cook for 5 minutes at 15 pounds, OR cover and cook regularly for 30 minutes, adding more liquid if the mixture becomes dry.

*1 pound whole wheat noodles (fresh) OR about 1 quart of cooked whole wheat noodles	*2-3 cups grated soft cheese (cheddar, muenster, mozzarella)
	*1 cup parmesan cheese, grated

(1) Cook the noodles in lightly salted water, and drain them.

(2) Now all you have to do is divide everything in half. There should be about 4 cups of sauce, so put 2 cups in a casserole mixed with half the noodles and half the total cheese. Place the casserole in the refrigerator, and tomorrow or the next day bake it for about 45 minutes at 350°F until it is bubbly and browned on the top.

(3) For tonight, stir the noodles, cheese, and sauce together. Heat it briefly over a medium flame, then eat!

* ───────────────────────────────

4 cups cooked whole wheat noodles : 1⅓ cups grated cheese
1⅔ to 2⅔ cups more grated cheese

Macaroni Crumb Custard
6 portions

1 portion = approx. 16 grams of usable protein
37% to 45% of average daily protein need

The top of the casserole will puff slightly as it bakes. The topping is light and crusty while the noodles are creamy. This is probably a dish that your children will really go for.

*1 cup whole wheat OR wheat-soy macaroni
*1 cup whole grain bread crumbs
*1½ cups hot milk
*3 eggs, beaten
½ cup chopped onion
*1 to 1½ cups grated cheese (combine your favorites—try blue, kuminost, parmesan, or cheddar)
½ tsp salt
pinch cayenne
2 tbsp mixed fresh herbs OR 1 tbsp mixed dry herbs (oregano, basil, parsley, rosemary)

(1) Cook the noodles in salted water until they are tender. Drain them and set aside.
(2) While the noodles are cooking, soak the bread crumbs in the hot milk.

(3)   After the crumbs are soft, stir in the eggs, onion, cheese, and seasonings.

(4)   Place the noodles in an oiled 1½-quart casserole. Pour the crumb-cheese mixture over all, and don't stir. Set the casserole in a pan of hot water and bake at 325°F for an hour, or until the custard is firm.

*_____

    1   cup whole wheat noodles : 1 cup milk
    1   cup bread crumbs : ⅓ cup grated cheese
    ⅔   to 1⅙ cup grated cheese
    ½   cup milk
    3   eggs

_____

Potato Kugel
a 7″ x 11″ or 9″ x 9″ pan—
about 15 squares

              2 squares = approx. 9 grams of usable protein
                  20% to 24% of average daily protein need

The kugel is delicious hot or cold. Decide before baking which topping you prefer (if not both), for when cold it can be easily eaten with your hands and will be better protein if all the cheese is already there.

 *6   average potatoes   ¼   cup whole grain
 2-3   carrots   bread crumbs
   1   big onion   *¾   cup milk powder
   1   clove garlic,   (1 cup instant)
       minced
 *2   eggs, beaten   **Topping:**
   3   tbsp oil   *1   cup grated cheese
   2   tsp salt   *OR 2 cups yogurt and ⅓
                                   cup grated cheese

(1) Grate the potatoes, carrots, and the onion into a large bowl. Drain off the liquid that will accumulate around the edges of the mixture before going on.

(2) Stir in all the remaining ingredients. But add the milk powder carefully to avoid lumps.

(3) Spread the mixture evenly in an oiled pan. Place it in a 350°F oven for 40 minutes to an hour. (The square pan will take longer than the 7″ x 11″.) When the kugel is nearly done it will test dry like a cake, the edges should be brown, and it will smell delicious. Before you remove it from the oven, add the grated cheese, either ⅓ or 1 cup. Leave it for about 5 more minutes, or until the cheese is completely melted.

(4) If you are using the smaller amount of cheese, serve the yogurt at the table using about 2 tablespoons per square. It is just as delicious with the full cup of grated cheese *and* yogurt. And for serving cold, the yogurt isn't necessary for complete protein.

---

*

3	potatoes : ¾ cup milk powder
3	potatoes : 1 cup grated cheese OR 2 cups yogurt and ⅓ cup grated cheese
2	eggs

Cheese Scalloped Potatoes
8 portions

> 1 portion = approx. 9 grams of usable protein
> 20% to 24% of average daily protein need

A luscious way to serve potatoes . . .

1 clove garlic, bruised	3 tbsp butter
oil	salt
	paprika
*6 large or 8 medium-sized potatoes	*½ cup sesame seeds (toasted—optional)
	*1¼ cups hot milk
*2 cups grated cheese (try Swiss)	

(1)   Rub a large shallow baking dish with the bruised garlic, then oil it lightly.

(2)   Without peeling the potatoes, slice them on the slicing side of a four-sided grater, or slice very thin with a sharp knife.

(3)   Place ½ of the slices on the bottom of the baking dish; sprinkle with 1 cup of the grated cheese, dot with 1½ tablespoons butter, and sprinkle the ½ cup of sesame seeds over. Add some salt and paprika. Repeat the layers (except there won't be another layer of sesame), using the remaining potatoes, cheese, and butter, plus more salt and paprika.

(4)   Pour the 1¼ cups of hot milk into the dish. Bake in the upper third of the oven at 425°F for about 25 minutes, until the potatoes are tender, and the top is lightly browned and crusty.

---

*

6 potatoes : 2 cups grated cheese
½ cup sesame seeds : ⅓ cup milk
slightly less than 1 cup milk

Potato Corn Cakes
about 20 cakes

> 2 cakes = approx. 6 grams of usable protein
> 14% to 16% of average daily protein need

These cakes are delicious with applesauce and yogurt. You may think that grating the potatoes and onion is a bother, but I'm convinced that grated vegetables make much lighter pancakes.

*4 medium potatoes, scrubbed, with skins	*2 tbsp whole wheat flour
1 large onion	*1 tbsp soy grits
*2 eggs, beaten	*1 cup milk powder (1⅓ cups instant)
*1 tbsp brewer's yeast	*2 cups corn, fresh, frozen, or drained canned
1 tsp salt	

(1) Grate the potatoes and the onions (and please leave the potato skins on); stir in the eggs, brewer's yeast, salt, flour, and soy grits.
(2) Carefully add the milk powder so that it doesn't lump too much (a few lumps don't matter).
(3) Stir in the corn, and your cakes are ready to fry.
(4) Fry on an oiled griddle, browning them well on each side.

*
_____

  2   cups corn
  2   eggs
  1   tbsp brewer's yeast
  2   tbsp whole wheat flour : ¼ tbsp soy grits
  ¾   tbsp soy grits
  4   potatoes : 1 cup milk powder

Potato Ginger Pudding
6 portions

> 1 portion = approx. 16 grams of usable protein
> 36% to 44% of average daily protein need

A dominant but not overpowering ginger flavor makes this dish delightfully different. If you are very fond of ginger, add 2 to 3 tablespoons more slices. Serve the casserole with a green vegetable or raw salad, or both.

*5	medium potatoes, cooked and mashed—about 3 cups	2	tbsp fresh ginger root, sliced thin
*2	eggs	1	tsp salt
*¾	cup milk	*¾	cup sesame seed meal
*1	cup cottage cheese	*1	cup raw cashew pieces
1	medium onion, quartered		

(1) Put the eggs and milk into a blender and buzz; add the cottage cheese and buzz again until smooth. Drop in the onion quarters and ginger; buzz again until the whole mixture is smooth.

(2) When you mash the potatoes, leave the skins on. The skins contain most of the vitamins in the potatoes, and their color and texture will make the casserole more interesting.

(3) Stir the blender mixture into the mashed potatoes along with the salt, sesame meal, and cashew pieces.

(4) Turn the mixture into an oiled 2-quart casserole. Bake at 350°F for 1 hour, until the top is lightly browned and a toothpick or skewer comes out clean.

* _____

```
5   potatoes : 1 cup cottage cheese
½   cup milk : ¾ cup sesame meal
¼   cup milk
2   eggs
1   cup cashews
```

The Staff of Life

Bread once was called the staff of life because it truly could sustain life. Because it was made from whole grain flours, it was an important part of the diet, not just a convenient holder for butter or cheese.

Today it's hard to find a loaf of bread that one could call the staff of life. Our food industry prefers to remove all of the life-giving qualities from the grain, after which it is mixed with preservatives, emulsifiers, stabilizers, and other chemicals, and then whipped full of air so we think that it's fresh. As the egg of a chicken contains in a simple package all the nutrients to make another chicken, foods derived *directly* from plant and animal tissues probably contribute most effectively to form a constructive environment for the development of cells and tissues of the creatures that consume them. The energy storehouses (carbohydrates and fats) that make up the bulk of our "miracle processed foods" cannot sustain life.[1] But the food industry keeps mak-

[1] Recently a test was done with commercial "enriched" bread. Weanling rats were fed this bread for 90 days, and they all died before the tests were completed. A low cost supplement consisting of vitamins, minerals, and an amino acid, lysine, enabled the rats to live through the test, and they also grew seven times as fast. The main criticism of the research was that bread is not eaten alone and that other single foods would provide similar results. The researchers then tested rats using other single foods, including milk, eggs, meat, and breakfast cereals. The results showed that eggs and milk alone seemed to be the best substances for sustaining life (although a copper and iron deficiency showed up in the milk-fed rats). "Enriched" macaroni and breakfast cereals fell at the bottom of the scale, but when they were supplemented as in the bread experiments,

195

ing them and advertising how they will build strong bodies, and we buy. Do we buy plastic foods because we are ignorant or because we have almost no choice?

Making bread regularly might seem like a lengthy, time-consuming chore (if it must be called a chore). Some people prefer to spend their time in the supermarket discovering new super-instant, everlasting products rather than hang around their own home doing a little creative cooking. I much prefer to spend the day in the garden, tending to the bread for a total of maybe an hour and a half. Most people think bread is an all-day job because you do have to be around every hour or so, but you don't have to knead all day; you just have to leave it alone for certain intervals.

Is there any odor more earthy than the fragrance that permeates your house while the loaves bake? A friend of ours once said, "I'm not really sure that homemade bread is so much better than the store-bought stuff, but I really dig the smell when it bakes." Our friend might be a bit deprived if he can't tell the difference in taste, but he proved that no one can ignore that smell that is almost edible itself (and is impossible to hide from the neighbors)!

I have included a Key Bread Recipe for those who have never gotten into bread before. The most enjoyable way to learn, however, is with an experienced bread-making friend at your side. The first loaf will take more time than subsequent enterprises with bread, so invite your friend to help you and you can talk about the bread, weather, life, or whatever . . . When you share the first bread you ever baked, "breaking

the rats gained weight quickly (except in the case of puffed rice, which I guess was beyond help).

—from Williams, Heffley, and Bode, "The Nutritive Value of Single Foods." *Proc. Nat. Acad. Sci. USA,* Vol. *68,* No. 10 (Oct. 1971), pp. 2361-2364.

bread" will mean something more than it ever did before.

Some specific suggestions for bread making:

(1) For the first bakings, make several loaves. You don't want to restrain your family, and until they are used to having good bread around all the time they will gobble up loaf after loaf before it has even cooled from the oven.

(2) I haven't had much luck with freezing unbaked bread dough, although I have read in several places that it can be done (thaw to room temperature, let rise, and bake as usual). What I usually do is freeze the already baked loaves. I take them from the freezer one at a time, as they dry out quickly after being frozen.

(3) You will be amazed at how long the loaves will keep without freezing. After they have cooled, wrap them in plastic bags and put them in your bread box or drawer. (The way to get dried-out bread is to put it in your refrigerator.) It will keep in your bread drawer for 10 days without preservatives! Imagine that. The food industry doesn't realize that people don't buy bread to keep it for years—most people buy it to eat it!

(4) You may make rolls from any bread recipe. Roll pinches of dough into 2-inch balls; place them next to each other in a shallow baking pan, or put 3 balls together in a muffin tin well. Let them rise and bake them ½ to ⅔ of the time required for loaves. Serve while hot and break apart.

(5) Add your own flourishes to bread: soaked dried or fresh herbs, or ground seeds, such as caraway or dill, can be kneaded in when you shape the loaves.

(6) Make sweet breads by rolling one of the loaves out flat; sprinkle with cinnamon, honey, raisins, nuts, and seeds, roll it up like a jelly roll, and shape it gently for the pan you're using. What scrumptious breakfast toast! You can do this with any type of bread, too. Let it rise, and bake as usual.

Bread goes everywhere with you, and it's so versatile: sandwiches, puddings, toppings, crusts, the substance for fruit or vegetable loaves, croutons for soup or salad. Bread can accompany dishes and meals of all kinds. It should always find its way to the table—breakfast, lunch, and dinner.

A Key Bread Recipe

Please check the Glossary for terms or foods unfamiliar to you. Assemble your ingredients and you're ready for an adventure!

Whole Wheat Soy Bread
4 loaves of 15 slices

What We Say . . . . is often different from **. . . . What We Mean**

4½ cups warm stock	The stock should be between 90° and 110°F for dry yeast. Fresh yeast requires cooler liquid, about 85°F. Check it with a candy thermometer, or if you can hold your finger in the liquid comfortably, it is close to your temperature (98.6).
2 tbsp baking yeast	If you prefer fresh yeast, substitute two ⅔-ounce cakes.
½ cup oil	
½ cup honey	
1 tbsp salt	

(2 tbsp crushed poppy seeds —optional)	You can use these or not, as you prefer.
*2½ cups soy flour *8-10 cups whole wheat flour	The type of flour, how it's ground, and the weather will determine the final amount.
Dissolve the yeast in the warm stock.	Put all of the stock in a large mixing bowl that will hold all of the bread when it is mixed. Sprinkle the yeast over the liquid and let it sit for about 5 minutes until it dissolves or puffs (different strains of yeast do different things). Then stir the mixture.
Add the oil, honey, and salt (and poppy seeds).	Stir the mixture until the salt and honey have dissolved.
Stir the whole wheat and soy flours together and add to the batter gradually	In a separate bowl blend the flours thoroughly. Add the flour to the liquid 1-2 cups at a time. After about 4 cups are added, stir the batter about 100 times to develop the gluten of the wheat.
... using enough to make a kneadable dough.	A kneadable dough can be handled easily and it will not stick to your hands once the kneading has begun. (Once you have a friend show you this consistency, it will be obvious to you each time you make bread.) You may add flour to the dough until it cannot absorb any more. Don't hesitate to add more while kneading if the dough gets sticky.
Let the dough rest about 15 min-	Cover the dough with a cloth while you prepare a floured board for

utes, then knead
until smooth and
elastic.

kneading. (You may knead the bread right in the bowl if it's big enough.) To knead: flatten the dough with your palms, pushing it away from you; fold it in half, turn it a quarter turn, flatten again, fold, and turn. Kneading can be a gentle matter; there is no need to pound the bread. Continue kneading until the bread becomes alive in your hands. When elastic, the bread will be more difficult to press out of shape and it will spring back when you try to flatten it.

Let rise until
double,

Place the bread back in the mixing bowl. You may oil the bread and/or the bowl, but I don't think it's essential to the rising. Place the covered bowl in a warm place (over a pilot light, or on a radio, or radiator) and leave it until its volume has doubled. This should take about an hour for loaves that are mostly whole wheat flour. It takes more time with rye or buckwheat flours.

shape into loaves,

Punch the dough down in the bowl, turn it onto the floured board, and knead for a few minutes until it is easy to handle. You may add a small amount of whole wheat flour if the dough is sticky. Divide the dough into four pieces. If you want to shape the loaves "officially," check any basic cookbook for details and drawings. I prefer to smooth and shape the dough until it is the right size for the pans and has no folds or creases.

and let rise again
in oiled pans.

There is no need to buy 4 bread pans when you make this recipe (or any other). Try the following instead of pans:

(1) Shape round loaves or braid the loaves. Let them rise on an oiled cookie sheet, cast iron frying pans, casseroles, or on any pan that you can put in the oven. The pan should be about twice the size of the dough before it rises.

(2) Shape loaves that you can drop into the bottom of oiled coffee cans or 46-ounce-size juice cans. The bread will rise as well as a flat loaf. Dust about 1 tablespoon of flour on the bread before placing it in the can. This helps avoid sticking. If it is still difficult to remove the bread from the can, you can remove the bottom after the baking is done, loosen with a knife, and then push the loaf through. (Then recycle that can!) Beautiful round slices for round sandwiches.

The loaves should increase their volume slightly less than double for this second rising.

Bake at 350°F for
about 35 minutes.

The oven should be preheated. Brush the loaves with oil for a soft crust, or with beaten egg for a hard, shiny crust. After baking for 35 minutes, remove one loaf from its pan. Tap the bottom, and if it sounds hollow and a broom straw comes out clean, it's done. The loaf should be golden brown, too.

EATEATEATEATEATEATEATEATEATEATEATEATEATEATEATEAT

More Breads

Whole Wheat Soy Bread[1]
4 loaves of 15 slices each

> 1 slice = approx. 2 grams of usable protein
> 5% to 6% of average daily protein need

A medium grained loaf that toasts well and makes delicious sandwiches.

4½	cups warm stock	(2	tbsp crushed poppy seeds-optional)
2	tbsp baking yeast		
½	cup oil		
½	cup honey	*2½	cups soy flour
1	tbsp salt	*8-10	cups whole wheat flour

(1) Dissolve the yeast in the warm stock. Add the oil, honey, and salt (and poppy seeds).
(2) Stir the whole wheat and soy flours together and add to the batter gradually, using enough to make a kneadable dough.
(3) Let the dough rest about 15 minutes, then knead until smooth and elastic.
(4) Let rise until double, shape into loaves, and let rise again in oiled pans.
(5) Bake at 350°F for about 35 minutes.

Note: This loaf can "cool rise." After the first kneading, let the dough rise in the refrigerator for several hours, or overnight. Bring it gradually to room temperature, shape into loaves, and proceed as in (4).

---
*
10   cups whole wheat flour : 2½ cups soy flour

---

[1] A Key Bread Recipe (See p. 198).

Wheat Grits Bread
3 loaves of 15 slices each

> 1 slice = approx. 3 grams of usable protein
> 8% to 9% of average daily protein need

An easy and delicious bread.

4	cups stock, hot	¼	cup honey
*1	cup plus 2 tbsp soy grits	2	tbsp oil
2	tbsp baking yeast	*9	cups whole wheat flour
2	tsp salt		

(1) Soak the soy grits in the hot stock.
(2) When the liquid is lukewarm, stir in the yeast, salt, honey, oil, and whole wheat flour.
(3) Knead the dough until smooth and elastic. If you need more flour, add 2 tablespoons of soy grits with each cup.
(4) Let rise until double, punch down, shape into loaves, and let rise again.
(5) Bake at 350°F for 45 minutes to 1 hour.

* _____

9 cups whole wheat flour : 1 cup plus 2 tbsp soy grits

Triple Rich Bread
3 loaves of 15 slices each

> 1 slice = approx. 4 grams of usable protein
> 8% to 10% of average daily protein need

Triple rich because of lots of milk powder, wheat germ, soy flour, and brewer's yeast . . .

Recipes for a Small Planet

3	cups stock, warm	2	tsp salt
2	tbsp baking yeast	*1	cup milk powder
½	cup honey		(1⅓ cups instant)
*2	eggs, beaten	*1	cup soy flour
*¼	cup brewer's yeast	*6-8	cups whole wheat
*1	cup wheat germ		flour

(1) Combine the stock, yeast, and honey; let it stand for about 5 minutes, then beat in the eggs.

(2) Stir together the brewer's yeast, wheat germ, salt, milk powder, and soy flour; beat this mixture into the dough, then beat about 100 strokes.

(3) Gradually add the whole wheat flour, then knead until smooth and elastic. Let rise until double, punch down and shape into 3 loaves; place them in oiled bread pans and let rise again.

(4) Bake at 350°F for 50 to 60 minutes.

* ——————————————————————————————————————

2	eggs
¼	cup brewer's yeast
1	cup wheat germ
4	cups whole wheat flour : 1 cup soy flour
3	cups whole wheat flour : 6 tbsp milk powder
10	tbsp milk powder

——————————————————————————————————————

Wheat Germ Bread
3 loaves of 15 slices each

> 1 slice = approx. 3 grams of usable protein
> 7% to 8% of average daily protein need

This is a slightly sweet loaf that makes delicious rolls too.

3 cups stock, warm	*3 cups wheat germ
2 tbsp baking yeast	*¾ cup milk powder
2 tsp salt	(1 cup instant)
¼ cup melted butter	*6 cups whole wheat
¼ cup honey	flour

(1) Dissolve the yeast in the stock; stir in the salt, butter, and honey.

(2) In a separate bowl stir together the wheat germ, milk powder, and whole wheat flour. Stir this into the liquid mixture gradually, until the dough is dry enough to knead.

(3) Knead until smooth and elastic; let rise until double. Shape into 3 loaves, place in well-oiled pans, let rise again.

(4) Bake at 325°F for 40 to 45 minutes.

* _____

    6 cups whole wheat flour : ¾ cup milk powder
    3 cups wheat germ

_____

Milk and Honey Whole Wheat Bread
3 loaves of 15 slices each

1 slice = approx. 3 grams of usable protein
7% to 8% of average daily protein need

A delectable loaf . . .

3 cups stock, warm	*1½ cups milk powder
2 tbsp baking yeast	(2 cups instant)
½ cup oil OR melted butter	2 tsp salt
½ cup honey	*7-8 cups whole wheat flour

(1) Dissolve the yeast in the stock. Add the oil and then the honey by measuring the oil first in a ½ cup scoop, then scooping the honey, which will slide right out without sticking.

(2) Stir the milk powder, salt, and 3 cups of the whole wheat flour together; add this mixture to the liquid.

(3) Beat the batter about 150 strokes, then add the remaining whole wheat flour, using enough to make a stiff dough for kneading.

(4) Knead for 5 minutes until smooth and elastic; let rise until double in a warm place.

(5) Punch down, shape into 3 loaves; place the loaves in oiled pans, let rise again, and then bake at 350°F for about 30 minutes.

* _____

  8 cups whole wheat flour : 1 cup milk powder
½ cup milk powder

_____

High-Protein Challah
3 loaves of 15 slices each

> 1 slice = approx. 3 grams of usable protein
> 8% to 9% of average daily protein need

A rich, but light loaf.

3	cups stock, warm	*4 eggs, beaten
2	tbsp baking yeast	*9 cups whole wheat
2½	tsp salt	flour
⅓	cup honey	*1 cup plus 2 tbsp
¼	cup melted butter	milk powder (1½
¼	cup oil	cups instant)

(1) Dissolve the yeast in the warm stock in a large mixing bowl. Add the salt, honey, butter, and oil and stir well.

(2) Beat in all but 2 tablespoons of the eggs. Set the 2 tablespoons of reserved egg aside.

(3) Stir the flour and milk powder together, then stir it gradually into the liquid until it is dry enough to begin kneading. You may not need it all.

(4) Knead until smooth and elastic, let rise until double, shape into 3 loaves and let rise again.[1] Brush the loaves with the 2 tablespoons of reserved egg just before baking. Bake at 350°F for 30 to 35 minutes.

---

* _____

4   eggs
9   cups whole wheat flour : 1 cup plus 2 tbsp milk
    powder

_____

Unusual Pickle or Olive Juice Bread
3 loaves of 15 slices each

> 1 slice = approx. 4 grams of usable protein
> 8% to 10% of average daily protein need

The dominant flavor of this bread depends on what your pickle or olive juice tastes like. If you don't have any juice, make the bread with regular stock. It slices thin to make crunchy toast. This bread proves that you really don't have to throw anything away!

---

[1] This bread is most beautiful when braided. Divide the whole dough into 3 parts, one part for each loaf. Divide each part into 3 parts again. Roll the small parts into strands that are 12 inches long and 1½ inches thick. Line them up and then braid them, pinching the ends together. Place each loaf in an oiled bread pan OR on an oiled cookie sheet. Let rise and continue as in (4).

1	quart warm stock, including 2 cups juice from pickles or olives	⅓	cup honey
		1	tbsp salt
		*3	cups rye flour
		*2½	cups soy flour
2	tbsp baking yeast	*6-7	cups whole wheat flour
⅓	cup oil		

(1) Dissolve the yeast in the warm stock; add the honey, salt and flours in the order given. Use as much whole wheat flour as you need to make a kneadable dough.

(2) Knead until smooth and elastic, let rise until double, punch down, knead again, and shape into 3 loaves.

(3) Place the loaves in oiled pans and bake at 350°F for 40 to 50 minutes.

* _____

10   cups whole grain flour : 2½ cups soy flour

_____

Cheese and Onion Bread
1 loaf of 15 slices

1 slice = approx. 5 grams of usable protein
11% to 13% of average daily protein need

This elegant loaf can be prepared the day before you serve it freshly baked (see below). It has a mild onion and cheese flavor that's mouth watering.

1	cup stock, warm	½	cup chopped fresh chives or scallions
1	tbsp baking yeast		
2	tbsp honey	*3	cups whole wheat flour
*1	egg, beaten		
1	tsp salt	*6	tbsp milk powder (½ cup instant)
*1	cup grated sharp cheddar cheese		

(1) Dissolve the yeast in the stock. Add the remaining ingredients in the order given after stirring the whole wheat flour and milk powder together.

(2) Knead the dough until smooth and elastic, let rise until double, punch it down, shape into a loaf, place in an oiled bread pan and let rise again.

(3) Bake the loaf at 350°F for 30 to 35 minutes.

To cool-rise the loaf: Knead as in (2); let it do its first rising in the refrigerator overnight. Next day let the dough stand in a warm place for a few hours until the dough is warm. Shape into a loaf, let rise until double, and bake as usual.

* _____

    3 cups whole wheat flour : 6 tbsp milk powder
    1 cup grated cheese
    1 egg

_____

Cornmeal Wheat Bread
4 loaves of 15 slices each

> 1 slice = approx. 4 grams of usable protein
> 10% to 12% of average daily protein need

A close-grained bread with a delectable crunch, this loaf will slice thin with ease.

    5   cups stock, warm   *1   cup soy flour
    2   tbsp baking yeast   *¾   cup milk powder
    1   tbsp salt   (1 cup instant)
    ⅔   cup oil   *1½   cups soy grits
    ½   cup molasses   *10-12 cups whole
    *3   cups yellow corn-   wheat flour
         meal

(1) Dissolve the yeast in the warm stock. Add the remaining ingredients in the order given, using as

much whole wheat flour as necessary to make a dough suitable for kneading.

(2) Knead the dough until smooth and elastic—about 15 minutes. If the dough is too bulky to knead comfortably, divide it into 2 pieces and knead each piece separately.

(3) Let the dough rise in a warm place until double, punch it down, shape into 4 loaves, place in oiled pans, and let rise again.

(4) Bake the loaves at 350°F for about 45 minutes.

*

3 cups cornmeal : 1 cup soy flour : ¾ cup milk powder
12 cups whole wheat flour : 1½ cups soy grits

High-Rising Bread
4 loaves of 15 slices each

1 slice = approx. 3 grams of usable protein
7% to 9% of average daily protein need

This bread is very light and rises high. The potato flour gives it a fine texture plus good keeping qualities. The peanut flour adds subtle sweetness.

5	cups stock	
⅓	cup butter	
*½	cup potato flour	
(1	cup sourdough starter—optional)	
2	tbsp baking yeast	
1	tbsp salt	
*¼	cup brewer's yeast	
*¾	cup milk powder (1 cup instant)	

*⅞	cup raw peanuts, ground (about 1⅛ cups meal)
*½	cup soy flour
*½	cup wheat germ
*2	cups rye flour
*8	cups whole wheat flour (more if needed)

(1) Heat the stock to lukewarm. Melt the butter in it, then add the potato flour 1 tablespoon at a time, whisking it in carefully to avoid lumps.

(2) Turn the mixture into a large mixing bowl; add the rest of the ingredients in the order given EXCEPT for 5 cups of the whole wheat flour. Beat the mixture 100 strokes, set it aside in a warm place and let it rise. The "sponge" will get quite massive in about an hour.

(3) Stir the sponge down, add the remaining 5 cups of whole wheat flour, plus any more you might need to make a kneadable dough.

(4) Knead the dough until it's smooth and elastic, let rise again until double, punch down and shape into 4 loaves.

(5) Place the loaves in oiled bread pans; let them rise until they're very high. Then bake at 325°F for 45 minutes.

*
_____

3¾	cups whole wheat flour : ⅞ cup peanuts : ¼ cup soy flour
1¼	cups whole wheat flour : ¼ cup brewer's yeast
3	cups whole wheat flour : 6 tbsp milk powder
1	cup rye flour : 2 tbsp milk powder
1	cup rye flour : ¼ cup soy flour
½	cup potato flour : ¼ cup milk powder
½	cup wheat germ

_____

Spicy Rye Bread
2 small loaves of 10 slices each

> 1 slice = approx. 3 grams of usable protein
> 7% to 8% of average daily protein need

It might seem that this would be a heavy loaf since it does not rise very high. Yet it is a fine-grained and very soft bread that will slice thin. It is strong flavored, so you will find it especially delicious spread with ricotta or with other mild cheeses.

1½	cups stock, warm	2	tbsp soft butter OR oil
2	tbsp baking yeast		
½	cup molasses	*2	cups rye flour
1	tbsp salt	*½	cup soy flour
2	tbsp dried grated orange rind	*2	cups whole wheat flour
1	tbsp fennel seeds, crushed or ground	*¼	cup milk powder (⅓ cup instant)
1	tbsp anise seeds, crushed or ground	2	tbsp cornmeal

(1) Dissolve the yeast in the warm stock. Stir in the molasses, salt, orange rind, seeds, butter or oil.

(2) Add the rye flour and soy flour and beat until smooth.

(3) Stir together the whole wheat flour and milk powder; add this mixture gradually to the dough, using enough to make a dough suitable for kneading.

(4) Knead until smooth and elastic; let "rise" 1½ to 2 hours. It won't rise very much. Shape into 2 round or oval loaves, place on a cookie sheet that's been oiled and dusted with cornmeal. Let rise, then bake at 350°F for 35 minutes.

---

*

2 cups rye flour : ½ cup soy flour
2 cups whole wheat flour : ¼ cup milk powder

Limpa Bread
2 small loaves of 10 slices each
or 1 large loaf

1 slice = approx. 3 grams of usable protein
7% to 9% of average daily protein need

Spicy and fragrant rye bread.

1	cup boiling stock	2	tsp salt
*6	tbsp soy grits	¼	cup oil
1	tsp fennel seeds, crushed or ground	⅓	cup molasses
1	tsp cumin seeds, crushed or ground	1	tbsp baking yeast
2	tsp grated dried orange peel OR 1 tbsp fresh peel	*1	cup milk
		*2	cups rye flour
		*2-3	cups whole wheat flour

(1) Pour the boiling stock over the grits, seeds, orange peel, salt, oil, and molasses. (Measure the oil first, then use the same cup to measure the molasses.)

(2) When the mixture has cooled to lukewarm, add the yeast, milk, and rye flour. Add enough whole wheat flour to make a stiff dough.

(3) Knead about 10 minutes until smooth and elastic. Let rise about 2 hours, or until double.

(4) EITHER shape into loaves, place in oiled pans, and let rise again; OR you may shape two small round loaves or one large round one. Place on an oiled cookie sheet to rise.

(5) Bake the loaves at 350°F for 35 to 45 minutes.

*

3 cups whole wheat flour : 6 tbsp soy grits
2 cups rye flour : 1 cup milk

Oat Rye Soy Bread
2 loaves of 15 slices each

> 1 slice = approx. 4 grams of usable protein
> 10% to 12% of average daily protein need

A fine-grained loaf that slices thin.

¼	cup warm stock	*(½	cup milk powder [⅔
1	tbsp baking yeast		cup instant]—
*2	cups stock or milk, hot		optional **only** if you used milk instead of stock, above)
*1	cup rolled oats		
2	tsp salt	*1	cup soy flour
¼	cup oil	*2	cups rye flour
¼	to ½ cup honey	*3-4	cups whole wheat flour
*2	eggs, beaten		
*½	cup wheat germ		

(1) Dissolve the yeast in the ¼ cup stock (or milk) and set aside.

(2) Pour the hot stock (or milk) over the rolled oats; stir in the salt, oil, and honey. Let the mixture sit until it is lukewarm.

(3) Stir in the yeast mixture and eggs. Stir together the wheat germ, (milk powder), soy flour, and rye flour. Then add the mixture to the dough. Blend well and then stir in enough whole wheat flour for kneading.

(4) Knead until smooth and elastic; let rise until double (1-1½ hours).

(5) Shape into loaves, place in oiled pans, let rise again until doubled. Bake at 350°F for 45 minutes to 1 hour.

Variations—

> *Oat Wheat Bread:* Use 2 cups rolled oats,

omit the rye flour, and use about 5 cups whole wheat flour in all.

Sourdough Oat Bread: Use 1 cup sourdough starter, 2⅔ cups rolled oats, omit the rye flour, and use about 4 cups whole wheat flour in all.

*
_____

1	cup soy flour : 4 cups whole wheat flour
1	cup rolled oats and 2 cups rye flour : 1½ cups milk
½	cup milk
2	eggs
½	cup wheat germ

_____

Caraway Rye Bread
2 small loaves of 10 slices each

1 slice = approx. 4 grams of usable protein
9% to 11% of average daily protein need

A fragrant, close-grained loaf.

¼	cup warm water	3	tbsp caraway seeds, crushed or ground
1	tbsp baking yeast		
1½	cups warm stock	*¼	cup milk powder (⅓ cup instant)
½	cup molasses		
2	tbsp oil	*6	tbsp soy grits
1	tbsp salt	2½	cups whole wheat flour
*2½	cups rye flour		

(1) Dissolve the yeast in the ¼ cup warm water, using a small bowl.
(2) In a large mixing bowl combine the 1½ cups stock, molasses, oil, and salt.
(3) Stir in the rye flour and beat until smooth; add

the yeast mixture, caraway seeds, powdered milk, and soy grits.

(4) Stir in enough whole wheat flour to make a soft dough suitable for kneading. Let rest 10 minutes.

(5) Knead the dough for about 10 minutes, until smooth and elastic. Set in a warm place and let rise 1½ to 2 hours.

(6) Punch the dough down, knead it briefly. Shape it into two round loaves, or place in two small oiled bread pans. Let rise another 1 to 1½ hours.

(7) Bake the loaves at 375°F for about 30 minutes. Brush the loaves with soft butter for a soft crust when they are done.

* _____

½ cup rye flour plus 2½ cups whole wheat flour : 6 tbsp soy grits

2 cups rye flour: ¼ cup milk powder

_____

Sourdough (SD) Starter

1 cup = approx. 10 grams of usable protein

1 tbsp baking yeast (omit if you live in the San Francisco area)	2 tsp honey
	2½ cups whole wheat flour
½ cup warm water	2 cups warm water

(1) Combine the yeast and ½ cup warm water. Add the honey and then gradually beat in the whole wheat flour and remaining warm water.

(2) Place the mixture in a large crock or gallon glass jar. Do not use any kind of metal container, because the starter will react chemically with the metal.

(3) Cover the container with a damp cloth secured with a rubber band.

(4) Keep the container at room temperature for 5 days. Stir it down each morning.

(5) On the 5th day, add ¼ cup more whole wheat flour and ¼ cup more warm water. Let it stay at room temperature until the 6th day.

(6) It is ready to use or refrigerate on the 6th day. To store, place in a small crock or jar (no metal here, either) and refrigerate.

(7) When you use 1 cup starter, replace it with 1 cup whole wheat flour and 1 cup water. Even if you do not use the starter weekly, be sure to discard 1 cup and replace it as above at least once a week to keep the starter fresh.

(8) Use a wooden spoon to stir down the starter daily. Stirring daily is advisable, but not altogether necessary.

Sourdough Whole Wheat Bread (SD)
3 loaves of 15 slices each

> 1 slice = approx. 3 grams of usable protein
> 8% to 9% of average daily protein need

This bread is nice if you add sweet spices, raisins, and nuts to one loaf, and different types of seeds to the others. The sweet loaf is especially delicious for breakfast toast.

1 quart stock, warm	1 tbsp poppy seeds
1 tbsp baking yeast	1 tbsp flax seeds
*1 cup sourdough starter	raisins
	honey
*¼ cup soy grits	sweet spices (cinnamon, nutmeg, cloves, ginger, et. al.)
*1 cup milk powder (1⅓ cups instant)	
1 tbsp salt	
*10 cups whole wheat flour	sunflower seeds or other nuts

(1)   Dissolve the yeast in the warm stock. Stir in the
      starter and soy grits; let sit for about 10 minutes.

(2)   Mix the milk powder and salt with 2 or 3 cups
      of the whole wheat flour; stir the mixture into the
      liquid. Then add enough of the remaining whole
      wheat flour for kneading.

(3)   Knead until smooth and elastic, let rise until dou-
      ble, punch the dough down.

(4)   Divide the dough into 3 parts. Knead the poppy
      seeds into one part and shape into a loaf. Knead
      the flax seeds into the second part, and shape.
      Finally, for the third loaf: roll the dough out flat,
      but not too thin; spread raisins all over the sur-
      face, sprinkle with sweet spices and sunflower
      seeds, then drizzle honey over all. Roll it up
      tightly like a jelly roll, then fold and shape it
      gently to fit into your oiled bread pan. Place the
      first 2 loaves in oiled pans also.

(5)   Let all the loaves rise until they are almost dou-
      ble. The loaf with the added fruit and seeds may
      get bigger than the others.

(6)   Bake at 350°F for about 1 hour.

*

8   cups whole wheat flour : 1 cup milk powder
2   cups whole wheat flour : ¼ cup soy grits
1   cup sourdough starter

Egg and Yogurt Bread (SD)
4 small loaves of 10 slices each

> 1 slice = approx. 5 grams of usable protein
> 11% to 13% of average daily protein need

Wheat germ and bran plus eggs make this bread especially high protein.

3	cups stock, warm	*1	cup wheat bran
1	tbsp baking yeast	*1	cup wheat germ
*1	cup sourdough starter	*1	cup soy grits
		*1	cup rye flour
1	tbsp salt	*6-8	cups whole wheat flour
*¾	cup yogurt		
*2	eggs, beaten		

(1) Dissolve the yeast in the warm stock. Stir in the starter, salt, yogurt, eggs, wheat bran, wheat germ, soy grits, and rye flour. Blend this mixture until it is smooth.

(2) Add the whole wheat flour gradually, using enough to make the dough easy to knead. Knead until smooth and elastic, then let rise until double.

(3) Punch down, shape into loaves (you may make 3 large loaves instead of 4 small), let rise again in oiled pans.

(4) Bake the loaves at 375°F for 40 to 45 minutes.

*

_____

1	cup soy grits : 8 cups whole wheat and rye flour
¾	cup yogurt
1	cup wheat germ
1	cup wheat bran
2	eggs
1	cup sourdough starter

_____

Sun Seedy Oatmeal Bread (SD)
3 loaves of 15 slices each

1 slice = approx. 3 grams of usable protein
6% to 8% of average daily protein need

Sourdough starter will make a mellow loaf, whether

you allow it to get sour or not. This bread is close grained, light in color, and of course, delicious.

3	cups stock, warm	*½	cup soy grits
1	tbsp baking yeast	*5	cups whole wheat
*1	cup sourdough		flour (more if
	starter		needed)
2	tsp salt	*½	cup sesame seeds
*2	cups rolled oats	*½	cup sunflower seeds

(1) Stir together the stock, yeast, starter, salt, oats, and soy grits; let the mixture sit for 15 minutes to allow the oats and soy grits to soften.

(2) Stir in 3 cups of the whole wheat flour and beat 100 strokes. Let this "sponge" rise for at least 1 hour. If you want a very sour bread, let it rise six hours or overnight.

(3) Stir down the sponge and add the remaining 2 cups of whole wheat flour. Knead, adding more flour if necessary, until smooth and elastic. Let rise 1 hour, or until double.

(4) Punch down; knead again, adding the sesame and sunflower seeds. Shape into 3 loaves. Let rise in oiled pans. Then bake at 350°F for 30 to 45 minutes.

*_____

2   cups rolled oats and 5 cups whole wheat flour : ½ cup soy grits : ½ cup sesame and ½ cup sunflower seeds
1   cup sourdough starter

Four Grain Bread (SD)
3 loaves of 15 slices each

1 slice = approx. 4 grams of usable protein
8% to 10% of average daily protein need

A close-grained bread that toasts nicely and is excellent for making rolls, too.

3 cups stock, warm	*1 cup rye flour
1 tbsp baking yeast	*1 cup cornmeal
*1 cup sourdough starter	*1 cup soy flour
⅛ to ¼ cup melted butter OR oil	*¾ cup milk powder (1 cup instant)
1 tbsp salt	*7 cups whole wheat flour
*¼ cup brewer's yeast	

(1) Stir the stock, yeast, starter, butter, salt, and brewer's yeast together. Add the remaining ingredients in the order given, using enough whole wheat flour to make a kneadable dough. Be sure to stir the milk powder into the rye, cornmeal, and soy flour so it won't lump.

(2) Knead the dough until smooth and elastic; let rise until double. Shape into 3 loaves, place in oiled pans, and let rise again.

(3) Bake the loaves at 350°F for 40 minutes.

* _____

1 cup cornmeal : ⅓ cup soy flour : ¼ cup milk powder
3 cups whole wheat flour : ⅔ cup soy flour
1 cup rye flour : ¼ cup brewer's yeast
4 cups whole wheat flour : ½ cup milk powder
1 cup sourdough starter

Nut and Seed Bread (SD)
3 loaves of 15 slices each

> 1 slice = approx. 4 grams of usable protein
> 9% to 11% of average daily protein need

This is a coarse-grained loaf, richly textured by the nut meal, seeds, and soy grits.

2½ cups stock, warm
1 tbsp baking yeast
*1 cup sourdough starter
*½ cup soy grits
*1 cup sesame seeds
*¼ cup milk powder (⅓ cup instant)
3 tbsp honey

2 tsp salt
*1 cup raw peanuts, ground (about 1½ cups meal)
2 tbsp caraway seeds
2 tbsp poppy seeds
*6 cups whole wheat flour

(1) Dissolve the yeast in the warm stock, then add all of the remaining ingredients in the order given, using only 3 cups of the whole wheat flour.

(2) Beat the dough about 50 strokes, then let the "sponge" rise until double in bulk.

(3) Add the remaining whole wheat flour, knead until smooth and elastic; let rise again in the bowl until doubled.

(4) Shape the dough into 3 loaves, place in well-oiled pans, let rise again, and bake at 350°F for 45 minutes to 1 hour.

*
1 cup peanuts : ¼ cup milk powder
6 cups whole wheat flour : ½ cup soy grits : 1 cup sesame seeds
1 cup sourdough starter

Mixed Grain Bread (SD)
4 small loaves of 10 slices each

> 1 slice = approx. 3 grams of usable protein
> 8% to 9% of average daily protein need

A soft, close-grained bread . . .

3½	cups stock, warm	*1	cup cornmeal
2	tbsp baking yeast	*1	cup rye flour
*1	cup sourdough starter	*1	cup wheat germ
*1⅓	cups rolled oats	*1	cup soy flour
2	tsp salt	*¾	cup milk powder (1 cup instant)
2-3	tbsp oil	*5	cups whole wheat flour
⅓	cup molasses		

(1) Dissolve the yeast in the warm stock. Add the starter, oats, salt, oil, and molasses; let the mixture stand 5-10 minutes until the oats are softened.

(2) Stir the grains together and add to the liquid gradually. You may want to add more whole wheat flour if the dough is sticky; just be sure to add 2 tablespoons of milk powder (about 3 tablespoons instant) for each cup of extra whole wheat flour.

(3) Knead until smooth and elastic, let rise until double. Shape into loaves, place in oiled pans, and let rise again. You may make 3 large loaves instead of 4 small.

(4) Bake at 350°F for 35 minutes.

*
_____

1	cup cornmeal : ⅓ cup soy flour : ¼ cup milk powder
1⅓	cups rolled oats : ¼ cup soy flour
1	cup rye flour : ¼ cup soy flour
4	cups whole wheat flour : ½ cup milk powder
1	cup whole wheat flour : ¼ cup soy flour
1	cup sourdough starter

Breads in a Flash

When you're out of yeast bread, there's nothing like a quick bread to round out a meal, be it lunch or dinner. The smell of freshly baked muffins or rolls will fill your kitchen and entice your family or guests.

Quick breads do not keep as well as yeast breads, but usually we don't make many loaves, and what we make almost always gets eaten right up!

Sweet quick loaves or coffee cakes are my favorite fast dessert. When friends drop in and we all get the munchies, it takes only about 15 minutes to assemble many of the quick recipes—especially when four or five trippy people pitch in to help!

Muffins

"Casserolls"
a 9" x 9" pan of 12 rolls

2 rolls = approx. 4 grams of usable protein
9% to 10% of average daily protein need

These are rich, buttery and crusty rolls. Serve them hot right out of your casserole dish.

*1 cup milk	1 tbsp baking yeast
1 tbsp honey	*1½ cups whole wheat
¼ cup butter, divided	flour
½ tsp salt	

(1) Heat the milk, honey, 1 tablespoon of butter, and the salt until the butter melts and the honey dissolves. Place the mixture in another bowl to cool to about 100°F.

(2) While the mixture cools, melt the remaining butter and then set it aside to cool.

(3) Add the yeast to the milk mixture. Stir to dissolve and then let it sit until it bubbles a little. Add the whole wheat flour; beat it 50 strokes, until smooth and elastic.

(4) It won't be dry like a bread dough, but it also does not require kneading. Let the dough rise about 30 minutes.

(5) Pour one-half the reserved melted butter on the bottom of a 9″ x 9″ baking pan or casserole. Stir the batter down, then drop it by heaping tablespoons into the buttery pan. Pour the remaining butter over the rolls; let rise until double.

(6) Bake at 400°F for 30 minutes. Serve hot from the pan.

---

*

1½   cups whole wheat flour : ¾ cup milk
¼   cup milk

Crunchy Nut Muffins
about 16 muffins

> 2 muffins = approx. 8 grams of usable protein
> 17% to 21% of average daily protein need

These muffins are a perfect accompaniment to soup and salad. Toast the leftovers and spread with ricotta cheese.

*1½	cups whole wheat flour	*¼	cup peanuts, chopped (and toasted)
*¼	cup soy flour	⅓	cup currants or raisins
1	tbsp baking powder	*1	egg, beaten
½	tsp salt	*1	cup milk
*¼	cup sesame seeds (toasted)	1-4	tbsp melted butter OR oil
*⅓	cup sunflower seeds (toasted)	1-4	tbsp honey

(1) Stir all of the dry ingredients together. This should include the seeds, nuts, and raisins.

(2) In a separate bowl beat the egg; add the milk, oil, honey, and blend.

(3) Make a well in the dry ingredients and add the liquid mixture all at once. Stir just enough to moisten the dry ingredients.

(4) Drop the batter into well-oiled muffin tins. Bake at 375°F for 15 to 20 minutes. And serve them hot.

Variation—Nutty Nut Muffins: For an even nuttier muffin, add up to 1½ cups more of chopped peanuts. The milk will complement them.

---

*

1½ cups whole wheat flour : ¼ cup soy flour : ¼ cup sesame seed
1 egg
⅓ cup sunflower seeds : ¼ cup peanuts
1 cup milk

Cheesies
40 balls

> 4 cheesies = approx. 7 grams of usable protein
> 16% to 20% of average daily protein need

These are great hors d'oeuvres or snacks, and excellent with soup, too. Serve them warm if possible.

*1 cup grated
   cheddar cheese
½ cup sherry
¼ tsp worcestershire
   sauce
*1 egg
1 tsp salt
¼ tsp each: onion
   powder, garlic
   powder, paprika

*2 cups whole wheat
   flour
2 tbsp oil
*1¼ cups sesame seeds,
   ground (about 1½
   cups meal)
(pecan or walnut
   halves—optional)

(1) Blend the grated cheese, sherry, worcestershire sauce, and egg with a wooden spoon. Be sure the cheese is separated rather than in a lump.

(2) Stir in the salt and seasonings, then add the whole wheat flour. Knead the mixture lightly.

(3) Add the oil, and knead; then knead in the sesame meal ⅓ cup at a time.

(4) Pinch off pieces of dough and roll them into balls about the size of a large marble.

(5) Place them on an unoiled baking sheet and flatten them gently with your finger. (You may press a walnut or pecan half into each one.)

(6) Bake at 400°F for 10 to 15 minutes.

Variation—Hot Cheesies: Add ¼ teaspoon cayenne pepper and omit the onion powder, garlic powder, and paprika. These

cheesies are warm even when
served cold!

* _____

2	cups whole wheat flour : ⅓ cup grated cheese
1¼	cups sesame seeds : ⅓ cup grated cheese
⅓	cup grated cheese
1	egg

Spiced Pear Muffins
12 muffins

> 2 muffins = approx. 6 grams of usable protein
> 15% to 18% of average daily protein need

This spiced muffin is delicious and fruity for breakfast, but not too sweet to accompany your dinner.

*1⅔	cups whole wheat flour	*1	egg, beaten
*⅓	cup soy flour	*1	cup milk OR 1 cup water plus ¼ cup milk powder (⅓ cup instant)
1	tbsp baking powder		
½	tsp salt	1-4	tbsp melted butter OR oil
½	tsp cinnamon		
¼	tsp nutmeg	1-4	tbsp honey
½	cup chopped pears (about ½"); use fresh or drained, canned pears		

(1) Stir the dry ingredients together with the spices in
a small bowl; add the chopped pears and distribute them gently throughout the flour mixture.

(2) Blend the liquid ingredients together and then
pour them into the dry all at once. Stir 12 times
or less to moisten.

(3) Fill oiled muffin tins ⅔ full; bake at 400°F for about 25 minutes, until nicely browned. Serve hot.

*

1⅔ cups whole wheat flour : ⅓ cup soy flour
 1   egg
 1   cup milk

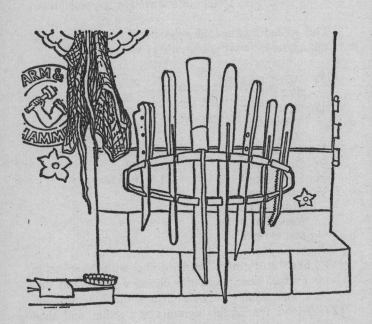

Basic Complementary Muffins
12 muffins

> 1 muffin = approx. 3 grams of usable protein
> 8% to 9% of average daily protein need

This is a basic, plain muffin, perfect with meals that have very spicy or distinctively strong-flavored dishes.

*1⅔	cups whole wheat flour	*1	cup milk OR 1 cup water plus ¼ cup milk powder (⅓ cup instant)
*⅓	cup soy flour		
1	tbsp baking powder	1-4	tbsp melted butter OR oil
½	tsp salt		
*1	egg, beaten	1-4	tbsp honey

(1) Stir the dry ingredients together, including any milk powder you are using.

(2) In a separate bowl beat the egg with the milk (or water), oil, and honey.

(3) Make a well in the dry ingredients and pour the liquid in all at once; stir just enough to moisten all of the ingredients, but don't worry about a few lumps.

(4) Fill oiled muffin tins ⅔ full. Bake at 400°F for 25 minutes, until well browned.

*
_____

1⅔	cups whole wheat flour : ⅓ cup soy flour
1	egg
1	cup milk

_____

Oatmeal Muffins
12-15 muffins

> 2 muffins = approx. 7 grams of usable protein
> 15% to 18% of average daily protein need

Delicious with honey and butter, these muffins are a fine addition to any meal.

*1	cup whole wheat flour		*1	cup sour milk, buttermilk, OR yogurt
*⅔	cup rolled oats		2	tbsp oil
*⅓	cup soy flour		1	tbsp honey
1	tsp baking soda		*⅔	cup sunflower seeds (toasted)
½	tsp salt			
*1	egg, beaten			

(1) If you have a blender, blend the rolled oats to make oat flour. If not, leave them whole for a muffin with a more distinctive texture.

(2) Stir all of the dry ingredients together in a small bowl.

(3) Combine the egg, sour milk, oil, and honey. Make a well in the dry mixture and pour in the liquid. Moisten with as few strokes as possible. Stir in the sunflower seeds.

(4) Drop into oiled muffin tins, bake at 400°F until nicely browned, about 25 minutes.

* _____

1	cup whole wheat flour plus ⅔ cup rolled oats : ⅓ cup soy flour
⅔	cup sunflower seeds : ½ cup sour milk
½	cup sour milk
1	egg

Sour Orange Muffins
24 muffins

2 muffins = approx. 5 grams of usable protein
10% to 13% of average daily protein need

These muffins are almost sweet enough for dessert, but they are delicious for breakfast or dinner. The sourdough starter is present mainly to react with the baking soda to make a light muffin, but it adds a tang of its own, too.

*1½ cups whole wheat flour
*½ cup soy flour
1 tsp salt
1 tsp baking soda
*¼ cup sesame seeds
*¾ cup sourdough starter (see p. 216)

½ cup honey
*2 eggs, beaten
*½ cup buttermilk OR yogurt
½ cup oil
2 tsp freshly grated orange peel OR 1 tsp dried peel

(1) Stir the flours, salt, soda, and sesame seeds together in a small mixing bowl.
(2) Combine the sourdough starter, honey, eggs, buttermilk, oil, and orange rind; pour this mixture into the first, stirring only enough to moisten.
(3) Fill oiled muffin tins ⅔ full. Bake in a 375°F oven for 20 to 25 minutes.

* _____

1½ cups whole wheat flour : ¼ cup soy flour : ¼ cup sesame seeds
¼ cup soy flour : ½ cup buttermilk
2 eggs
¾ cup sourdough starter

Quick Breads

Pancake, Waffle, or Camping Bread Mix
about 6½ cups

> 1½ cups mix = approx. 20 grams of usable protein
> 47% to 56% of average daily protein need

This mixture is ready to use with the addition of water and a few other ingredients. For camping, water and powdered eggs can make you a good campfire bread.

*4	cups whole wheat flour	1	tbsp salt
*1	cup soy flour	*½	cup milk powder (⅔ cups instant)
2	tbsp baking powder		

(1) Stir these dry ingredients together and store in a tightly covered jar or can. Put in a plastic bag for camping.

(2) When you're at home, add the following to 1½ cups of the mix:

1-2	eggs	water (or milk) to make a thick batter for pancakes or a thin batter for waffles
2	tbsp oil	
2	tbsp honey	

(3) For camping, if you have the four above ingredients you can add them, but you may want to use powdered eggs and raw sugar. We usually take honey and oil with us when we go backpacking, so we use them. Whatever you add, you know that the mix itself is high protein; and since there

is extra milk powder, you can add peanuts or sesame seeds.

*
___

1 cup soy flour : 4 cups whole wheat flour
½ cup milk powder

___

Irish Soda Bread
1 small round loaf of 12 slices

> 1 slice = approx. 3 grams of usable protein
> 7% to 8% of average daily protein need

This bread is so easy to make, and superb when served hot from the oven with butter. It can also be sliced like yeast bread for sandwiches or toast.

*2	cups whole wheat flour	*1 egg, beaten
½	tsp salt	1 tbsp honey
1	tsp baking soda	*1 cup yogurt OR buttermilk
(⅛	tsp ground carda-mom—optional)	

(1) Stir the dry ingredients together.
(2) Beat the honey and buttermilk into the beaten egg; gradually pour this mixture into the dry ingredients. The combined mixture will be dry like a yeast bread dough. Blend it with your hands to work all of the flour in. If it is too dry, add a little buttermilk; if too wet, add more whole wheat flour.
(3) Knead the bread for about 5 minutes, then shape into a flat but round loaf.
(4) Place the loaf on an oiled baking sheet; cut two parallel slashes in the dough about ½ inch deep. This allows the dough to rise during baking without cracking.

(5) Bake the bread at 375°F for 25 to 30 minutes, until it is well browned and tests done like yeast bread. (See the Key Bread Recipe, p. 198, for testing doneness.)

Variations—

> *Currant Soda Bread:* Add 1 cup currants or raisins to the dry ingredients.
> *Caraway Soda Bread:* Omit the cardamom. Substitute 1 teaspoon of crushed caraway seeds.

*

───────────────────────────────

2 cups whole wheat flour : 1 cup buttermilk
1 egg

───────────────────────────────

Sourdough Corn Bread
a 10″ round pan of 12 pieces

> 1 piece = approx. 4 grams of usable protein
> 9% to 11% of average daily protein need

The sourdough starter adds an interesting taste and texture to traditional cornbread.

*1 cup sourdough starter (see p. 216)	*2 eggs, beaten
*1 cup cornmeal	2 tbsp honey
*1/3 cup soy flour	1/4 cup melted butter
1½ cups water	1/2 tsp salt
*6 tbsp powdered milk (½ cup instant)	1 tsp baking soda

(1) Blend the ingredients in the order given.
(2) Turn the batter into a 10″ oiled round cake pan or cast iron frying pan. Bake at 400°F for 25 to 30 minutes.

(3)   Slice the bread into wedges and serve hot.

* _____

    1   cup sourdough starter
    1   cup cornmeal : ⅓ cup soy flour : ¼ cup milk powder
    2   eggs
    2   tbsp milk powder

_____

Moist Corn Bread
a 7" x 11" or 9" x 9" pan;
about 15 pieces

> 2 pieces = approx. 7 grams of usable protein
> 15% to 18% of average daily protein need

This cornbread is moist and rich, a perfect accompaniment to soups, salads, or bean dishes.

*1 cup cornmeal	½ tsp salt
*1 cup whole wheat flour	*1 egg, beaten
*3 tbsp soy grits	*3 cups buttermilk OR yogurt
2 tsp baking powder	¼ cup oil
½ tsp baking soda	¼ cup honey

(1)   Stir together all of the dry ingredients in a large bowl.

(2)   Stir the liquid ingredients together in a separate bowl and then stir them into the dry ingredients, mixing only enough to combine the ingredients thoroughly. Less mixing will make a more tender bread.

(3)   Pour the batter into an oiled pan and bake at 350°F for 40 to 50 minutes. The top will spring back when the bread is done, and a tester should come out clean, although it may be somewhat wet—*i.e.*, there shouldn't be any uncooked batter

on it, but it may be wetter than you would normally expect.

This cornbread is most delicious when eaten warm with butter or honey, or both!

* _____

1	cup cornmeal : 3 tbsp soy grits : 1 cup buttermilk
1	cup whole wheat flour : ½ cup buttermilk
1½	cups buttermilk
1	egg

_____

Quick Wheat Soy Bread
1 loaf of 15 slices

> 1 slice = approx. 4 grams of usable protein
> 9% to 10% of average daily protein need

A dark, rich-tasting loaf, good with cream cheese when it's hot from the oven. Toast it with butter and cinnamon for breakfast.

*2½	cups whole wheat flour	½	tsp salt
*½	cup plus 2 tbsp soy flour	*2	cups sour milk or buttermilk
2	tsp baking soda	2	tbsp oil
		¼	cup honey

(1) Stir the dry ingredients together.
(2) Blend the liquid ingredients; pour them into the dry and blend well.
(3) Pour the batter into a well-oiled loaf pan and bake at 325°F for about 1 hour, until a toothpick comes out clean.

* _____

2½ cups whole wheat flour : ½ cup plus 2 tbsp soy flour
2 cups milk

_____

Quick Molasses Bread
1 loaf of 15 slices

1 slice = approx. 3 grams of usable protein
8% to 9% of average daily protein need

Thickly sliced and crumbly, this loaf is perfect with soup as well as fruit.

*2 cups whole wheat flour	¼ cup oil
*½ cup soy flour	¼ cup molasses
½ tsp cinnamon	3 tbsp honey
¼ tsp salt	1 tsp grated orange rind
2 tsp baking powder	
*2 eggs, beaten	*¾ cup milk

(1) Stir together the dry ingredients.
(2) In another bowl beat the eggs, oil, molasses, honey, orange rind, and milk together.
(3) Stir the liquid mixture into the dry ingredients and combine carefully. The batter will be stiff.
(4) Turn the batter into an oiled loaf pan; bake at 375°F for 30 minutes, until a toothpick comes out clean.

Variations—

Dark Molasses Bread: Omit the honey and use in all ½ cup molasses.
Molasses Fruit Nut Bread: Add 1 cup raisins and ½ to 1 cup chopped nuts to the original recipe.

* ———————————————————

¾ cup milk
2 cups whole wheat flour : ½ cup soy flour
2 eggs

Wheatless Flat Bread
12 pieces

1 piece = approx. 3 grams of usable protein
7% to 8% of average daily protein need

The first time I made this bread I couldn't believe that I had really made it with rye flour. It was so tender and sweet. Do serve it hot with cream cheese, ricotta, or butter.

*2	cups rye flour	*1	cup double milk
½	tsp salt		(see glossary for
2	tsp baking powder		explanation)
1	tbsp honey	2	tbsp melted butter OR oil

(1) Combine the dry ingredients, including any milk powder that you might be using for double milk.

(2) Stir the liquid ingredients together, then stir them into the dry mixture until a smooth dough forms.

(3) Oil and flour a cookie sheet or large baking pan (I use a cast iron frying pan). Place the dough on the pan, flour your hands, and pat it into a large circle (or square) that is ½ inch thick.

(4) Prick the dough with a fork many times, bake it at 450°F until lightly browned—about 10 minutes.

---

*

2 cups rye flour : 1 cup milk
1 cup milk

Quick Coconut Bread
1 loaf of 15 slices

> 1 slice = approx. 3 grams of usable protein
> 6% to 8% of average daily protein need

A marvelous aroma will fill your kitchen when you bake this loaf. Serve the bread to accompany an elegant buffet, or for a potluck. Try spreading it with peanut butter for a new taste in peanut butter sandwiches!

*2	cups whole wheat flour	½	tsp baking soda
1	cup unsweetened grated coconut	*3	eggs, beaten
*¼	cup soy grits	¼	cup oil
1	tbsp baking powder	¼	cup honey
1	tsp salt	¼	tsp almond extract
		1	tsp lemon juice
		*1	cup milk

(1) Stir all of the dry ingredients together.
(2) In another bowl beat the eggs with the oil, honey, almond extract, lemon juice, and milk.
(3) Stir the wet ingredients into the dry and beat well. The batter will be stiff.
(4) Turn the batter into an oiled loaf pan or ring pan. Bake at 350°F for 30 minutes, until a toothpick comes out clean and the bread is lightly browned.

---

*

2　cups whole wheat flour : ¼ cup soy grits
3　eggs
1　cup milk

Coffee Cakes

Cheese-Filled Coffee Cake
two 9″ rings of 10 pieces each

> 1 piece = approx. 7 grams of usable protein
> 16% to 20% of average daily protein need

This is a most elegant dessert. Toast the leftovers if there are any. When I make it everyone keeps eating and eating until it's all gone. If you make it in a ring mold or spring-form pan that has a fancy bottom, it's especially attractive, since you turn it over before serving.

2 tbsp baking yeast dissolved in . . .	*6⅓ cups whole wheat flour
½ cup warm water	*1⅙ cups soy flour
1 cup melted butter	
¾ cup honey	**Filling:**
*1 cup yogurt OR buttermilk	*1 cup ricotta cheese
*5-6 egg yolks, beaten until thick and light	*2 whole eggs, beaten
	1 tsp vanilla
	½ cup honey

(1) Blend the melted butter, honey, and yogurt into the beaten egg yolks; stir in the dissolved yeast.

(2) Stir together the whole wheat flour and soy flour in a large mixing bowl. Remove about 3 cups of the mixture and set it aside (to add later during the kneading).

(3) Pour the yeast and egg mixture into the large bowl full of flour; blend the ingredients together. It should be wet and soft, but not sticky. Knead for about 5 minutes until the dough is smooth, adding the reserved 3 cups of flour if it *is* sticky.

(4) Put the dough back in the bowl, set in a warm place, and let rise until double.

(5) While the cake is rising, prepare the filling: Put the ricotta cheese through a sieve or beat it vigorously with an electric mixer until it is smooth; blend in the whole eggs, vanilla, and honey.

(6) Punch down the dough, knead a few times, and divide it into 2 pieces. Roll each piece into a 13-inch circle. Fit each circle over a ring mold, gently lifting it to rest on the bottom, and letting some of the dough hang over the outside edge. Pour ½ the filling into the well of dough in each pan. Lift the outside edges of the dough, bring them over the filling, and seal them by pinching them to the inside ring. Cut a cross in the dough that covers the center ring, then fold those flaps down over the dough covering the filling. Pinch to seal. The fillings should be completely sealed.

(7) Let the cake rise until the dough reaches the top of the pans. Bake the cakes at 350°F for 30 minutes. Test with a toothpick for a completely baked cake.

(8) Cool the rings 10 minutes in the pan, then turn onto racks top-sides down. Serve at room temperature (top-side down).

---

*

1	cup yogurt : 1⅔ cups whole wheat flour
5-6	egg yolks and 2 whole eggs
2⅔	cups whole wheat flour : ⅔ cup soy flour
2	cups whole wheat flour : ½ cup soy flour
1	cup ricotta cheese

Sunflower-Topped Coffee Cake
a 7" x 11" pan of 15 pieces

2 pieces = approx. 7 grams of usable protein
17% to 20% of average daily protein need

The topping for this cake is super-crunchy and gives an exciting texture to the finished cake. Serve it warm or cold.

*2 cups whole wheat flour	*1 cup buttermilk OR yogurt
1 tsp baking powder	⅔ cup honey
*2 tbsp milk powder (3¼ tbsp instant)	3 tbsp melted butter OR oil
½ tsp baking soda	
1 tsp salt	**Topping:**
½ tsp each: cinnamon, nutmeg, ginger	*⅔ cup sunflower seeds, coarsely chopped and toasted with ...
¼ tsp each: cloves, allspice	1 tbsp butter
*2 eggs, beaten	2 tbsp honey

(1) Stir all of the dry ingredients together using only one-half of all the spices. Set aside the remaining ¼ teaspoons of cinnamon, nutmeg, ginger and ⅛ teaspoons of cloves and allspice for the topping.

(2) In a separate bowl combine the eggs, buttermilk, honey, and melted butter.

(3) Stir the wet ingredients into the dry with as few strokes as possible, then turn the mixture into an oiled baking pan.

(4) Prepare the topping as follows: melt the butter (1 tablespoon) in a small frying pan; add the chopped sunflower seeds and heat until they are

toasty brown and fragrant with butter. Remove from the heat; stir in the honey and remaining spices.

(5) Spread the topping carefully over the batter in the baking pan.

(6) Place in a 350°F oven for about 25 minutes, until the cake tests done.

*

⅔ cup sunflower seeds : 2 tbsp milk powder
2 cups whole wheat flour : 1 cup buttermilk
2 eggs

Walnut-and-Raisin-Filled Coffee Cake
an 8″ x 8″ pan of 9 pieces

> 1 piece = approx. 5 grams of usable protein
> 11% to 14% of average daily protein need

Serve this cake slightly warm. I had never made a quick cake with a filling before this one, but it works deliciously.

Filling:
1 tbsp cornstarch
½ cup water, cold
*½ cup chopped walnuts
3 tbsp to ⅓ cup honey
1 cup raisins
grated peel of 1 lemon
OR ½ tsp lemon extract

Cake:
½ cup butter
⅔ cup honey
*2 eggs
½ tsp vanilla
1⅔ cups whole wheat flour
*⅓ cup soy flour
2 tsp baking powder
½ tsp salt
*½ cup milk
¾ tsp cinnamon

(1) Prepare the filling: Dissolve the cornstarch in the cold water; mix in the walnuts, honey, raisins, and lemon flavoring. Bring to a boil and cook over low heat until the mixture has thickened. Set aside to cool.

(2) For the batter: Cream together the honey and butter. Add the eggs and beat until the mixture is slightly fluffy; beat in the vanilla.

(3) Stir together the whole wheat flour, soy flour, baking powder, and salt. Add this mixture to the creamed mixture alternately with the ½ cup milk.

(4) Spread one-half the batter in an oiled baking pan; cover carefully with the raisin filling. Spread the remaining batter on the top. Sprinkle with the ¾ teaspoon cinnamon.

(5) Bake at 350° F for 25-30 minutes.

*_____

  1⅔ cups whole wheat flour : ⅓ cup soy flour
   ½ cup milk
   ½ cup walnuts
  2   eggs

_____

Orange Coffee Cake
a 9" x 9" pan of 9 pieces

                  1 piece = approx. 4 grams of usable protein
                    9% to 11% of average daily protein need

Because of its fresh orange flavor, I prefer this coffee cake for breakfast, but it's just as tasty at other times of the day, of course!

Cake:
*1⅔ cups whole wheat flour
*⅓ cup soy flour
½ tsp salt
1 tbsp baking powder
½ cup honey
2 tsp grated orange peel
½ cup orange juice

¼ cup melted butter OR oil
*2 eggs, beaten
1 tsp vanilla

Topping:
2 tbsp grated orange peel
¼ cup honey
1 tsp cinnamon
1 tbsp melted butter

(1) Stir together the flours, salt, and baking powder.
(2) In a separate bowl combine the honey, orange peel, orange juice, melted butter, eggs, and vanilla.
(3) Mix the liquid ingredients with the dry with a minimum of strokes.
(4) Pour into an oiled and floured cake pan.
(5) Combine the orange peel, honey, cinnamon, and butter for the topping; drizzle the topping over the batter in the pan.
(6) Bake at 400°F for 30 minutes, until the cake pulls away from the sides of the pan.

*

1⅔ cups whole wheat flour : ⅓ cup soy flour
2 eggs

Buttermilk Raisin Coffee Cake
an 8″ x 8″ pan of 9 pieces

1 piece = approx. 6 grams of usable protein
13% to 16% of average daily protein need

This cake is delightfully light and easy to assemble.

You could make it in larger pans (such as an 11″ x 7″) for more but smaller pieces.

*2 cups whole wheat flour	1 tsp baking powder
*¼ cup soy grits	½ cup raisins
½ tsp salt	¾ cup honey
2 tsp cinnamon	¼ to ½ cup oil
1 tsp baking soda	*1 cup buttermilk
	*2 eggs, beaten

(1) Stir the raisins and the dry ingredients together.
(2) In a separate bowl beat the honey, oil, buttermilk, and eggs together. Stir in the dry ingredients enough to blend them, but don't overblend. The littlest blending makes the tenderest cake.
(3) Pour into an oiled pan and bake at 350°F for 30-35 minutes.

*
_____

2 cups whole wheat flour : ¼ cup soy grits
1 cup buttermilk
2 eggs
_____

Familia Cake
a 9″ tube pan of 20 pieces

1 piece = approx. 5 grams of usable protein
12% to 14% of average daily protein need

A quick cake to prepare if you have some familia cereal around (see page 49). It has a delicate texture but is hearty like a light fruit cake.

*2 eggs
¾ cup honey
¼ cup butter
*½ cup milk
1 tbsp rum or brandy
*1 cup whole wheat flour
*1½ cups familia (p. 49)

1 tbsp baking powder
½ tsp salt

Glaze:
*1½ cups cottage cheese honey and rum (or brandy)

(1) Put the eggs, honey, butter, milk, and rum into your blender and buzz until smooth.

(2) Stir together the whole wheat flour, familia, baking powder, and salt. Pour in the liquid mixture and stir until they are well mixed.

(3) Pour the batter into an oiled spring form with a tube (or use a casserole with a custard cup in the middle).

(4) Bake the cake at 350°F for about 45 minutes, until it's nicely browned and a tester comes out clean.

(5) Glaze the cake with the cottage cheese, which has been whipped smooth in the blender with honey and rum.

---

*

2 eggs
½ cup milk: 1 cup whole wheat flour
1½ cups familia
1½ cups cottage cheese

Sweet Loaves

Date and Orange Loaf
1 loaf of 15 pieces

> 1 piece = approx. 4 grams of usable protein
> 9% to 10% of average daily protein need

If you use pitted, very sweet dates such as deglet noir, your loaf will be very rich, like a fruit cake. Adjust the amount of honey that you use according to your sweet tooth and your dates.

⅓ cup fresh orange juice	1 tsp vanilla extract
*⅔ cup hot milk	(¼ tsp orange extract— optional)
1 cup chopped dates	
*¼ cup soy grits	*2 cups whole wheat flour
the rind of one orange, ground or finely chopped	1 tsp baking powder
	½ tsp baking soda
2 tbsp oil	½ tsp salt
½ to ¾ cup honey	*¾ cup chopped walnuts
*2 eggs, beaten	

(1) If your orange has more than ⅓ cup of juice, reduce the amount of hot milk so that the total liquid is 1 cup.

(2) Pour the hot mixture over the dates and soy grits; let the mixture soak while you prepare the batter.

(3) Cream the oil and honey; beat in the eggs and vanilla (and orange extract).

(4) Stir the dry ingredients together (except the walnuts) and add them alternately with the soaked date mixture to the creamed honey.

(5)   Stir in the orange rind and walnuts.

(6)   Turn into an oiled loaf pan (5″ x 9″); bake at
      325°F for one hour for a moist bread, 1½ hours
      for a drier loaf.

* _____

⅔   cup milk
¼   cup soy grits : 2 cups whole wheat flour
2   eggs
¾   cup walnuts

_____

Carob Date Loaf
a small loaf pan of 12 slices

> 1 slice = approx. 2 grams of usable protein
> 4% to 6% of average daily protein need

This recipe, dark and rich, can be made into muffins
as well. See the variation below.

3   tbsp butter   ¾   cup chopped dates
½   cup honey   ⅓   cup carob powder
*2 eggs   2   tsp baking powder
½   tsp vanilla   *1 cup whole wheat
¼   tsp salt   flour
*2 tbsp soy grits

(1)   Cream together the butter and honey; beat in the
      eggs, vanilla, and salt. Stir in the soy grits.

(2)   Add the chopped dates to the liquid mixture and
      beat it gently to separate all of the lumps.

(3)   Add the carob powder, baking powder, and whole
      wheat flour in the order given.

(4)   Turn the mixture into an oiled loaf pan. Bake at
      325°F for 20 to 25 minutes. Check for burning
      in the last 10 minutes of baking and reduce the
      heat if the loaf is too brown.

Variation—Carob Date Muffins: Use ¾ cup whole wheat flour instead of one. Drop the batter into oiled muffin tins and bake at 375°F for about 10 minutes.

---

* ———————————————————————————————

1　cup whole wheat flour : 2 tbsp soy grits
2　eggs

Lemon-Sesame Bread
a small loaf pan of 10 slices

1 slice = approx. 4 grams of usable protein
9% to 11% of average daily protein need

Both tart and sweet . . .

Cake:
¼　cup oil
½　cup honey
*2　eggs
juice of one lemon
grated rind of 2
　　lemons
*½　cup sesame seeds
*1　cup whole wheat
　　flour

*¼　cup soy flour
*1½　tbsp milk powder
　　(2 tbsp instant)
2　tsp baking powder
½　tsp salt

Topping:
juice of one lemon
3　tbsp honey

(1)　Beat the oil and honey until they are blended; beat in the eggs, lemon juice, and rind.
(2)　Stir the dry ingredients together and then stir them into the first mixture.
(3)　Bake in a small oiled loaf pan (preferably smaller than 5″ x 9″) at 350°F for 45 minutes, until a tester comes out clean.

(4) Combine the lemon juice and honey for the topping, heating it if your honey has crystallized; pour this over the warm loaf when it comes out of the oven. You may poke several holes with a toothpick first, if you like; this will make it soak in more.

(5) Cool for 10 minutes, then remove it from the pan.

* _____

>   2   eggs
>   1   cup whole wheat flour : ¼ cup soy flour
>   ½   cup sesame seeds : 1½ tbsp milk powder

_____

Banana Bread
a 5" x 9" loaf of 12 slices

> 1 slice = approx. 4 grams of usable protein
> 9% to 11% of average daily protein need

This is a rich loaf, and delicious served warm. Cut it carefully and spread with ricotta or cream cheese. And if there's any left over, toast it for breakfast.

¼ cup butter	*¼ cup milk powder (⅓ cup instant)
⅔ cup honey	1 tsp salt
*3 eggs, beaten	2 tsp baking powder
1 cup mashed banana pulp (from about 3 small bananas)	1 tsp baking soda
	*2 cups whole wheat flour
⅓ cup water	(walnuts and raisins —optional)
1 tsp vanilla	

(1) Cream the butter and honey (with an electric mixer, if possible) until light; beat in the eggs, banana pulp, water, and vanilla.

(2)   Stir together the dry ingredients; stir them into the first mixture, blending with as few strokes as possible.

(3)   Stir in 1 cup walnuts and ½ to 1 cup raisins, if desired.

(4)   Turn the batter into an oiled loaf pan; bake at 325°F for about 1 hour, until well browned and a tester comes out clean.

---

*

2   cups whole wheat flour : ¼ cup milk powder
3   eggs

Carrot Bread
1 ring of 12 slices

> 1 slice = approx. 4 grams of usable protein
> 10% to 12% of average daily protein need

This is a slightly heavy but sweet loaf, wonderful when sliced thin and served with yogurt or ricotta cheese. The larger amount of honey makes a very sweet bread, so adjust the amount according to your sweet tooth (or your honey supply).

*2 cups whole wheat flour	*2 eggs, beaten
2 tsp cinnamon	½ cup oil
1 tbsp baking soda	2 tsp vanilla
1 cup raisins	⅔ to 1 cup honey
*¼ cup soy grits	2 cups ground or grated carrots
*½ cup nuts or seeds	

(1)   Stir the first six ingredients together in a large mixing bowl, making sure the raisins are separated and not in clumps.

(2) Blend the next five ingredients in the order given. Stir them into the first mixture using a minimum of strokes.

(3) Turn the batter into an oiled and floured ring and bake at 325°F for about 1 hour, until a tester comes out clean. You might also try baking this bread for 35 minutes in 6-ounce juice cans to make small gifts or just more decorative slices.

*

    2 cups whole wheat flour : ¼ cup soy grits
    ½ cup nuts or seeds
    2 eggs

Pumpkin Bread
a 5″ x 9″ loaf of 12 slices

> 1 slice = approx. 4 grams of usable protein
> 10% to 12% of average daily protein need

This not-too-sweet bread is excellent with ricotta cheese spread over it, with yogurt, or with any hard cheeses. We took this bread camping, and the raccoons ate it all!

⅓ cup oil	1 tsp fresh ginger, grated
⅔ cup molasses	
⅔ cup pureed, cooked pumpkin	*2 tbsp brewer's yeast
	*¼ cup milk powder (⅓ cup instant)
*2 eggs, beaten	
½ tsp each: cinnamon, nutmeg	*¼ cup peanut meal
	*1¾ cups whole wheat flour
¼ tsp each: mace, cloves, and salt	
	1 tbsp baking powder

(1) Blend the oil, molasses, pumpkin, eggs, and all of the spices in a large bowl.

(2) Stir the remaining ingredients together and add to the first mixture.

(3) Bake in a well-oiled loaf pan at 325°F for about 1 hour. If the loaf gets too brown before the end of the baking time, lower the heat to 300°F.

*

   2 eggs
   ¼ cup peanut meal : 2 tsp milk powder
   1¾ cups whole wheat flour : 3 tbsp plus 1½ tsp milk powder
   2 tbsp brewer's yeast

Thanksgiving Cranberry Bread
a 5″ x 9″ loaf of 12 slices

> 1 slice = approx. 5 grams of usable protein
> 11% to 13% of average daily protein need

We had this loaf at our "House Thanksgiving" last fall. It's pleasingly tart but cakelike in texture, and beauty-full of bright red cranberries.

   ¼ cup butter
   ⅔ to 1 cup honey
   *2 eggs
   1 cup orange juice
   *2 cups whole wheat flour
   *¼ cup milk powder (⅓ cup instant)
   1 tsp baking powder
   1 tsp baking soda
   ½ tsp salt
   *1 cup chopped nuts
   2 cups of fresh whole cranberries

(1) Cream the butter and honey; beat in the eggs and orange juice.

(2) In a separate bowl stir together all of the dry ingredients (not the cranberries); add them gradually to the liquid mixture. Fold in the cranberries.

(3)   Turn the batter into an oiled and floured loaf pan.
       Bake at 325°F for 1 to 1¼ hours.

* _____

   2   cups whole wheat flour : ¼ cup milk powder
   2   eggs
   1   cup nuts

_____

Pineapple Walnut Bread
a 5″ x 9″ loaf of 12 slices

> 1 slice = approx. 4 grams of usable protein
> 10% to 12% of average daily protein need

Pineapple juice, as the major liquid ingredient, really
gives this bread a full fruit flavor.

2 tbsp oil	*3 tbsp wheat germ
½ cup honey	*3 tbsp milk powder
*2 eggs, beaten	(¼ cup instant)
1 cup pineapple juice	2 tsp baking powder
	½ tsp salt
*1¾ cups whole wheat flour	*¾ cup walnuts, chopped
*¼ cup soy flour	

(1)   Beat together the oil, honey, and eggs; stir in the
       pineapple juice.
(2)   Stir the dry ingredients together, then add to the
       liquid using just a few strokes.
(3)   Spoon the batter into an oiled loaf pan; bake at
       350°F for about one hour, until a toothpick
       comes out clean.

* _____

   2   eggs
   1   cup whole wheat flour : ¼ cup soy flour
  ¾   cup whole wheat flour : 3 tbsp milk powder
  ¾   cup walnuts
   3   tbsp wheat germ

_____

Short and Sweet (Cookies and Bars)

Cookies are a favorite munchie of ours. We have a yellow cookie man whose fat belly holds our baked delights. All of our young visitors know where he stands, empty or full, laughing in the kitchen.

Many of the following recipes will not be as sweet as "boughten" cookies. I am convinced that the food industry uses even more sugar in their cookies than they did ten years ago. But then maybe my taste has changed, because if you chew whole grains well, they will be sweet even without honey or sugar. Feel free to increase the amount of honey in the following recipes up to ⅓ more. I can't guarantee that the recipe will be exactly the same with more honey, so use your instinct to determine a safe addition. Also, in comparing recipes remember that you need only about ½ as much honey as sugar. When you try out mine for the first time, chew them thoroughly and you will taste the subtle sweetness of the grains and honey.

And munch on . . .

Gorp Cookies
11 dozen cookies

> 2 cookies = approx. 2 grams of usable protein
> 5% to 6% of average daily protein need

Gorp is a traditional camping mix for high-energy snacks, consisting of raisins, peanuts, and M & M's or chocolate chips. Before one of our camping trips I realized I could increase the protein by adding sunflower seeds to complement the peanuts, and also make the mix easy to eat by making cookies. Every cookie is full of protein and energy.

1	cup butter	*1	cup sunflower seeds
1½	cups honey		
*2	eggs, beaten	*1½	cups peanuts, roasted and coarsely chopped
½	tsp salt		
2	tsp vanilla		
1	tsp baking powder	1½	cups raisins
*3¾	cups whole wheat flour	1½	cups chocolate or carob chips
*¼	cup milk powder (⅓ cup instant)		

(1) Cream the butter, with an electric mixer if possible, until it's creamy and light; add the honey and cream them together.

(2) Beat in the eggs, salt, and vanilla.

(3) Stir together the baking powder, milk powder, and whole wheat flour; add it to the creamed mixture, and blend.

(4) Stir in the seeds, nuts, raisins, and chips.

(5) Drop by teaspoons onto an unoiled cookie sheet.

(6) Bake for 10 to 12 minutes at 375°F.

---

*

¾	cup peanuts : 1 cup sunflower seeds
3¾	cups whole wheat flour : ¾ cup peanuts : ¼ cup milk powder
2	eggs

Kitchen Sink Cookies
4 dozen cookies

> 2 cookies = approx. 3 grams of usable protein
> 6% to 7% of average daily protein need

These delicious cookies contain all those wonderful things that cookies should have!

*1 cup whole wheat flour	⅔ cup raisins
*¼ cup soy flour	⅔ cup chocolate chips
*1⅓ cups rolled oats	*¼ cup peanuts, chopped
¾ cup unsweetened flaked coconut	*⅓ cup sunflower seeds
*¼ cup milk powder (⅓ cup instant)	¼ cup oil OR melted butter
½ tsp salt	¼ cup molasses
1 tsp cinnamon	¼ cup honey
½ tsp powdered ginger	*2 eggs, beaten

(1) Stir together all of the dry ingredients (*i.e.* everything except the oil, honey, molasses, and eggs).

(2) Beat the eggs in a small bowl; measure the oil, then the honey and molasses in the same measuring cup. Beat all the liquid ingredients together thoroughly.

(3) Pour the liquid into the dry ingredients and combine until the dry ingredients are moistened. If the mixture seems too dry add some milk or water until the dough is of drop cookie consistency.

(4) Drop the cookies onto an unoiled cookie sheet. Bake at 350°F for 10 to 12 minutes.

Variation—Oatmeal Cookies: Omit the ⅔ cup choco-

late chips and you will have delicious oatmeal cookies.

*_____

2	eggs
1	cup whole wheat flour : ¼ cup soy flour
1⅓	cups rolled oats : 2 tbsp milk powder
2	tbsp milk powder
¼	cup peanuts : ½ cup sunflower seeds

_____

Chocolate Coconut Cookies
10 dozen cookies

> 2 cookies = approx. 2 grams of usable protein
> 4% to 5% of average daily protein need

You should go for these—especially if you happen
to be a chocolate freak (use the larger amount of chocolate chips). They're great for quick energy when
you're hiking, too.

¾	cup butter	1½	cups unsweetened
1	cup honey		coconut shreds
*2	eggs	*2½	cups whole wheat
1	ounce un-		flour
	sweetened baking	*¾	cup soy flour
	chocolate, melted	1-2	cups chocolate
1	tsp vanilla		chips
¼	tsp salt	*1	cup toasted
½	tsp baking powder		sunflower seeds
½	tsp baking soda	*¾	cup chopped
			roasted peanuts

(1) Cream the butter and honey; beat in the two eggs,
     melted chocolate, vanilla, and salt.
(2) Stir together the baking powder, soda, coconut,
     wheat and soy flours; blend this mixture into the
     creamed mixture.

(3) Stir in the chocolate chips, sunflower seeds, and peanuts. If you have only raw peanuts, they will toast lightly when the cookies are baked, so use them.

(4) You may chill the batter or roll it right away. Make large marble-sized balls; place them on an unoiled cookie sheet. They won't spread, so place them close together.

(5) Bake at 350°F for about 10 minutes.

* _____

2	eggs
2½	cups whole wheat flour : ½ cup plus 2 tbsp soy flour
2	tbsp soy flour
1	cup sunflower seeds : ¾ cup peanuts

_____

Banana Peanut Butter Cookies
4 dozen cookies

2 cookies = approx. 3 grams of usable protein
8% to 10% of average daily protein need

An unusual combination that's surprisingly delicious.

*1 egg, beaten	*3 tbsp milk powder
½ cup honey	(5 tbsp instant)
1 large ripe banana, mashed (about ½ cup)	½ tsp baking powder
	1 tsp baking soda
	½ tsp salt
*½ cup crunchy peanut butter	1½ tsp cinnamon
	½ tsp nutmeg
*1½ cups whole wheat flour	*1 cup sunflower seeds

(1) Blend the egg, honey, banana, and peanut butter thoroughly.

(2) Stir together the dry ingredients, then combine them with the liquid mixture.

(3) Drop by teaspoons onto an oiled cookie sheet. Bake 10 to 12 minutes at 350°F.

---

*
1	egg
½	cup peanut butter : 1 cup sunflower seeds
1½	cups whole wheat flour : 3 tbsp milk powder

Pumpkin Cookies or Bars
2 dozen cookies

> 2 cookies = approx. 3 grams of usable protein
> 7% to 8% of average daily protein need

Substitute yams or other winter squash for the pumpkin.

*1¼	cups whole wheat flour	½	cup butter
		⅔	cup honey
*5	tbsp soy flour	*1	egg
1	tsp baking soda	1	cup cooked and pureed pumpkin
½	tsp salt		
½	tsp cinnamon	*1	cup chopped walnuts
½	tsp nutmeg		
¼	tsp cloves	½	cup chopped raisins
		½	cup chopped dates

(1) Stir together the dry ingredients and spices.
(2) In another bowl cream the butter and honey; beat in the egg until the mixture is smooth. Stir in the pumpkin puree, and don't worry if the texture is strange.
(3) Add the dry ingredients to the pumpkin mixture; blend, then stir in the nuts and dried fruit.
(4) Drop by heaping tablespoons onto an oiled cookie sheet.

(5) Bake at 325°F for 15 minutes, until they are golden.

Variation—Pumpkin Bars: Pour the cookie batter into an oiled 8″ x 8″ pan. Bake at 350°F for 25 minutes. Cool and cut into squares.

*

1¼ cups whole wheat flour : 5 tbsp soy flour
1 egg
1 cup chopped walnuts

Fruit Bar Crunch
18 bars

2 bars = approx. 6 grams of usable protein
14% to 17% of average daily protein need

An elegant treat—not too sweet, but somewhat unusual tasting . . .

1½ cups unsulfured dried apricots OR dried peaches

Crust:
*1 cup wheat germ
*⅓ cup soy flour
*⅔ cup whole wheat flour
⅓ cup honey
¼ cup butter
¼ cup oil

Topping:
*⅔ cup whole wheat flour
1 tsp baking powder
½ tsp salt
*2 eggs
½ cup honey
¼ tsp almond extract
*½ cup chopped walnuts

(1) Snip the dried apricots or peaches into small pieces; drop them into about 1½ cups boiling water. Simmer them about 20 minutes OR just until they're soft.

(2) While the apricots simmer, stir the wheat germ, soy flour, and ⅔ cup whole wheat flour together; pour in the honey and stir, cut in the butter, and pour in the oil. Mix it all up using your hands. You should have a mixture that will press into a 7″ x 11″ or 9″ x 9″ pan.

(3) Press 2 cups of the mixture into your baking pan. Set the rest aside. Bake the crust at 350°F for 10 minutes.

(4) Stir together the ⅔ cup whole wheat flour, baking powder, and salt.

(5) In another bowl beat the eggs, honey, and almond extract; stir in the flour mixture, chopped walnuts, and the apricots that have been snipped and cooked. Spread this mixture over the baked crust. Sprinkle the reserved crust mixture over the top, pressing it in lightly.

(6) Bake in a 350°F oven for 25 minutes. Cool and cut into bars.

*

1	cup wheat germ
1⅓	cups whole wheat flour : ⅓ cup soy flour
2	eggs
½	cup walnuts

Carob Nut Brownies
an 8″ x 8″ pan—12 brownies

1 brownie = approx. 5 grams usable protein
11% to 14% of average daily protein need

These are delicious brownies, rich but not too rich. Try them with yogurt or ice cream. And if you like them less cakey, make them in a 7" x 11" or 9" x 9" pan.

½	cup butter OR oil	*⅔	cup whole wheat flour
½	cup honey		
*2	eggs	*2	tbsp milk powder (3½ tbsp instant)
½	tsp salt		
1	tsp vanilla	1	tsp baking powder
⅓	cup carob powder	*⅔	cup sunflower seeds
		*½	cup roasted peanuts, chopped

(1) Cream the butter (or oil) and honey; beat in the eggs, salt, and vanilla.
(2) Stir together the carob powder, whole wheat flour, milk powder, and baking powder; blend into the creamed mixture.
(3) Stir in the sunflower seeds and peanuts.
(4) Turn into an oiled baking pan; bake at 325°F for 20 to 25 minutes. Cool and cut into bars.

* _____

2	eggs
⅔	cup whole wheat flour : 4 tsp milk powder
2	tsp milk powder
⅔	cup sunflower seeds : ½ cup peanuts

Honey Almond Bars
40 1" x 2" bars

> 2 bars = approx. 3 grams of usable protein
> 8% to 10% of average daily protein need

The filling of these bars is made like cream puffs. They are a rich delight for dessert (cut them big) or snacks. We find them quite elegant with custard or ice cream.

Crust:

⅓ cup oil	*⅓ cup soy flour
*1 cup whole wheat flour	3-4 tbsp water

(1) Stir the flours together and mix in the oil, distributing it as evenly as possible.

(2) Add enough water to enable you to gather the dough like a pie crust.

(3) Press the dough into an oiled 9″ x 13″ pan.

Filling:

1 cup water	*1 cup whole wheat flour
⅓ cup butter	
*2 tbsp soy grits	*3 whole eggs at room temperature
½ cup honey	
1½ tsp almond extract	½ cup chopped almonds (or other nuts)
¼ tsp salt	

(1) In a 2- to 2½-quart saucepan heat the water, butter, and soy grits until the butter melts.

(2) Bring the mixture to a boil and add the honey, almond extract, salt, and finally the whole wheat flour. When the flour is added the mixture will thicken immediately and form a dryish glob. Continue to heat this glob for about one minute over medium heat. Remove from the stove.

(3) The next step must be done quickly. Make a depression in the dough that will hold an egg. Drop in one egg and beat it immediately into the dough. The mixture will be slimy, but then the

egg will suddenly be incorporated. The need for speed here is so the egg will not cook (as in scrambled eggs) before it is beaten in. Add the second and third eggs one at a time following the same procedure.

(4) Hold on to the chopped nuts and spread the filling over the prepared crust. Bake the bars for 20 minutes at 375°F. Spread the nuts over the top (they will just sit on top) and bake 5-10 minutes until the nuts are nicely toasted.

Icing:

3	tbsp honey	*½	cup milk powder (⅔
1-2	tbsp soft butter		cup instant)
¾	tsp almond extract	*1-3	tsp milk (or more)

(1) In a small bowl stir the honey, butter, and almond extract together.

(2) Add milk powder and milk alternately, stirring until you have a nice thick mixture. Add enough liquid milk so that you can drizzle the icing over the cooled bars. When this is done, cut them into bars and eat!

*————————————————————

1 cup whole wheat flour : ¼ cup soy flour
1 cup whole wheat flour : 2 tbsp soy grits
3 eggs
½ cup milk powder
a few tsp milk and soy flour

Banana Spice Bars
two 9″ x 9″ pans—18 bars

> 1 bar = approx. 5 grams of usable protein
> 11% to 13% of average daily protein need

These bars are light as cake, but solidly full of the crunch of sunflower seeds, peanuts, and soy grits.

1½	cups mashed very ripe bananas	2	tsp cinnamon
*2	eggs	1	tsp allspice
⅔	cup honey	½	tsp nutmeg
¼	cup oil	½	tsp salt
*½	cup buttermilk OR yogurt	¼	tsp cardamom
¼	tsp almond extract	1	tbsp baking powder
*2	cups whole wheat flour	1	tsp baking soda
*¼	cup soy grits	*½	cup chopped peanuts
		*⅔	cup sunflower seeds

(1) Put the bananas, eggs, honey, oil, buttermilk, and almond extract into your blender; buzz until smooth.

(2) In a large mixing bowl stir together all the remaining ingredients; make a deep well and pour in the blender mixture. Combine the mixtures completely, but don't overmix.

(3) Pour the batter into two well-oiled pans. Bake at 350°F for 30 to 35 minutes, until the cake is well browned on top, dark around the edges, and pulls away from the sides of the pan.

(4) Cut into bars while the cake is still warm; set the pans on racks to cool.

---

*
2 eggs
2 cups whole wheat flour : ¼ cup soy grits
½ cup peanuts : ⅔ cup sunflower seeds
½ cup buttermilk

Peanut Bars
36 bars

2 bars = approx. 7 grams of usable protein
15% to 18% of average daily protein need

The peanuttiest . . .

*½	cup peanut butter	*¼	heaping cup milk powder
½	cup butter		(⅓ heaping cup instant)
1	cup honey		
*2	eggs	1	tsp salt
2	tsp vanilla	2	tsp baking powder
*1	cup chopped peanuts, roasted or raw	*½	cup milk (OR ½ cup water plus 2 more tbsp milk powder)
*2	cups whole wheat flour		

(1) Use a large mixing bowl. Cream together the peanut butter and butter. When the mixture is light, cream in the honey. Beat in the eggs one at a time, then beat in the vanilla.

(2) Stir together the peanuts, whole wheat flour, milk powder, salt, and baking powder; add this mixture alternately with the ½ cup of milk to the creamed mixture.

(3) Turn the mixture into two 9″ x 9″ oiled pans (or into pans of equivalent size).

(4) Bake at 350°F for 25 minutes. Cool and cut into bars.

---

*

2	cups whole wheat flour : ¼ cup peanut butter : ½ cup milk
¼	cup peanut butter : 1 heaping tbsp milk powder
1	cup peanuts : 3 tbsp milk powder
2	eggs

Gingerbread
a 9" x 9" pan of 12 pieces

> 1 piece = approx. 4 grams of usable protein
> 9% to 10% of average daily protein need

A dark molasses gingerbread—delicious with yogurt and fruit.

*1¾ cups whole wheat flour	2 eggs, beaten
*½ cup soy flour, scant	⅓ cup oil OR melted butter
½ tsp salt	1 cup unsulfured molasses
1 tsp baking soda	¾ cup hot water
2 tsp baking powder	
1 tbsp freshly grated ginger root	

(1) Stir the dry ingredients together (include the fresh ginger root here, too).

(2) Stir the remaining liquid ingredients together. They won't blend very well, but we just want them to be together.

(3) Add the liquid to the dry mixture and blend with a few swift strokes. Immediately place the mixture in a well-oiled baking pan.

(4) Bake at 325°F for 30 to 35 minutes, until the cake tests done.

---

*
1¾ cups whole wheat flour : ½ cup soy flour (scant)
  2 eggs

Spiced Sesame Bars
an 8″ x 8″ pan of 9 pieces

1 piece = approx. 3 grams of usable protein
7% to 8% of average daily protein need

Soft cake with the crunch of sesame . . .

*2	eggs, beaten	½	tsp salt
½	cup honey	¼	tsp baking soda
3	tbsp sesame oil	¼	tsp allspice
*½	cup whole wheat	¼	tsp mace
	flour	½	tsp cinnamon
*1	tbsp soy grits	*¼	cup toasted sesame
*1	tbsp milk powder		seeds
	(1½ tbsp instant)		

(1) Combine the eggs, honey, and oil.
(2) Stir the dry ingredients together (EXCEPT the sesame seeds), add to the egg mixture, and blend.
(3) Oil an 8″ x 8″ pan; sprinkle ½ of the sesame seeds on the bottom, pour in the batter, and top with the remaining seeds.
(4) Bake at 350°F for 20 minutes. Cool and cut into bars.

* ———————————————————————

2 eggs
½ cup whole wheat flour : 1 tbsp soy grits
¼ cup sesame seeds: 1 tbsp milk powder

———————————————————————

Just Desserts

When I was little I always asked "what's for dessert?" before we had eaten our main course. Children, and adults too, enjoy ending meals on a sweet note, and we also like to snack on sweet things. There is nothing wrong with eating sweets IF they occur in balance with other foods. Our ancestors instinctively ate grapes. The sweetness attracted them, but they didn't know that it was the vitamins and minerals in the grapes that they really needed. With modern technology we extract all of the vitamins and minerals out of grapes or beets, and what we have left is pure chemical sugar. Man has not lost his instinct for sweets, but the sweets he eats have no food value remaining.

Many people think that sugar will give them a lot of energy. This is true, but only for a short time. When you eat something very sweet, your blood sugar level goes up. Your insulin level then increases to metabolize the sugar. However, huge quantities of sugar overstimulate the pancreas, too much insulin is produced, and the blood sugar drops to a new low. Suddenly you are feeling tired again. So you gain nothing (except maybe a few extra pounds) if you eat sugary foods for instant energy. High-protein foods, however, will raise your blood sugar slowly, and the level will be maintained for a longer time.

In the following recipes I have combined sweets with high-protein combinations of grains or dairy products—constructive alternatives to destructive desserts.

Peanut Puree Soufflé
6 portions

> 1 portion = approx. 13 grams of usable protein
> 29% to 35% of average daily protein need

A new experience in taste from the flavor of cooked peanuts makes this soufflé truly exotic, but extremely delicious.

*1 cup raw peanuts, cooked and pureed with 1 cup of their cooking water— about 1¾ cups puree	¼ cup honey 1 tsp vanilla a pinch of salt
*¼ cup milk powder (⅓ cup instant)	*5 egg whites OR 4 extra large egg whites, at room temperature ¼ tsp cream of tartar

(1) Cook the peanuts until they are very tender. To make a smooth puree easily: buzz the milk powder in a blender with the 1 cup of cooking water; add the peanuts, and buzz again until smooth.

(2) Pour the puree into a small bowl; stir in the honey, vanilla and salt. Be sure the puree is at room temperature before going to the next steps.

(3) Put the egg whites in a deep bowl; using a clean wire whisk or an electric mixer, beat them until they are stiff, but not dry. Beat in the cream of tartar.

(4) Fold the egg whites into the puree: stir a small blob of whites into the puree first to lighten it; then fold in the remaining whites completely, but don't fold more than you need to make the mixture homogeneous.

(5) Pour the mixture into a buttered 1½- to 2-quart soufflé baker or deep casserole with straight sides.

(6) Bake at 350°F for about 30 minutes, when the soufflé should be puffed with a lightly browned top. It will shimmer as if very wet. It should not be dry like a cake.

(7) Serve it at once, for it will only be beautiful for a few minutes.

*

1 cup raw peanuts : ¼ cup milk powder
5 egg whites

Cottage Cheese Cake
a 10″ pie of 8 portions

1 portion = approx. 12 grams of usable protein
29% to 34% of average daily protein need

A rich cheesecake, but not as rich as those made with sour cream and cream cheese. A lot of protein for dessert!

Cake:

*4 eggs	cinnamon
*2 cups cottage cheese	
½ cup honey	**Topping:**
½ tsp salt	*1½ cups yogurt
1 tsp lemon juice	2 tbsp honey
OR ½ tsp vanilla	½ tsp vanilla

(1) Prepare a whole wheat pie crust (or make your favorite graham cracker or cookie crumb crust), or granola crust (p. 293).

(2) Put the eggs into your blender and buzz until they're whipped; add the cottage cheese ½ cup at a time and blend until smooth.

(3) Pour the mixture into a small bowl; stir in the honey, salt, and lemon juice.

(4) Turn it into the pie crust, which has been partially baked. Dust with cinnamon and bake at 350°F for about 20 minutes.

(5) Stir together the topping ingredients, pour it over the partially baked pie, and bake another 10 to 15 minutes.

(6) When it is done, a knife inserted in the center will come out clean. Cool the pie on a rack for an hour; then chill several hours or overnight before serving.

*───────────────────────────────

    1½ cups yogurt
     2 cups cottage cheese
     4 eggs

─────────────────────────────────

Frozen Cream Cheese and Yogurt Pie
a 9″ pie of 8 portions

> 1 portion = approx. 5 grams of usable protein
> 11% to 14% of average daily protein need

A luscious pie that's easy to assemble. Keep it frozen or it will turn to soup. Garnish with any fresh fruit that's in season.

*1 9″ pie crust made from ½ recipe Whole Wheat Pie Crust (p. 292)

  1 cup cream cheese, softened to room temperature—try to obtain cream cheese without additives like vegetable gum

*⅔ cup yogurt

*¼ cup milk powder (⅓ cup instant)

  ½ cup honey

(vanilla or almond flavoring—optional)

fruit in season

(1) Bake the pie crust at 375°F for about 15 minutes. Cool it while you make the filling.

(2) Beat the cream cheese and yogurt together with a wire whisk (or electric mixer, if you prefer) until the mixture is smooth. Whisk in the milk powder 2 tablespoons at a time; then whisk in the honey.

(3) (Add a few drops of flavoring if you wish. You might try lemon or orange, too.) Pour the filling into the cooled pie shell and put it into the freezer.

(4) If you are fond of frozen fruit, you may garnish the pie before freezing. Otherwise, when the pie is firm, garnish with fruit and then serve.

*

1	whole wheat pie crust : 2 tbsp milk powder
⅔	cup yogurt
2	tbsp milk powder

Buttermilk Pie
a 9″ pie of 6 portions

1 portion = approx. 5 grams of usable protein
12% to 14% of average daily protein need

What can you say about a buttermilk pie?

6	tbsp butter	2	tsp lemon juice
¾	cup honey	1	tsp grated fresh
*2	eggs, separated		lemon rind
*¼	cup whole wheat flour		nutmeg
*1½	cups buttermilk	1	9″ whole wheat pie crust (p. 292)

(1) Cream the butter with an electric mixer, if possible; cream in the honey, then beat in the egg YOLKS one at a time. Beat in the flour, then

slowly add the buttermilk, beating constantly. The texture of the mixture might be very strange at this point, but it won't affect your pie, so don't worry.

(2) Stir in the lemon juice and rind.

(3) Beat the egg whites until stiff; fold them into the batter.

(4) Pour the filling into an unbaked whole wheat pie crust and bake at 325°F for about 45 minutes, until the filling is firm and puffed, and very brown. Although it is beautiful when puffed and hot, it's best to let it cool to room temperature, then serve.

---

*

    1 cup buttermilk : 2 cups whole wheat flour (for filling
       and crust)
    ½ cup buttermilk

Bread Pudding with Lemon Sauce
8 portions

> 1 portion = approx. 8 grams of usable protein
> 18% to 22% of average daily protein need

Make this pudding with whole wheat bread or whole protein bread that has dried out a little.

*2	cups dry whole wheat bread cubes	*4	eggs, slightly beaten
*4	cups hot milk	1	tsp vanilla
½	to ⅔ cup honey	(½	cup raisins— optional)
1	tbsp butter		
½	tsp salt		

(1) Pour the hot milk over the bread cubes; while they soak, stir in the honey, butter, vanilla, and salt (and raisins).

(2) When the mixture has cooled slightly, beat in the eggs.

(3) Pour into an oiled 1½-quart baking dish. Place in a pan of hot water and bake at 350°F for about 1 hour, until firm.

(4) Serve warm with lemon sauce:

1	tbsp cornstarch	¼	to ⅓ cup honey
dash salt		1½	tbsp lemon juice
dash nutmeg		2	tbsp butter
1	cup boiling water		

(1) Combine the cornstarch, salt, and nutmeg in a small saucepan; stir in the hot water gradually and cook over low heat until thick and clear.

(2) Blend in the honey, lemon juice, and butter.

* _____

2	cups dry bread cubes : ½ cup milk
4	eggs
3½	cups milk

_____

Chocolate Peanut Pudding
6 portions

> 1 portion = approx. 11 grams of usable protein
> 24% to 29% of average daily protein need

Real pudding that is nothing like any instant you might buy—delicious and nutritious, too.

1	ounce un-sweetened baking chocolate	*2	eggs, beaten and at room temperature
*½	cup crunchy peanut butter	*2	cups milk
¼-½	cup honey	½	tsp vanilla
		(¼-½	cup raisins—optional)

(1) Melt the chocolate in the top of a double boiler; stir in the peanut butter and honey to make a nice thick goo.

(2) Stir in the milk and beat with a wire whisk until the mixture is blended and very warm.

(3) Add ½ cup of the liquid to the beaten eggs; mix well and return them to the double boiler. (Stir in the raisins.)

(4) Cook the mixture in the double boiler until it is thick like a custard or cream sauce—about 5 minutes.

(5) Stir in the vanilla, pour into custard cups or one serving dish, and chill several hours.

*_____

½	cup peanut butter : ¾ cup milk
1¼	cups milk
2	eggs

_____

The Very Best Yogurt
1 quart

1 cup = approx. 9 grams of usable protein
20% to 24% of average daily protein need

See Appendix D for methods of keeping yogurt at 110°F so the culture will develop. This homemade yogurt has 2 more grams of usable protein than commercial types, and of course lacks the chemicals that preserve and thicken them.

The longer you keep it in the refrigerator, the tarter it becomes. And a tart starter will produce tart yogurt. So when your starter is too tart, buy a new one for your next batch of yogurt.

The flavoring possibilities for yogurt are vast, so use the suggestions below to spark your own imagination.

Always add the flavoring after the yogurt is done and cold.

*1 cup whole milk	1 cup warm water
*2 tbsp high quality commercial yogurt, or some you saved from your last batch (this = starter OR culture)	*1 cup NON-INSTANT milk powder (instant just doesn't work)
	2 cups warm water

(1) Put the whole milk (somehow a little bit of fat is necessary to make the yogurt "yog" well), the culture, and 1 cup warm water into your blender. Buzz until the mixture is smooth. Add the powdered milk, about ¼ cup at a time, while the blender buzzes, and incorporate all of it. (If you don't have a blender or any electricity, shake all of the ingredients in a tightly covered jar, or whisk the powdered milk into the liquid in a large bowl.)

(2) Add the 2 cups of warm water and blend, shake, or stir again.

(3) Pour the mixture into small pyrex bowls, or into one large bowl or crock.

(4) Keep the yogurt at 110°F until the culture has "yogged." This may take anywhere from 3 to 8 hours. You will find that yogurt gets there quicker in different types of weather. See Appendix D for several methods of keeping the culture at 110°F.

(5) When the yogurt is thick, refrigerate it. When it's cold, eat it plain or flavor it with any of the following:

Yogurt Flavors:
    honey

honey and carob powder
molasses
honey and cinnamon
rhubarb marmalade
any fruit preserves or conserves or jams
apple butter
(home) canned apricots or other fruits
chopped fresh bananas and strawberries
any fresh fruits or berries
frozen unsweetened fruits or berries
soaked dried fruits
cocoa and honey
chopped nuts or toasted seeds
toasted coconut

Note: see the Glossary for more information about yogurt.

* ——————————————————————————————

1   cup milk
1   cup milk powder
2   tbsp starter

Fruit Cheese Kuchen
a 9″ cake of 8 portions

> 1 portion = approx. 13 grams of usable protein
> 30% to 36% of average daily protein need

A delicious cheesecake with a sweet bread-like crust—it gives you more protein than you really need from a dessert!

Cake:
- *¼ cup milk
- ¼ cup honey
- ½ tsp salt
- ¼ cup butter
- 1 tbsp baking yeast
- *2 egg whites
- *2-2½ cups whole wheat flour

- 1 tsp grated fresh lemon peel OR ⅛ tsp lemon extract

Filling:
- *2 cups cottage cheese
- *2 egg yolks
- ⅓-½ cup honey

Topping:
- 1½ cups drained fruit—canned, fresh or frozen cherries, peaches, plums, berries, et al.
- ⅔ cup fruit juice that's compatible with the fruit
- 2 tbsp cornstarch
- 2 tbsp honey
- 2-3 drops almond extract

(1) Heat the milk, honey, salt, and butter over low heat until the butter melts; turn it into a mixing bowl and allow to cool to lukewarm.

(2) Dissolve the baking yeast in the lukewarm mixture; stir in the egg whites and 2 cups of the whole wheat flour. Knead until smooth and elastic (about 5 minutes), adding the remaining ½ cup of whole wheat flour, if necessary. Set in a warm place to rise until double.

(3) For the filling, blend the cottage cheese until smooth in a blender OR put it through a sieve or strainer. Stir in the egg yolks, honey, and lemon flavoring; set it aside.

(4) Punch down the dough and pat it into an oiled 9-inch round cake pan, making a rim around the edge. Spread the cheese filling over the dough inside the rim. Let rise again while the oven preheats OR about 15 minutes.

(5) Bake at 400°F for 25 minutes, until the crust has browned and the cheese is firm. Cool in the pan until you can handle it (or even until it is completely cold); remove it from the pan and place on a serving plate.

(6) In a small saucepan combine the cornstarch with the fruit juice; heat over a medium flame and add the honey and almond extract. Stir constantly until the mixture has thickened and cleared. Stir in the fruit, then cool the topping. Pour it over the cooled cake, slice, and eat!!

*

2	eggs
¼	cup milk
2½	cups whole wheat flour : 5 tbsp cottage cheese
1	cup plus 11 tbsp cottage cheese

Elegant Yogurt Compote
about 1½ quarts

> 1 cup = approx. 4 grams of usable protein
> 10% to 12% of average daily protein need

This is an example of how easily you can make an elegant dessert from your own fresh yogurt. Try serving the compote in cream-puff shells, with cookies or cake.

*2½ cups plain yogurt, preferably homemade fresh yogurt

⅓ cup honey

1 cup toasted unsweetened coconut

2 cups sliced apricots (fresh,

soaked-dried, or home canned)[1]

1 cup grated apples

2-3 drops almond extract

*1 cup broken walnuts (or other nuts)

(1) Stir the ingredients together in the order given. You may reserve part of the toasted coconut to sprinkle on each individual serving.

(2) Chill several hours before serving.

* _____

2½ cups yogurt
1 cup walnuts

_____

Churned Ice Cream
about 4 quarts

1 cup = approx. 4 grams of usable protein
10% to 12% of average daily protein need

There is no ice cream like the kind you make at home. We always wait until we have a lot of friends together. We all sit on the kitchen floor, passing the smokes and the bucket around for churning.

*5 cups milk

½ tsp salt

1-1½ cups honey

*4 eggs, beaten and at room temperature

(1 vanilla bean— optional)

*1 cup half-and-half

*1 cup whipping cream

flavoring (see below)

[1] You may use any fruit that's in season, or that you have frozen or canned.

(1) Heat the milk and salt in a large saucepan until the mixture is very hot, but not boiling.

(2) Stir in the honey and dissolve it completely.

(3) Beat the eggs in a quart bowl; continue beating them while you add 1 cup of the hot honeyed milk. Add 1 more cup of the hot milk to make sure the eggs are hot and won't curdle when you add them back to the saucepan. Do this and whisk constantly while you pour them in.

(4) Keep the heat low (and add the vanilla bean, which has been cut into 4 pieces). Cook the custard, stirring almost constantly with a wooden spoon until the mixture thickens. This process may take longer than 30 minutes, so you must be patient. The extra time will be worth having extra-delicious ice cream. When done it should be as thick as partially whipped cream. Cool the custard in the refrigerator (and as soon as you can handle them, slit the pieces of vanilla bean and scrape the tiny seeds into the custard).

(5) When the custard is very cold, flavor it and stir in the half and half, and the whipping cream. It's now ready to freeze. Do this according to the directions that come with your ice cream freezer.

Flavorings:

  (a) 2 tbsp instant coffee dissolved in a small amount of water, plus 3 tbsp rum

  (b) 4 ounces baking chocolate melted carefully in the saucepan before you heat the milk

  (c) ¼ to ½ cup carob powder

  (d) 2 tsp vanilla extract (or vanilla bean)

  (e) ¼ cup rum, brandy, sherry, or any liqueur

  (f) 3-4 cups chopped fresh fruit (or soaked dried fruit)

  (g) ¾ to 1 pound unsweetened frozen fruit (do

not thaw, but add to custard just before
freezing)

(h)   3-4 mashed bananas and 2 tbsp lemon juice

Use any combination of flavorings that strikes your
fancy, and try your own ideas. Once the flavor is cho-
sen, choose one or more of the following for texture
and contrasting flavor:

Texturizers:

(a)   1-2 cups chopped raw or roasted nuts
       (peanuts, sunflower seeds, and sesame
       seeds would be complemented by the
       milk

(b)   1 or more cups toasted unsweetened
       coconut

(c)   1-2 cups chocolate or carob chips or shaved
       semi-sweet chocolate

(d)   1-2 cups chopped dates

(e)   1-2 cups crushed fresh pineapple

* _____

5   cups milk
4   eggs
1   cup half-and-half
1   cup whipping cream

Baked Custard
5 small portions

1 portion = approx. 6 grams of usable protein
            14% to 17% of average daily protein need

Any custard recipe with milk and eggs is a good protein dessert. Try different flavorings to surprise your
family.

*2 cups milk plus 2 tbsp powdered milk (or 3 tbsp instant)

*2 eggs, well beaten

2-4 tbsp honey

1 tsp vanilla (or other flavoring—see below)

(1) Beat the powdered milk into the whole milk OR you may use all powdered milk and water.

(2) Beat the eggs into the milk with a wire whisk; add the honey and vanilla.

(3) Pour the mixture into lightly oiled or buttered custard cups, or one baking dish. Place them in a pan of hot water filled to halfway up the sides of the cups or dish.

(4) Bake at 325°F for about 50 minutes, until a knife inserted in the center comes out clean.

Other Flavors:

(a) Add 2 tsp rum or brandy to the basic recipe, and omit the vanilla.

(b) Add 1 tbsp carob powder to the basic recipe.

(c) Add a few drops peppermint extract; omit vanilla.

(d) Add a few drops almond extract; omit vanilla.

(e) Stir in ¼ to ½ cup lightly toasted unsweetened coconut. Add ½ cup chocolate or carob chips, too.

---

*

2 cups milk
2 tbsp milk powder
2 eggs

Spiced Fruit Rice Pudding
6 portions

> 1 portion = approx. 9 grams of usable protein
> 20% to 24% of average daily protein need

A rice pudding with a difference...

*1½	cups raw brown rice	¼	tsp powdered ginger
*2½-3	cups milk	2	cups of fruit—fresh or soaked dried apples, apricots, or oranges—coarsely chopped
	pinch of salt		
½	cup honey		
*1	egg, beaten		
½	tsp cinnamon	2	tbsp lemon juice
½	tsp nutmeg	*1	cup yogurt

(1) Cook the rice in a pressure cooker or regular saucepan, using milk instead of water. Use 2½ cups milk in the pressure cooker OR 3 cups for regular cooking.

(2) When cooked the rice should be tender but will look soupier than rice cooked with water. Stir in the honey, egg, cinnamon, nutmeg, and ginger.

(3) Oil a 1-quart casserole and spread one-half of the rice mixture over the bottom. Gently place one-half of the fruit chunks on top of the rice. Repeat the two layers and place in a 350°F oven.

(4) Bake the pudding for 25 minutes. Remove from the oven and spread the 1 cup yogurt over the top. Chill several hours before serving.

---

*

1½	cups raw brown rice : 2 cups milk
1	egg
1	cup yogurt
½-1	cup milk

Whole Wheat Pie Crust
two 9″ single crusts

*when complemented with dairy products,
1 crust = approx. 14 grams of usable protein

This crust is a plain whole wheat crust that you can use for quiches or sweet cheese desserts. Any dairy product or even a bean pie will complement it.

*2   cups whole wheat   ½   cup soft shortening
     pastry flour   about ½ cup water
½   tsp salt

(1)   Stir the salt and whole wheat pastry flour to-
      gether.
(2)   Work the shortening in with a knife or pastry
      blender, but don't work it in too much. The
      pieces may be quite lumpy, but it will make a
      flakier crust.
(3)   Add about ⅓ cup of water and move the crust
      mixture around so the water will soak in. Gather
      the dough gently and add more water if there is
      some flour that won't gather.
(4)   Divide the dough in half, roll each half and fit
      into pie plates OR you may use half of the crust
      for an upper crust.
(5)   If you are making an unbaked pie, bake the crust
      at 375°F for 10 to 15 minutes. Prick the bottom
      with a fork so it will stay flat OR put about ¼
      cup of raw rice over the bottom to hold the crust
      down.

---

*
  2   cups whole wheat flour : 1 cup milk OR ⅓ cup
      grated cheese

Crunchy Granola Pie Crust
a 9- or 10″ crust

1 crust = approx. 23 grams of usable protein
53% to 64% of average daily protein need

Of course, you're not going to serve a pie crust all by itself, but I have included this recipe for you to use with any pies or cheesecakes that you like to make. You can see how much protein you are adding to the whole pie.

*2	cups Raw All Protein Crunchy Granola (see recipe p. 48)	*½	cup whole wheat flour
		*1	tbsp milk powder (1½ tbsp instant)
		¼	cup melted butter

(1) Stir the flour and milk powder into the raw granola. Pour the melted butter over and mix well.

(2) Press the crust into a pie plate and use it according to the type of pie you are making.

---

*

2   cups All Protein Crunchy Granola (recipe p. 48)
½   cup whole wheat flour : 1 tbsp milk powder

Wholesome Whole Wheat Pie Crust
a 9- or 10″ double crust

1 crust = approx. 34 grams of usable protein
79% to 95% of average daily protein need

Remember that you will be dividing the crust into several portions, so divide the protein in your mind also. Use this crust for any sweet pie or cheese quiche.

*2 cups whole wheat pastry flour	⅓ to ½ cup soft butter OR other shortening
*¼ cup milk powder (⅓ cup instant)	(1 tablespoon lemon juice—optional)
½ tsp salt	¼ cup or more cold water
*1 egg, beaten	

(1) Stir the flour, milk powder, and salt together in a small bowl.
(2) Make a well in the center and add the remaining ingredients EXCEPT the water; cut them in with a knife or pastry blender, then add enough water to enable you to gather the dough into 2 balls.
(3) Roll 1 ball and fit it into a pie plate. Chill while you prepare the filling. Roll the top crust when the pie is filled, fit it over the top, or make a lattice crust (especially for fruit pies).

* _____

1 egg
2 cups whole wheat flour : ¼ cup milk powder

Cheddar Cheese Pie Crust
a 9″ bottom crust

> 1 crust = approx. 29 grams of usable protein
> 67% to 81% of average daily protein need

Use this crust for sweet fruit pies, main dish vegetable pies, or even cheese pies.

*¾ cup whole wheat flour	*1 cup grated cheddar cheese
½ tsp salt	*¼ to ⅓ cup water
(¼ tsp dry mustard— optional)	

(1) Stir together the dry ingredients; add the cheddar cheese and enough water to allow the dough to gather.
(2) Gather the dough, roll it out, and then place in an oiled 9-inch pie plate. It is ready to fill and bake.

* _____

¾ cup whole wheat flour : ⅛ cup grated cheese
⅞ cup grated cheese

Dairy Delights

The following beverages are delightful and refreshing summer drinks (that are good any time of the year). A nutritious substitute for high-calorie milkshakes, a "lassi" (made with a banana and unsweetened fruit juice) will "cost" you only about 200 calories for 2 cups. The same amount of an ice cream shake is about 750 calories, as well as little protein to boast about.

In the following recipes, use the freshest fruit juices you can get. Did you ever taste apple juice that was pressed or juiced before your eyes? Although the supermarket offers mostly sugary carbonated beverages and juice drinks, you still can usually find some real fruit juice that's been processed without sugar.

Serve these luscious beverages to your kids (and to yourself) with some whole grain cookies when they ask for a snack. And if they ask for more, you won't have to say no!

Homemade Buttermilk
about 1 quart

> 1 cup = approx. 9 grams of usable protein
> 20% to 24% of average daily protein need

It's as easy, if not easier, to make homemade buttermilk as it is to make yogurt. Check Appendix D for ways of keeping yogurt at 110°F. I find the pilot light of my stove perfect for buttermilk culture.

*½ cup commercial cultured buttermilk	*1 cup milk powder (don't use instant, please)
*½ cup regular whole milk	4 cups warm water

(1) Put the buttermilk, regular milk, and 1 cup of water into your blender; buzz a few seconds to mix them.

(2) Add a second cup of warm water and the milk powder; buzz to mix the powder in completely.

(3) Add the remaining water, mix, then pour the milk into a glass jar. You will probably need a jar larger than a quart, because your blender will make about a cup of foam. Keep the mixture at 110°F until it clabbers—about 8 hours or overnight.

* _____

½ cup buttermilk
½ cup milk
1 cup milk powder

_____

Hot or Cold Carob Froth
4 portions

> 1 portion = approx. 7 grams of usable protein
> 16% to 20% of average daily protein need

A delicious hot or cold milk shake . . .

*4 cups cold milk	½ tsp cinnamon
3 tbsp carob powder	2 tbsp honey
½ tsp vanilla	

(1) For a cold froth: blend all ingredients in a blender until smooth and foamy, then serve.

(2) For hot froth: process the ingredients as above; pour the mixture into a saucepan and heat over a medium flame. As you heat the mixture, the volume of the foam will increase as the air inside the bubbles heats, so watch carefully to avoid boil-overs. Test the liquid, not the foam, for the best drinking temperature.

Variation—Banana Carob Froth: Omit the honey and blend a whole ripe banana with all of the ingredients in the blender.

*

    4   cups milk

___

"Tiger's Milk"
2 portions

> 1 portion = approx. 9 grams of usable protein
> 21% to 25% of average daily protein need

This is a thick, thick drink—breakfast all by itself.

*¾	cup yogurt	½ to ¾ cup orange,
*1	whole egg	pineapple, or other
1-2	tbsp honey	fruit juice
1	banana	*3-4 tbsp brewer's yeast

Process all ingredients until smooth in a blender. Be sure you use delicious brewer's yeast!

*

    ¾   cup yogurt
    1   egg
    3-4   tbsp brewer's yeast

Homemade Instant Breakfast
1 portion

> 1 portion = approx. 14 grams of usable protein
> 33% to 39% of average daily protein need

Notoriously expensive commercial "instant break-fasts" are mainly milk powder, flavorings, sugar, and chemicals added to thicken and preserve. You can create a large variety of flavors in your own kitchen, sweetened exactly as your taste demands.

*1   cup double milk . . .
        (use 1 cup cold milk
        and ¼ cup milk
        powder (⅓ cup
        instant) OR
        use 1 cup water and
        ½ cup milk powder
        (⅔ cup instant)

Blend in the blender with any flavoring that follows:

Flavorings:

(1)   1 tbsp carob powder, ¼ tsp vanilla, a dash cinnamon, ½ tsp honey

(2)   1 tsp postum (cereal beverage), 1 tbsp honey

(3)   ¼ tsp almond extract, ¼ to ½ tsp nutmeg, honey to taste

(4)   1 tsp instant coffee, 1 tbsp honey

(5)   1 tbsp molasses

(6)   ½ tsp vanilla and 1 tsp honey

(7)   1 tbsp homemade jam or preserves

And use your own imagination too.

* _____

   1   cup double milk

_____

BanApple Lassi
2 portions

> 1 portion = approx. 4 grams of usable protein
> 8% to 11% of average daily protein need

*½ cup yogurt   *2   tbsp brewer's yeast
 ½ cup apple juice   cinnamon to taste
 1 banana

Buzz in the blender until smooth.

---
*
½ cup yogurt
2 tbsp brewer's yeast

The Quick Lassi
1 portion

> 1 portion = approx. 4 grams of usable protein
> 8% to 10% of average daily protein need

Easy, easy—no blender necessary.

*½ cup buttermilk   any fruit juice

Pour the buttermilk into a tall glass; fill the glass with
your favorite fruit juice and stir.

---
*
½ cup buttermilk

Apricot Lassi
2 portions

> 1 portion = approx. 2 grams of usable protein
> 4% to 5% of average daily protein need

The perfect refresher on a summer day.

*½	cup buttermilk OR yogurt	½	cup of ice (about 3 large cubes)
½	cup apricot nectar	¼	tsp nutmeg
1	banana		(honey to taste—optional)

Process in the blender until the ice is broken up and the consistency is smooth. Add a couple more cubes of ice if you prefer a thinner, icier shake. Enough to serve three.

Variation—Pineapple Lassi: Substitute ½ cup unsweetened pineapple juice for the apricot nectar—delicious.

* _____

½   cup buttermilk or yogurt
_____

Egg Nog
12 portions

> 1 portion = approx. 5 grams of usable protein
> 11% to 13% of average daily protein need

A beautiful drink for a holiday, or any day that deserves to be celebrated.

*6   eggs, separated   *4   cups milk
*1   cup heavy cream,   (whiskey, brandy, or
     whipped   rum—optional)
½   cup honey

(1)   Beat the egg yolks until they are light and lemon-colored; add the honey and beat again. Blend in the milk.

(2)   Beat the egg whites until stiff, but not dry; fold them into the milk mixture, then fold in the whipped cream.

(3)   Spike it if you like, pour into small glasses, and sprinkle with freshly grated nutmeg.

* _____

6   eggs
1   cup whipping cream
4   cups milk

_____

Lemon Zest
2 portions

> 1 portion = approx. 4 grams of usable protein
> 8% to 10% of average daily protein need

Icy and tangy to make you pucker . . .

*1   cup yogurt OR but-   2-3   tbsp honey
     termilk   4   ice cubes
6   tbsp lemon juice

Buzz in the blender until the ice is broken up, but not completely liquified.

* _____

1   cup yogurt or buttermilk

_____

Violet Froth
2 portions

> 1 portion = approx. 4 grams of usable protein
> 8% to 10% of average daily protein need

mmmmmmmmmmmm . . .

¾ cup pineapple juice	1 ripe banana
¼ cup grape juice	½ cup ice (about 3
*1 cup buttermilk OR	large cubes)
yogurt	

Buzz in a blender until smooth.

---

* 1   cup buttermilk or yogurt

Banana Orange Royale
2 portions

> 1 portion = approx. 4 grams of usable protein
> 8% to 10% of average daily protein need

1 orange, peeled, sectioned, and seeded	*1 cup yogurt OR but-termilk
1 banana	honey to taste

Process in a blender until smooth, for a thick drink. If you prefer a lighter "shake," add a couple of ice cubes before blending.

---

* 1   cup yogurt or buttermilk

Purple Devil
3 portions

> 1 portion = approx. 2 grams of usable protein
> about 4% of average daily protein need

If you don't drink this right away, it will separate into a layer of froth and a clear layer, but it's still refreshing.

⅔ cup pineapple juice	⅔ cup apple juice
⅔ cup grape juice	*⅔ cup buttermilk

Buzz in the blender until smooth and foamy.

---

* _____

⅔ cup buttermilk

_____

Banana Strawberry Delight
2 portions

> 1 portion = approx. 4 grams of usable protein
> 8% to 10% of average daily protein need

If you like bananas and strawberries...

*1 cup buttermilk OR yogurt	3-4 ice cubes
1 banana	(1 tbsp honey—optional)
3-4 large strawberries	

Blend all ingredients in a blender until smooth.

---

* _____

1 cup buttermilk or yogurt

_____

Orange Breakfast Wake Up
2 portions

1 portion = approx. 4 grams of usable protein
8% to 10% of average daily protein need

This will wake you up for sure . . .

*1   cup buttermilk OR
      yogurt

½   orange, peeled, sec-
      tioned, and seeded

½   lemon, peeled, sec-
      tioned, and seeded
      OR 1 tbsp lemon
      juice

½   tsp grated fresh or-
      ange rind

1-2   tbsp honey

Process everything in the blender until smooth.

* _____

1   cup buttermilk or yogurt

Appendices

Appendices

Appendix A

Basic Cooking Instructions

In the recipes the measurements generally indicate dry ingredients. You may be taken back by terms such as "½ cup dry soy beans, cooked" or "1 cup raw brown rice, cooked." However, the dry measure is more accurate for obtaining maximum protein complementarity, and although it may be confusing at first, I think that it is clearer than expressions like "½ cup soybeans, cooked." Does this mean ½ cup of cooked soybeans or ½ cup of dry soybeans, cooked, which would be about 1½ cups of cooked beans? It might make quite a difference in the final dish.

A. Cooking Beans

1. *Regular Cooking:* Place the amount of beans to be cooked in a strainer and rinse with cold water. Then cover the beans with 3 to 4 times their volume of water and:
   (a) Soak them overnight (in the refrigerator, if possible, so they will not ferment) OR
   (b) Place the beans and water in a large saucepan, bring to a boil, simmer for 5 minutes, and remove them from the heat. Cover tightly and let them soak for 2 hours. (This process is the same as soaking them overnight.)

Bring the beans to a boil after following (a) or (b). Lower the heat and simmer them, partially covered, according to the timetable below (regular cooking). Add water when necessary. Drain the stock and the beans are ready for your recipe.

2. *Pressure Cooking:* Rinse the beans in cold water in 1. Bring water (3 to 4 times the volume of beans) to a boil.

Add the beans, cover, and bring to 1g pounds pressure.

Cook the beans according to the timetable below (pressure cooking). Cool the pressure cooker under cold running water, open it, and drain the stock from the beans.

TIMETABLE FOR COOKING BEANS

	Regular Cooking (soaked beans)	Pressure Cooking (unsoaked beans)
Black beans, kidneys, peanuts, black-eyed peas, pintos, and soy beans	2 hours	20 to 25 minutes
Mung beans, small red beans (azuki, aduki)	3 hours	30 to 35 minutes
Garbanzos (chick peas)	4 hours	40 to 45 minutes
Lentils, split peas	1 hour	10 to 15 minutes

The advantage of a pressure cooker is obvious!

B. Cooking Grains

1. *Regular Cooking:* Rinse the grain under cold water and drain.

(a) Use twice as much water as grain (4 cups water for 2 cups of rice). Bring it to a boil, stir in the grains, and bring the mixture to a second boil. Lower the heat to simmer, cover tightly, and cook until all the liquid is absorbed and the grains are tender. Don't uncover the pan until the cooking time is up (see timetable for grains), and don't stir until all of the liquid is absorbed. If the rice is not tender when all of the liquid is absorbed, add hot water and simmer again, OR

(b) An unorthodox but viable method, which produces a grain texture preferred by some: Use twice as much water as grain, as above. Place the water (cold) and the grain in a saucepan, bring to a boil, lower to a simmer, cover, and cook as in (a). This method produces a more sticky rice, but if you let it stand about 15 minutes after cooking it will fluff some. We always use this cooking method while we're camping, OR

(c) The sauté method is most commonly used when cooking bulgur or buckwheat groats, but is delicious with rice also: Put about ⅛ inch of oil in the bottom of the cooking pot. Place the pot over a low flame and when the oil crinkles add the grain you plan to cook. Sauté the grain for about 5 minutes, adding more oil if it sticks. Stir often. You may continue the process until the grain is well browned, but the main purpose of the

method is to heat each grain and coat
it with oil. You may also add more
oil and sauté onions, garlic, celery,
etc. Finally, add hot or boiling water
(2 times the volume of grain), bring
to a second boil, lower the heat,
cover and simmer as in (a).

2. *Pressure Cooking:* Rinse the grain under cold
   water and drain.
   (a) Generally speaking, the volume of
       water needed to cook grains in a
       pressure cooker is less because of the
       efficiency of pressure cooking, *i.e.*
       very little water escapes as steam.
       There is no specific formula for water
       reduction, as the amount needed de-
       pends on the quantity of grain to be
       cooked. For instance, for 1 cup of
       rice, 2 cups of water is needed; but
       for 2 cups of rice, 3½ cups of water
       makes perfect rice. So the more rice
       you cook the more you reduce the
       water. Experiment with this to find
       the right ratio for the amount of grain
       you usually cook. Bring the water to
       boil in the pressure cooker, stir in the
       grain, cover and bring to 15 pounds
       pressure. Lower the heat and cook
       according to the timetable below.
       Cool the cooker as soon as the time is
       up or your grains may be black on
       the bottom, OR
   (b) Frankie's method to avoid sticking,
       and other tricks: Put 2 to 3 inches of

water into the pressure cooker and start it heating. Put the grain in a small stainless steel bowl (or even in a tin can or two) that will fit easily into the cooker without obstructing any vents. Fill the bowl with water to an inch above the grain. Put the bowl in the cooker, cover and bring to 15 pounds pressure. Cook as in (a) above. When it's done you will have a bowl of rice! The trick when using this method is to put beans in the 2 to 3 inches of water that are on the bottom of the cooker. Your beans and grain are both cooked! OR

(c) The sauté method can be used with the pressure cooker as in (c) for regular cooking. But reduce the volume of water as in regular pressure cooking (2 a).

TIMETABLE FOR COOKING GRAINS

	Regular Cooking	Pressure Cooking
Brown rice, barley, and other medium grains	40 to 45 minutes	20 minutes
Bulgur, cracked wheat, and soft or partially cooked grains	20 to 30 minutes	5 to 10 minutes
Whole wheat berries, whole rye, whole oats, and hard grains	1 hour or more[1]	35 minutes[2]

---

[1] Hard grains may be soaked overnight or simmered and then soaked for two hours. This will shorten the cooking time.

[2] For pressure cooking use twice as much water for hard grains so they will be as soft as possible when cooked.

C. Cooking Nuts and Seeds

1. *To Roast or Toast Raw Nuts or Seeds*[3] *(or Cooked Beans):*

    (a) Use a dry pan (no oil) and a medium flame. Add the seeds and cook, stirring often until they brown lightly. Move the seeds to a cool place (or they will continue to brown in the hot pan). Grind them if desired using a blender or mortar and pestle.

    (b) Spread the seeds or nuts on a shallow baking pan, heat the oven to 200°F and toast them until browned. Grind as in (a).

2. *To Roast Raw Nut or Seed Meals:* Buying nut meals rather than the whole nut or seed is expensive and unnecessary. But you may want to grind your nuts or seeds before toasting when you are mixing several types of meals together.

    (a) Use a dry pan and a medium flame. Stir the meal constantly until it is browned. Remove it from the hot pan immediately to avoid burning.

    (b) You can also toast nut and seed meals in a 200°F oven.

---

[3] Since most seeds are very small they are difficult to chew thoroughly. I recommend that they be ground for optimum digestibility.

Appendix B

Useful Utensils

In our modern world there is no end to the number of "time and work saving" appliances that industries and advertisers have convinced us we cannot live without. How could we have gotten along for so many years without electric can openers and electric knives? Is it "progress" that says women and men should not exercise their muscles for more than button pushing? In preparing natural foods there is little need for many appliances, but there are a few items that will speed up processes that took our grandmothers many hours or even days to complete.

1. Pressure Cooker. Besides being a fuel and time saver (see the cooking timetables in Appendix A), the pressure cooker locks vitamins into fresh vegetables and cooks legumes to a tenderness not possible in regular cooking. Once you have a pressure cooker, the trick is to alleviate your fears of "applesauce on the ceiling" by understanding that the chances of this are slight and can be reduced to nearly nothing by using small stainless steel refrigerator bowls or tin cans for cooking "dangerous substances." Just put the split peas or chopped apples in the bowls, add water (and cover with tin foil if you wish). Put about 1 inch of water in the bottom of the cooker, bring to 15 pounds pressure, and cook as usual. Also be aware of what your pressure cooker is saying as it cooks: it should rock gently as a small amount of steam escapes under the pressure gauge. When the cooker goes silent and still and the automatic air vent is up, turn off the heat and cool the cooker, then open and remove the clogging substance. If you don't turn off the heat, pressure builds up inside because of the clog; then the automatic air vent blows, followed by the food inside. The top of the pressure cooker will not blow off except in highly unusual circumstances!

2. *Blender.* A simple one- or two-speed blender will fulfill all of your needs quite adequately. Not only can it whip up high-protein beverages with yogurt, fruit juice, and ice, but it can grind nuts and seeds for fresh nut and seed meals. It will also grind small amounts of whole grain flour. You can purée soups and cooked beans, and make salad and vegetable dressings. You can even make peanut butter in a blender.

Of course, if you don't have electricity or you don't want to use any, you can use a mortar and pestle or a flour mill to grind grains and seeds, and a food mill to purée tender cooked substances.

3. *Other items* that are useful include *cast iron* pots and frying pans. There is no modern "improved" cookware that will serve you as well as cast iron. It conducts heat well, so it will cook long and slow without burning your food, and it will keep food warm at the table. Food hardly sticks to it and you barely need to wash it. In fact, it is generally recommended that you only wipe cast iron clean. If it is quite dirty use water, and if scrubbing is necessary use salt. Rinse it, wipe it dry, and oil it lightly. Never scour it with harsh cleansers or steel wool. The only cookware that I know that improves with age!

Use *wooden spoons* to stir stews in cast iron pots without scratching. They are gentle for delicate sauces and soft vegetables, and you can use them for everything from frying to bread making. I also like them because they're cool to the taste and they're quiet . . .

The only other major piece of equipment I would recommend is a *wok*. I bought one for one dollar without the stand or the cover. It works beautifully for frying rice, sautéing vegetables, and also for cooking eggs. My wok is carbon steel, so it ages like cast iron and needs little care (*i.e.* scrubbing). It is thin, so my vegetables cook fast (thus retaining vitamins), as if they were being cooked directly over the flame.

For *bakeware* be your own judge and buy according to your needs. I prefer iron, pyrex, cast or heavy aluminum baking pans to the lighter stainless steel or rolled or extruded aluminum. For using the recipes in this book you will need a minimum of baking pieces—one 8″ x 8″ OR 9″ x 9″ OR 7″ x 11″ pan. The differences among these sizes are so slight (64, 77, or 81 square inches) that you can choose the type of quick bread you prefer when you buy the pan. That is, the small pan will give you a higher bread or cake than the large. My preference is the 7″ x 11″ pan, which is in between and gives you lots of pieces that aren't too flat. You will also need a muffin tin, a cookie sheet, bread pans, and a casserole or two.

Appendix C

Kitchen Trickery OR How to Make Your Kitchen Meet the Needs of Cooking Natural Foods

All kitchens can be beautiful. If a place reflects joyous activity it is beautiful. If it is a place where daily drudgery is carried on, or where food is only defrosted and boiled, it will not have any glamour even if it is the most modern and well-equipped kitchen.

A window is the sun, giving energy and light to the activities within. Besides providing light and fresh air, it offers a sill for small green plants to grow on. Even in the city, even in winter, something will grow on your window sill—herbs or lettuce, tea or avocado trees will keep healthy by the dampness of the sink, the sun's energy, and your singing, of course.

Decorate your kitchen with pictures of things that you like, that give you pleasure and some peace too. Use the front of your cabinets, the refrigerator, stove, and the empty wall space for your kitchen gallery.

Now that your kitchen reflects you, here are several of my tricks for ease in the preparation of natural foods:

1. Keep grains and dry goods in cannisters that you can handle easily, and that you can label or see through. Three-pound coffee cans hold about five pounds of flour. Gallon glass jars are my favorites because natural food is beautiful to look at, and you don't have to guess what's

inside. Ask restaurants for their empty mustard and pickle-relish jars. Collect from your local recycling center. Use old apple cider jars for small seeds or whole grains, but for flours and things that need to be scooped, use wide-mouth containers.

2. For scooping flour, have handy different-sized measuring cups. No pouring and measuring is necessary; just scoop the right amount.

3. Use measuring spoons that will fit inside your spice jars. We all know what it's like to have twice (or more) the ginger we intended for a recipe!

4. Keep everything that you possibly can in glass jars, and you won't have to go through a dozen bags to find the tea that you want.

5. Keep old coffee measures (2-tablespoon, usually) in your cannisters of soy grits and milk powder. These measures are convenient when a recipe calls for 1 tablespoon up to ½ cup.

6. Keep a small jar of oil beside or on top of your stove, with a pastry brush in it. It's always ready to oil a griddle, frying pan or baking pan.

7. Put salt in a pointed-spout-top container, the kind usually used for dispensing ketchup. Just pour the salt into your measuring spoon, without a big mess.

8. Keep your compost container right next to your cutting board. When you chop vegetables, drop the waste right in. Carry out the compost daily to your garden heap.

9. Keep two bins under your sink for cans and bottles. After they are rinsed you can store them there until they are recycled.

10. When you measure honey or molasses for a recipe, first measure the oil in the same scoop.

Pour out the oil, then pour in the honey. The honey will slide right out without any sticking!

11.   When making soups or stews, put whole spices and herbs in a tea ball or egg. When the soup is cooked, remove the ball and you can be assured that no one will bite into a peppercorn.

12.   To mix non-instant powdered milk for baking, stir it into the whole wheat flour and other dry ingredients rather than trying to make it into liquid milk first. With this method you will never have lumps of milk powder in your cakes or breads. To make non-instant milk into liquid milk, use a blender to make it smooth or add just enough water to the milk powder to make a thick paste. Stir it until there are no lumps, then add more water. A wire whisk is useful for mixing non-instant milk, too.

13.   Instant milk is good for making milk quickly with cold water, but some brands of instant do not mix at all with hot liquid. Test out your instant before adding it to a hot drink!

Appendix D

Keeping Yogurt at 110°F

Yogurt is a sensitive culture, but it is possible to make delicious yogurt with a little care and patience. On some days it will take 3 hours for the culture to grow; other times it may take 8 hours or more. The factors I have discovered that make the difference are the weather, the kind of container used, the type of whole milk, and of course the method of maintaining the heat at 110°F. Be sure you can leave the yogurt in one place for all of those hours, because jiggling the culture while it is developing will only delay (it won't destroy) the final product. Be sure all the items that will touch the milk at any stage are scrupulously clean.

See the dessert section of the recipes for yogurt flavorings. Always stir in the flavoring after the yogurt is fully cultured and cold. You will probably find that you like plain yogurt too, once you taste it fresh and homemade.

The methods of maintaining heat are listed in the order of probability of success. Don't let this discourage you. All the methods work, but the last couple of ideas may not *always* be successful. If the culture fails, use it in bread in place of stock or milk.

1. A *yogurt maker* will do everything for you. Just plug it in, set the covered dishes on top, and let it stand 3 to 8 hours until thick. These devices are made to maintain 110°F heat, so they work 99.9 percent of the time.

2. A *hot tray* or *electric food warmer* can also maintain a constant temperature. The trick is to find a way to keep that temperature at 110°F. Put a bowl of warm water on the hot tray and place a candy thermometer in the water. Leave it for an hour, then check the temperature. Place several thicknesses of cloth on the tray if the water is too hot. Put the bowl of water over the cloth and test again.

3. The *oven* will maintain regular heat too, but often it is too hot. The temperature gradings on my oven start at 200°F, so I put the dial half way between 200°F and "on." Test the internal temperature with a bowl of water as in 2, and turn the dial accordingly. In order for the warmth to be close to the dishes of culture it is best to create a double boiler effect:

    Use a large pot or frying pan with a lid. This pot should be able to hold comfortably the smaller containers that will contain the culture. These small containers needn't have lids, since the large pan will cover everything. You can use custard cups, pyrex casseroles, or glass canning jars. Place the small containers inside the large pan; pour warm water all around the outside of the containers inside the large pan. Cover and leave it in the oven for about 3 hours or until set.

4. A *heating pad* often has temperature readings right on the switch. If not, check the temperature as in 2. Put the filled containers, covered and dry on the heating pad, and leave 3 to 8 hours.

5. A *thermos* will keep a culture warm in most situations. Fill it with the culture (after rinsing

with hot water), but don't cover it tightly so a vacuum won't develop. Leave it in a warm place overnight and you should have yogurt by morning.

6. *Down* will keep us warm, so it can keep yogurt warm too. Use a sleeping bag, jacket, or vest. Cover the culture tightly, then wrap it up in the down bag. Put it where it will be cozy and undisturbed for 8 to 12 hours.

7. Everyone has some warm places around the house or kitchen. Test the places with the bowl-of-water method as in 2. Try these: *radiator, heating duct, pilot light* on top of the stove, *sunny window,* on top of a *radio* or *TV!*

Appendix E

Tips for Freezing

Your freezer can be a useful time-saving device. You can freeze just about any cooked food. Eat fresh vegetables in season (but do freeze bumper crops from your garden) when possible. For any time-consuming recipe make twice as much as you would eat at one meal and freeze the leftovers. This way, you have made two meals in the time it takes to prepare one! Casseroles, patties, soups, loaves, yeast breads and quick breads all freeze well.

You can also freeze parts of casseroles or loaves. Cook a large batch of beans, use part of them today and freeze the rest in several containers. Use one for bean soup, another for a bean loaf, and another for stew or to add to rice. You can also freeze cooked rice or other grains.

In freezing anything be sure to keep excess air away from the food. Air surrounding frozen food will dry out the food and drain away the nutrients and flavor. Put the food into plastic bags and then suck or squeeze (gently) all the air out until the bag clings to the food. Fasten tightly with wire twists. Convenient as well as reusable are the 2-cup plastic containers from ricotta cheese or some types of ice creams or sherberts. Glass jars may be used as well. Just be sure with both of these to leave ½ to 1 inch of space for expansion.

Freeze the following:

Main-dish casseroles
grain dishes
loaves or patties
vegetable casseroles
soups
sandwich spreads

baked breads (yeast)
coffee cakes
loaf cakes
cookies
quick breads

Appendix F

Putting More Protein in Your Family's Diet*

1. Have on hand these high-protein foods to "toss in" to any recipe. In order from least to most expensive:

cheapest

1. Dry milk powder
2. Cottage cheese
3. Soy flour
4. Soy grits (partially cooked, cracked soy beans)
5. Hi-Protein Baby Cereal
6. Egg
7. Wheat germ
8. Grated cheese·
9. Peanut butter
10. Seeds: sunflower seeds, meal; sesame seeds, meal or butter
11. Peanuts
12. Brewer's yeast
13. Other nuts, especially pumpkin and squash kernels, cashews, black walnuts

costliest

---

* Based on Frances Moore Lappé. See p. 19.

II. With these ingredients you can make any dish protein rich:

A. To make protein-rich CASSEROLES, LOAVES AND CROQUETTES with

Beans, peas or lentils...add...

grated cheese   nuts
or cheese   extra milk
sauce   powder
egg   soy grits
seeds   soy flour

noodles or potatoes....add...

cheese   milk powder
cottage   egg
cheese   brewer's yeast
wheat germ

meat or vegetables or cheese... add...

soy grits or   seeds
flour   nuts
brewer's yeast

B. To make protein-rich VEGETABLE dishes, choose from among the following vegetables (they have more protein than other vegetables):

limas
peas ...and sprinkle on
corn top ....

brewer's yeast   toasted sesame seed
wheat germ   or meal
nuts
seeds   crumbled egg
grated cheese

broccoli
greens ...or serve with a
mushrooms protein-rich
asparagus sauce, for example
cauliflower ....

a white sauce with extra milk powder, or an herbed yogurt dressing, or cheese sauce

C. For protein-rich GRAIN dishes
such as ...

rice, barley, etc.,
as a main dish ....add....
- 2 tbsp soy grits per cup of raw rice
- *or*
- sesame seed, nuts, brewer's yeast, cheese or cottage cheese (added to cooked grain)
- *or*
- cook the grain in milk

oatmeal or other
hot breakfast cereal ....add...
- 2 tbsp soy grits per serving
- extra milk powder, milk, yogurt brewer's yeast, wheat germ

hot or cold cereal ......add...
- wheat germ
- Hi-Protein Baby Cereal
- crunchy granola
- yogurt or milk

D. For higher-protein BREAD:

In any basic bread recipe
use whole wheat flour and add ...
- any (or all?!) of the thirteen foods listed on page 326

For example:
To whole wheat bread
recipes . . . . add...
- ¼ cup soy flour OR 2 tbsp soy grits per cup whole wheat flour; sesame seed, nuts, brewer's yeast, milk powder, wheat germ

In cornbread recipes, use
whole wheat flour and add...
- soy flour or grits
- extra milk powder
- cooked beans

E. To increase the protein value
of SOUPS, such as . . .

cream of tomato,
cream of asparagus,
black bean, pea,
lentil, etc.

. . . add . . .

nuts, seeds, grated cheese
extra milk powder, cooked beans
or peas, soy flour or Hi-Protein
Baby Cereal (especially for thickening) brewer's yeast,
egg (take small amount of liquid
from soup pot, mix with beaten
egg and return to pot)

F. To increase the protein
value of DESSERTS, use . . .

any basic cake or
cookie recipe and
substitute whole wheat
flour for white flour and add . . .

any of the thirteen foods listed
on page 326
For example: nuts and seeds
(sesame cookies, banana nut
bread, chocolate chip cookies
with sunflower seeds and peanuts)
soy flour, eggs, extra milk powder, etc.

For cakes, make milk powder/
honey frostings or glazes.
Or serve DESSERTS already rich
in protein, such as: rice pudding (made with milk and eggs), cheese
cake (made with cottage cheese instead of cream cheese), custards,
or candy made from peanut butter or sesame seeds.

G. To increase the protein content
of SALADS such as ...

a green salad .... add ...
> Cheese, sunflower seeds, toasted
> sesame seed meal, egg, crou-
> tons of whole grain bread, nuts,
> seeds, dressings of cottage
> cheese or yogurt

a fruit salad .... add ...
> nuts, crunchy granola, cottage
> cheese, yogurt, wheat germ

a gelatin salad .... add ...
> nuts, cottage cheese, yogurt

H. SNACKS don't have to be "empty calories" if you follow these
suggestions.

High-protein DIPS for crackers or fresh vegetables:
—Cottage cheese blended with herb seasonings
 (Cottage cheese can be combined with yogurt for tanginess.)
—Cheese dips
—Bean dips (Mexican style or Middle Eastern style)
High-protein SANDWICHES with whole grain bread and ....
—Peanut butter plus milk powder (1 tsp milk powder for every
 tsp of peanut butter)
—Sesame filling (sesame meal blended with honey and milk pow-
 der)
—Leftover bean loaves.
Other high protein SNACK ideas:
—Any of the high-protein beverages
—Combination of sunflower seeds, peanuts and raisins
—Crunchy granola
—An "instant pudding" made by mixing cottage cheese, apple-
 sauce, nuts and raisins

III. Try this protein cooking trick—replace common lower-protein foods with other higher-protein foods.

When a recipe calls for...

sour cream
or ....substitute....
cream cheese

> cottage cheese (blended smooth, if desired)
> cottage cheese + yogurt for tanginess
> skim milk ricotta cheese (thinned with yogurt or butter-milk, if desired)

white flour........substitute....

> whole wheat flour, rye flour, or other whole grain flour OR in place of part of the flour use combinations of wheat germ, brewer's yeast, soy flour, seed meal, ground nuts, Hi-Protein Baby Cereal

fatty gravies.....substitute....

> white sauce rich in dry milk powder
> miso-based sauce (Chinese soy bean paste)

mayonnaise. ......substitute....

> If for a green salad...
>   yogurt (or part yogurt, part mayonnaise)
> If for macaroni or potato salad...
>   skim milk ricotta cheese thinned with milk, yogurt, or mayonnaise

Glossary of Foods

BEANS or **LEGUMES** can be purchased dry and sometimes in cans. To obtain their full protein value one should complement them with grains, seeds, or dairy products. The beans most frequently used in the recipes in this book are: black, garbanzo (sometimes called chickpeas or ceci beans), kidney, black-eyed peas, mung, small red (also called azuki or aduki), and soybeans. Beans are good protein because they contain all the essentials for their own reproduction and growth. See Appendix A for cooking instructions.

BREAD CRUMBS used in the recipes should be whole grain crumbs (from any whole grain bread) or whole protein crumbs (from the bread recipes). Although the bread is dry, it still contains protein that can be complemented by dairy products, beans, or seeds. Save crumbs from slicing, stale pieces, crusts, or even burnt toast. Dry the crumbs and pieces of bread by keeping them in an open jar or tin. Before using, crush them inside a towel with a rolling pin, or buzz them in the blender for fine crumbs. You can also use cookie, cake, or cracker crumbs.

BREWER'S YEAST. See YEAST.

BULGUR WHEAT, BULGHUR or **BURGHUL** is partially cooked (parboiled) or parched cracked wheat, a grain commonly used in many Middle Eastern countries. Cracked wheat may be substituted for bulgur in the recipes since its protein quality as well as its texture is the same. The protein in bulgur should be complemented by beans, dairy products, or beans and seeds. See Appendix A for cooking instructions.

BUTTER. Real butter makes all the difference in flavor whether you are using it to cook an egg or creaming it for a cake. Without the cholesterol from meat in our diet, we feel that using butter is not a health hazard. If you prefer not to use butter, substitute oil in equal amounts. In quick breads and cakes this will change the taste and texture only insignificantly. If you want to use margarine, read the label first and then decide. If the label says hardened vegetable oil, you can probably assume that it is coconut oil, a very cheap, highly saturated fat used by the food industry in many imitation dairy products.

BUTTERMILK, contrary to its name, contains little butterfat. The name was given because it can be a by-product of butter-making. The recipes refer to cultured buttermilk, which, like yogurt, is made by introducing friendly bacteria to regular milk. See the section on high-protein beverages (Dairy Delights) for a recipe for making your own. Buttermilk, like skim or whole milk, is high-quality protein by itself, but it is also useful (and delicious) for complementing grains, beans, and seeds. Yogurt may be substituted for buttermilk in baking, in beverages, and in casseroles. (See **YOGURT.**)

CAROB POWDER or **ST. JOHN'S BREAD** is a chocolate-like flour made from carob pods, which are ground and roasted to produce a cocoa-like substance. Carob is sweeter than cocoa and has a pleasant fruity flavor. It also lacks the caffein-like stimulant found in chocolate. It is alkaline, low in fat (2% as compared to 52% in chocolate), does not inhibit calcium absorption as does chocolate, and can be readily used by those who are allergic to chocolate.

CHEESE is high-quality protein like milk. Less fatty cheeses contain more protein than high-fat products like cream cheese. In the recipes, use the specific cheeses mentioned. If not specified, the cheese may be any natural cheese, NOT processed cheese. Be daring and try new flavors. (See the introduction to the cheese recipes, and **COTTAGE CHEESE** and **RICOTTA CHEESE** below.)

CORNMEAL is dried whole corn that has been ground. Undergerminated cornmeal not only has slightly more protein than degerminated, but it contains essential vitamins and minerals that are destroyed in the process of degermination. You may use white or yellow, fine or coarse meal.

COTTAGE CHEESE is one of the most concentrated sources of high-quality protein. In 1 cup of cottage cheese there are about 32 grams of usable protein. Compare this to a cup of milk, which has 7 grams of usable protein. Although it makes little difference in the amount of protein, I usually use low-fat cottage cheese. Use cottage cheese, like other milk products, to complement grains, seeds, or beans. (See also **RICOTTA CHEESE.**)

CRACKED WHEAT is simply whole wheat that has been cracked coarsely. It may be used as a substitute for bulgur wheat in any recipe. (See **BULGUR** above.)

DOUBLE MILK is a term I invented for milk that has the protein content of two cups of milk and the water content of one cup. To make 1 cup of double milk add ½ cup of milk powder (⅔ cup instant) to one cup of water OR use 1 cup of milk and ¼ cup of milk powder (⅓ cup instant). One cup of canned evaporated milk would also be equivalent in protein.

DRIED FRUIT is any kind of fruit that has had about ⅔ of its water removed. Most commercial dried fruit is treated with sulfur dioxide to make it look pretty and keep it soft. If you buy unsulfured fruit it will taste surprisingly like the original fresh fruit instead of the sulfur, and you can easily soften it by soaking (not cooking) in water.

EGGS are the most perfect source of protein known to fit human needs. They are also an inexpensive source. The recipes in this book require large eggs, but if you use extra-large you will be increasing the amount of "perfect protein" at low cost. An organic egg, fertilized or not, will provide you with more egg and less water. The test is in the tasting.

GOMASIO or **SESAME SALT.** See under **SEEDS.**

HERBS were discovered eons ago when man found they could flavor water in a delightful way. Soon it was discovered that certain herbs had curative powers and could dispel the symptoms of various ailments. Today our medicine men offer us drugs that do the same but at much greater expense. I have included herbs in the recipes not in order to cure anything, however; they are used to bring out and complement the subtle flavors of natural foods. Try growing herbs on your kitchen windowsill, or just outside the back door. You can plant dill, caraway, anise, cumin, coriander, and fennel seeds in tiny pots. Just pinch off what you need for cooking or tea. In any recipe use twice as much fresh herb as dried. (See the section "Growing Your Own" for more information.)

HONEY is the only sugar that does not have to be manufactured or refined. (It is illegal to sell unrefined sugar in the United States. What is commonly called brown, raw, or kleenraw sugar is white sugar that has had molasses added back in.) Buy unheated, unfiltered honey when possible. It may crystallize, but then it is even easier to cook with than liquid honey. Unheated honey contains glucose oxidase, an enzyme added to the honey by worker bees. Glucose oxidase attacks glucose, one of the sugars in honey, and hydrogen peroxide, which destroys bacteria, is released. But this bactericidal effect of hydrogen peroxide is inactive in undiluted honey. In undiluted honey, however, bacteria cannot flourish because of the high osmotic pressure; if bacteria are introduced they either die or remain without growing. And if the osmotic pressure is reduced by dilution, the glucose oxidase effect occurs—so either way, honey is kept bacteria-free. The natural acidity of honey also protects it from bacteria. There are yeasts that can live in a medium of high osmotic pressure, but if the honey doesn't contain more than 19 percent water, it will not ferment even though it contains the yeast.[1] With

---

[1] Roger Morse, "Environmental Control in the Beehive," *Scientific American*, Vol. 226, No. 4 (April 1972), pp. 92-98.

so many protective devices built in, it seems rather point-
less for honey to be processed.

If you find the flavor of some honey too strong, try the
mild ones like alfalfa, thistle, avocado, lima bean, orange
blossom, sage, or tupelo. Honey keeps baked goods fresh
for a long time (if you can keep them from being eaten).

LEGUMES. See **BEANS.**

MILK used in the recipes can be raw whole milk, any
type of pasteurized milk (regular, low-fat, or non-fat),
reconstituted powdered milk, or diluted canned milk (evaporated). You may substitute soy milk or goat's milk as
well. Milk and milk powder complement grains, seeds, and
beans, as well as being high-quality protein (and inexpensive) by themselves.

MILK POWDER is milk without the water. Usually it is
non-fat. You can buy instant or non-instant powdered
milk. For the recipes in this book, non-instant milk powder is all you need. (The measurements for instant are
given in parentheses.) Non-instant milk powder is easily
stirred into the dry ingredients of any recipe. If you want
to mix it for drinking, you can use a blender, whisk it, or
mix it into a smooth thick paste, then add more water.

MISO is fermented soybean paste, sometimes mixed with
rice or barley. It can be found in health food stores and
also in oriental groceries. Excellent as a seasoning, it can
also be stirred into hot water or stock to make delicious
broth. When you use miso, be sure to make it into a thin
paste with a small amount of hot water before adding it to
a large amount of liquid (or it will remain in one lump).
Miso paste varies from very light to dark. The lighter the
paste, the milder the taste. Light miso is delicious as a
sandwich spread or as a moistener for sandwiches instead
of mayonnaise.

Most **NUTS** are not good sources of protein because of
their high fat content. Many nuts are expensive. Peanuts

(which are actually legumes) are a good source of protein when complemented by milk or sunflower seeds. I often use the nut-seed combination in recipes calling for nuts. Other nuts are delicious for their own special flavor and texture, so I occasionally have included walnuts, almonds, and cashews in the recipes although they have not been experimented with for complementarity. (See **PEANUTS** below.)

OIL may be pressed from seeds (sesame, sunflower, safflower), beans (soybeans, peanuts), nuts (almond, walnuts), or other foods (olives, avocados, corn germ, wheat germ). There are only two foods that will yield a reasonable amount of oil when pressed without heating—sesame seeds and olives. Since there is no legal definition of "cold pressed," many oils are given that misnomer plus a high price. Most commercial oil is processed by solvent extraction: cooked material is mixed with a solvent which dissolves out the oil and also the "impurities"—such as Vitamin A, Vitamin E, and natural lecithin—which keep the oil from becoming rancid. After processing, preservatives are added to keep the oil tasteless, odorless, and colorless. If you buy crude or unrefined oil you may be surprised to find that it actually is flavorful.

PEANUTS are actually legumes that grow under the ground. When the recipes call for raw peanuts you may use Spanish or Virginia. In cases where just peanuts are required, you may use raw or roasted nuts according to your own taste. Complement peanuts with milk, with sunflower seeds, and with combinations of grains, beans, and seeds.

PEANUT BUTTER that you use in the recipes should be either raw or from roasted ground nuts. Rather than using the commercial "peanut butter," which contains maltodextrin, dextrose, mono- and di-glycerides, and hardened vegetable oil, make your own in a blender: use a little oil to "start" the butter, then grind roasted peanuts a few at a time, scooping out the butter as it reaches the consistency you prefer. Complement peanut butter the same as peanuts. (See **PEANUTS** above.)

RICE combines with brewer's yeast, beans, seeds, dairy products, and combinations of all of these to make high-quality protein. Use short or long grain brown rice, or you may substitute converted enriched white rice, as their protein quality is nearly the same. The potassium content of the white rice, however, is only 30% that of brown rice. If you want to use white rice, substitute equal amounts of converted rice for brown rice in the recipes. Since it is processed, converted rice will cook up to a greater volume than brown rice, so your dishes will be somewhat ricier. See Appendix A for cooking instructions.

RICOTTA CHEESE is similar to cottage cheese. It is mild flavored and has a light creamy texture. You can spread it on bread or mash it until it is smooth for mixing in cheese dishes. Ricotta is high in protein (20 grams of usable protein per cup). Substitute ricotta for cottage cheese in any of the recipes; in recipes where I suggest either, the final amount of protein in a portion is based on an average between the two. In recipes where I suggest only cottage cheese, substituting ricotta would result in slightly less usable protein per portion. (See also **COTTAGE CHEESE,** and the following recipe for making your own ricotta.)

Ricotta So Easy
about 1 cup

½ cup = approx. 10 grams of usable protein
23% to 28% of average daily protein need

The ricotta that you make yourself is mellower and fresher than you can buy. The first time I made it I was shocked at how easy it was to do. And though you're getting only one cup from a quart of milk, no waste is necessary. The whey may be used instead of water for making yogurt (see page 282), or as stock for bread or soup.

1 quart whole milk (may be reconstituted from non-instant powdered whole milk available in some health food stores)	the juice of one lemon (about 2 tbsp) some cheesecloth and a strainer or colander

(1) Put the milk over low heat and bring it to the scalding point (150°F). Remove from heat.

(2) Stir in the lemon juice and the milk will curdle.

(3) Let the mixture sit (without refrigeration) for 2 to 12 hours. I call this the mellowing process, and it seems that the more patient you can be, the mellower the cheese.

(4) Place 2 thicknesses of cheesecloth in your strainer or colander, then place this draining device over a bowl.

(5) Pour the cheese mixture into the drainer and allow the whey to drain several hours until the curd is dry. Refrigerate the first whey that you pour through, and if you happen to be on your way out, you can allow the draining processes to happen in the refrigerator, too.

And there you have it!

ROLLED OATS, also called oatmeal, are whole oats that have been rolled flat. Rolled oats used in the recipes should be regular oats rather than quick or instant oatmeal. Oatmeal has an amino acid make-up similar to whole wheat, so you may substitute 1⅓ cups of rolled oats for 1 cup of whole wheat flour. Regular oatmeal purchased in bulk, rather than in boxes is very inexpensive. Complement oats with dairy products, seeds, and beans, as you would whole wheat products.

SEA SALT contains trace minerals that are not found in processed salt commonly found in the supermarket. Check the label the next time you buy salt; you will find that you have also purchased sodium silico aluminate, dextrose, and potassium iodide. Iodine is important for those who live far from the sea, but are the other chemicals necessary? A grain or two of rice in the shaker will keep your salt pouring without extra chemicals.

SEEDS high in protein are **SESAME** and **SUNFLOWER.** Sunflower seeds are easiest to use in cooking when they are purchased hulled. But use unhulled sesame seeds if at all possible—they are brown and are not costly when purchased in bulk. The greatest rip-off around is a two-ounce spice jar full of hulled sesame seeds sold for 80 cents or more! Sesame and sunflower seeds have similar amino acid make-up and can probably be interchanged in recipes with the same quality of protein resulting. Complement seeds with dairy products, grains, and beans. See Appendix A for toasting seeds and seed meals. For gomasio, grind roasted sesame seeds and add salt.

SESAME BUTTER or **TAHINI** is unhulled sesame seeds ground into a smooth butter. Sesame butter is made from roasted seeds; tahini is from the raw seeds. You may interchange them in the recipes according to your own taste, as their protein make-up is the same. Complement sesame with dairy products, grains, or beans.

SOY FLOUR, also called soybean flour or soya flour, is made from ground raw soybeans. It is a good source of protein, like soybeans, and when combined with grains, seeds, or dairy products it makes high-quality protein. In baking, soy flour will tend to make the batter taste bitter, but once the baking is done the bitter taste is eliminated.

Soy powder is soy flour that has been partially cooked to remove the bitter taste; it can be mixed with water to make soy milk. To make your own soy powder, roast soy flour in a dry pan until lightly browned.

SOY GRITS are raw or partially cooked soybeans that have been cracked into 10 pieces. In the recipes you may substitute equal amounts of soy grits for soybeans, but expect a change in texture.

STOCK is one of my best refrigerator friends. Every time vegetables are cooked, the water they leave, whether they were steamed or boiled, is lightly flavored vegetable stock. Stock from cooked beans is especially rich. There is no need to throw this flavored water down the drain—keep it in the refrigerator and re-use it each time you cook vegetables, and it will become more and more delicious. Stock will keep for about one week if refrigerated, but don't throw it away after the time has passed. Bring it to a boil and simmer for about 10 minutes and it will keep for another week! Use stock in breads, for soups, and even for cooking grains.

TOFU is soybean cheese, also known as bean curd. It is made by making a milk from soybeans, then making a cheese from the milk. Some supermarkets carry tofu, and you can also get it in health food stores and oriental groceries and restaurants. Like soybeans, tofu may be complemented by grains, seeds, or dairy products.

WHEAT GERM is actually the embryo of the wheat. It contains most of the vitamins, minerals, and especially the protein of the wheat. In fact, wheat germ is what is removed from whole wheat to make white flour. Refrigerate raw wheat germ so that it does not become rancid. The recipes refer to raw wheat germ, which is very inexpensive if purchased in bulk rather than in jars or boxes. Wheat germ (raw or toasted) is also delicious by itself as a cereal, or with yogurt, fresh fruit, and nuts. Although it has not been experimented with for protein complementarity, from its amino acid make-up and high NPU we can see that it is a good source of protein by itself and probably excellent if complemented. Two tablespoons (level) of wheat germ have 2 grams of usable protein!

WHOLE WHEAT FLOUR is ground whole wheat berries. Graham flour is somewhat more coarsely ground whole wheat. If possible, grind whole wheat flour fresh before using, for it will become rancid (see **WHEAT GERM** above) if ground and not refrigerated. Stone ground whole wheat flour is superior to flour ground with steel blades, for the heat generated by the friction of the grains against the blades destroys most of the vitamins in the wheat. Whole wheat makes high-quality protein when combined with beans, dairy products, and combinations of beans and seeds.

YOGURT is a cultured milk product that can be made easily at home (see the dessert recipes). Making yogurt at home is much less expensive than commercial yogurt; what's more, YOU decide what goes into it, so you can avoid such substances as emulsifiers, modified starches (and who knows what they're modified with), guar gum, carrageenan, locust bean gum, and cellulose, plus all the sugar of flavored yogurt. Read those labels! Yogurt should be pure milk into which friendly bacteria are introduced—they make the milk thick while they actually partially digest the milk sugar. This is why many people who are allergic to milk are able to eat yogurt and buttermilk. Yogurt in the recipes always means plain yogurt. It will, like milk, complement grains, beans, and seeds. It has the same quality (and quantity) of protein as milk, cup for cup. (Also see **BUTTERMILK** above.)

YEAST for baking may be dry granulated yeast or fresh cakes. Dry yeast can be purchased in bulk from health food stores, and you can get fresh yeast from your neighborhood bakery. Refrigerated dry yeast will keep six months, and fresh yeast may be frozen for two months.

Fresh yeast should be dissolved in 80°F liquid, dry yeast in liquid at 110°F. Yeast feeds on the sugars of the grains you use, and also on the honey that you add to bread. Carbon dioxide and alcohol are produced, and the bread rises. Substitute 1 cake (⅔ ounce) of fresh yeast for 1 tablespoon of dry yeast in the recipes.

BREWER'S or **NUTRITIONAL YEAST** does not have rising properties like baking yeast. It is a good source of high-quality protein by itself (1 tablespoon has 2 grams of usable protein), and it also increases the protein quality of brown rice when used in combination. The one problem most people have with brewer's yeast is the taste. It is unfortunate that a lot of the packaged (and thus the most commonly available) brewer's yeast tastes like rotten hay. I can only recommend that you find a health food store run by organic merchants who will have high-quality and delicious brewer's yeast available for you.

INDEX

347

Recipes

Recipes

Recipes

Recipes

Recipes

Recipes

Recipes

Recipes

About the Author

ELLEN BUCHMAN EWALD was born in Chicago, Illinois, in 1946, and now lives in Berkeley, California, with her husband. She works with the Berkeley Organic Food Association (known as the Food Conspiracy). She is also involved with organic gardening and modern dance. At present, Mrs. Ewald is working on a new book—her goal in this work is to inspire creativity in the kitchen.

5 *of the best reasons to eat nutritiously.*

25   AL-1

You are
what you
EAT...

Women of all ages *can look and feel their best with these bestselling guides to wardrobe, weight loss, exercise and skin care.*

Make Your House a Home

Ballantine's domestic guides are the best ways to keep you house in order—and to save money doing it! From energy and economy to flowers and food, these are books for home and apartment alike.

25